William McKinley
Apostle of Protectionism

WILLIAM MCKINLEY
APOSTLE OF PROTECTIONISM

QUENTIN R. SKRABEC, JR.

Algora Publishing
New York

ISBN-13: 978-0-87586-576-8 (trade paper)
ISBN-13: 978-0-87586-577-5 (hard cover)
ISBN-13: 978-0-87586-578-2 (ebook)

Library of Congress Cataloging-in-Publication Data —

Skrabec, Quentin R.
  William McKinley, apostle of protectionism / Quentin R. Skrabec, Jr.
    p. cm.
  Includes bibliographical references and index.
  ISBN-13: 978-0-87586-576-8 (trade paper: alk. paper)
  ISBN-13: 978-0-87586-577-5 (hard cover : alk. paper)
  ISBN-13: 978-0-87586-578-2
  1. McKinley, William, 1843-1901. 2. Presidents—United States—Biography. 3. United
States—Politics and government—1897-1901. I. Title.
  E711.6.S57 2008
  973.8'8092—dc22

                        2007035155

Front Cover: President William McKinley speaks on a reviewing stand at the Pan
American Exposition in Buffalo on September 6, 1901. Later that day he was shot and he
died a week later. New York, USA.
    Image: © CORBIS
    Photographer: Frances Benjamin Johnston

Printed in the United States

To my grandmother Eleonora Skrabec
and Our Lady of Grace

ACKNOWLEDGEMENT

The Canton and Niles Museums and archives are wonderful resources for research on President McKinley, as well as the congressional papers. I would particularly like to credit the help and vast knowledge of Janet Metzger at the William McKinley Presidential Library and Museum. The staff at both the Canton and Niles memorials are outstanding and passionate. Special thanks also to the outstanding research of the Stark Historical Society. Background research is critical to the success of a focused biography, and I wish to highlight several excellent organizations that helped me, including the Benson Ford Research Center in Dearborn, the Clement Library of American History at the University of Michigan, the Ohio Historical Museum in Columbus, and Heinz Historical Center in Pittsburgh.

Table of Contents

INTRODUCTION

Many of the terms used in this book have changed in meaning, some dramatically, after two world wars, a worldwide depression, and the cold war. The Republican and Democratic Parties of today are far different than those of McKinley's day, and the reader must resist framing the parties of this biography into those of today. The term "American System" as used throughout the book refers to a specific economic blending of capitalism, government, and democracy as defined by Henry Clay in the 1830s and adopted by William McKinley. The full history of the term "American System" is discussed in Chapter 2.

Terms such as socialist, communist, and anarchist were not as clearly defined. The socialist movement was undergoing its own growing pains; even the followers of Karl Marx were split on the definition and what to call themselves. The conventional view of "socialism" in McKinley's day was that it was some kind of hodge-podge of anarchism. And clandestine foreign agents who made vague promises of a better life for workers, in fact, were supposedly acting to undermine the "holy" foundations of American capitalism. This pitted the workers against the barons of capitalism. Also, at the time there was no practical example of a functioning socialist government; socialism was only a political movement, which included a collection of anti-establishment planks.

Anarchists might be considered the terrorists of McKinley's day. Historically and politically they split from Marx's socialist movement and wanted no government at all. On the very fringe was a violent movement of anarchists who saw violence as a tool for change. The public, the press, and the government often used the terms "anarchist" and "socialist" interchangeably to make a political statement.

Some caution is therefore needed in extrapolating the meaning of the terms socialism and capitalism into today's broader sense. Both terms were still evolving in the 1890s. I use them in the timeframe of the 1890s, as they apply to the evolution of American industry. Today we see a blending of socialism and capitalism in the United States and Europe, but such examples were unknown in the 1890s.

The world of McKinley lacked basic protections such as social security and unemployment insurance. Capitalism and socialism were almost mutually exclusive terms at the economic level. They stood at different ends of the spectrum of business models. As noted, socialism was commonly linked in the press with anarchism and worker revolutions. To the average American, it was a little-understood and threatening foreign idea being brought to the country by European radicals. Politicians and the press often played on this fear to achieve political goals. The capitalists — the investor class — feared loss of power because of socialism's concept of shared ownership. Workers often turned to the various socialist parties because of abuse by the owners and bankers, who squeezed them to the bone. Probably neither the workers nor the owners had read Karl Marx or had any real idea of the political philosophy underlying the economic models. In the end, America took its own way of blending systems and ideas.

William McKinley is remembered as an Ohio Republican who supported tariffs and got assassinated. Beyond those minimal well-known facts, however, one thing had always struck me as odd. I grew up in Pittsburgh and worked in management in the steel industry. A few Republican steelworkers (mostly German), such as my grandfather, traced their party allegiance to the days of McKinley and Teddy Roosevelt. This remnant of Republicanism was highly unusual for union members, most of whom were strict Democrats in a Democratic town and a Democratic industry. Even more striking was that these Republican steelworkers were also Catholic, and until Ronald Reagan, Catholics had been almost exclusively Democrats. The steelworkers of my day looked to the Republican Party as the party of the bosses. It was thirty years before I gave it much thought.

My childhood history books portrayed McKinley as Big Business and a puppet of the robber barons, hardly a president who would have inspired a group of immigrant steelworkers. Perhaps the story was buried in the other brief lines given to McKinley as the "Napoleon of Protection." Researching this peculiar twist, I found myself writing this book. The picture of McKinley that emerges is strikingly different from the common template. This biography is focused primarily on McKinley's economic beliefs.

The Republican remnant of steel workers was part of a great political alliance built on American manufacturing in the 1800s. It was an alliance unique to McKinley's vision of a manufacturing American empire. McKinley had come from a middle class family of ironworkers. As a politician, he followed in the footsteps of Henry Clay, putting manufacturing above all other political roads. He believed that a strong industry was the beating heart of US democracy. He had fought for protective tariffs from the beginning of his political career. No matter how hard the criticism, even from his home congressional district, he never wavered from his position on protective tariffs. He found tariffs so central to industrial health that he often tied other issues to it. Many saw this as simpleminded and naive; however, the growth of US industry in the latter part of the 19th century bears him out. He found few allies in colleges, the merchant class, bankers, and farming areas, but he built new alliances in the middle class and working class, manufacturing owners, and wealthy capitalists. He politically united labor and the bosses for the good of the nation. It was a somewhat short-lived but strong alliance that left roots for decades.

The McKinley legacy has been reduced to a few lines in most history books. The view is often that of his political opponents of the 1890s who saw McKinley as the puppet or pawn of Big Business, a simplistic one-position president. A president who, without Mark Hanna, was unable to find the Oval Office each morning. His policy on tariffs was considered an umbilical cord to the robber barons and their trusts. This view distorts the meaning and value of McKinley's service. In fact, it was evolved from a stream of political debate going back to the Jeffersonians and Hamiltonians.

Both American political parties of today are free traders. Most free trade academicians see McKinley's protectionism as nothing more than a shortsighted form of nationalism. To support this view, they portray McKinley as unread and capable only of emotional arguments for protectionism, when just the opposite is true. The fact is that his speeches were peppered with statistics, his arguments factual and lacking emotion. Today's attacks vary little from the 1896 campaign themes of the Populists, Democrats of the period, and the "yellow press." It is only recently that McKinley is being considered for the second tier of "near-great presidents," but the historical branding of insignificance and lower tier runs deep. A serious look at McKinley's economic policy as a continuum of those of Alexander Hamilton and Henry Clay is still lacking.

Over the last ten years, I've written about a pantheon of industrialists and capitalists, great and small. These include the powerful, such as Andrew Carnegie and George Westinghouse, as well as the lieutenants such as Michael Owens and Bill Jones. I imagined these gods united in such a pantheon, and wondered who would occupy the seat of Jupiter. For years, I believed that Andrew Carnegie must have been the world's greatest capitalist, but research for this book leaves no doubt that the seat belongs to William McKinley.

Henry Clay Frick would have to be considered, but his reputation was even more tarnished by union strife than Carnegie's. It is only McKinley who could rise above criticism. His love of America and capitalism is as unequaled as it is pure. He had no personal gain from his stubborn belief in America's economic manifest destiny. He believed that American capitalism and Henry Clay's "American System" were the answer to the growth of anarchism. He made no excuses in his shameless support of American business. He believed that socialism and anarchism could not take root if American factories ran at capacity. It was a one-faceted (some might say naive) policy, and though he was often criticized by the muckraking press as a puppet of Big Business, his political alliance included the worker, foreman, owner, capitalist, and union leader. McKinley was well aware of the abuses of capitalism, but he believed with government oversight it could function better than the options offered by the socialists of the time. It should be noted that McKinley cared little for spreading theories or political philosophies but was focused on America's economic health and the growth of the nation. Like Henry Clay, McKinley had spent many hours studying the 900-page book of Adam Smith, the *Wealth of Nations*, non-fiction's version of *War and Peace*.

McKinley was middle class in everyway, and this leads to the historical view of a limited presidency. His father had been a foreman and manager and earned enough to make some investments in the industry. The family experienced unemployment, layoffs, reorganizations, and relocation. McKinley preferred family dining to state dinners, and his homes were typical of Midwestern America. He practiced an ecumenical Christianity and an inclusive pluralism. He lived in middle class homes all his life. His last home in Canton was not known as the President's mansion, as most presidents' were, but the McKinley "cottage." He had worked in the mills, experienced unemployment in his family, and knew the fear of job loss; he had carried a dinner pail to work and even experienced business failure and bankruptcy late in life. His father had lost his middle management job in an economic downturn. His $50,000 salary as President was a huge pay increase over his best years. He dedicated his life to the care of his invalid wife, putting her welfare ahead of his career. He believed in equal rights for women and Blacks far before it was in vogue. McKinley believed that inclusiveness was the foundation of capitalism and maintained that mobility into the middle class had to be a cornerstone of capitalistic democracies. He felt let down by capitalists who put profits before the overall good of the nation. He was cut down before he got his hands firmly on the reins to control this damaging propensity of capitalists.

While many claim he idolized these capitalists, just the opposite is true. And the capitalists of the time had a hard time understanding his commitment to the theory of capitalism without the great rewards. These robber barons could not understand him but admired his belief of what capitalism could really be. He touched the hearts of cold capitalists such as Henry Clay Frick, changed the hearts of others such as Mark Hanna, and found common ground with capitalists such as George Westinghouse. Furthermore, he realized that both the worker and the mill owner were invested in the full capacity operation of the mill. He found no common ground with Big Banking, which he saw as part of what's wrong in the system. His death brought these capitalists to tears, and they bound together to build one of the first presidential libraries in Niles, Ohio.

As a manager of the Republic Steel (LTV) in Canton, I had visited the McKinley monument often. I loved to take my two daughters to the museum there on Saturdays. The McKinley Monument at Canton was by and for the people. The Niles Library Memorial was different. My first visit to the Niles Library was in 2005 as I started this book, and it was there I saw a real life pantheon of capitalists. The Greek architecture and the bronze statues of capitalists related to my own vision of the period. It was striking to see a bronze statue of fellow Pittsburgher, Henry Clay Frick, in such a prominent position as the major donor. In Pittsburgh, Frick still represents the noxious side of capitalism and still brings anger in the hearts of many union leaders. Other Pittsburghers such as George Westinghouse, Andrew Mellon, Benjamin Jones, and the "Boys of Braddock" (Carnegie Veterans Association) were there. It was in my research on biographies of these Pittsburghers that McKinley's name was so prevalent. There were the busts of many Mahoning Valley steel makers and Ohio industrialists such as Mark Hanna. As a metallurgist, I recognized some greats in bronze such as John Battelle, who rolled the country's first tinplate and founded Battelle Institute in Columbus where I had once studied. It is in visiting both memorials that you sense the McKinley alliance of labor and capital.

I've been to many presidential memorials and libraries, but McKinley's Niles and Canton memorials, while beautiful and inspiring, lack tourists and visitors. The Canton memorial has faired a bit better than Niles with funding, but more is needed. Both sites reflect the stately past of American industry that today awaits a renaissance. The staff of the Niles Memorial is outstanding, but the Library (now part of the Niles public library system) and Museum lack funds. In so many ways McKinley has been forgotten and even overlooked. The building and bronze statues are beautiful pieces of art, but the great bronze faces could probably not be identified by the nation's youth. This site, like Canton, should be one of national pilgrimage. Its pantheon is a tribute to the "American System" of production and American capitalism. It should be a required stop for the nation's leaders. McKinley embodied the American dream and its place in our society. He saw America like George Washington, as the light of the world, exceptional in nature and destined by God. My research opened my eyes to a new view of McKinley, so that now I place him on the same heights with Thomas Jefferson.

McKinley remained scandal free in a time of political corruption. While he lacked the intellectual muscle of a Jefferson, his democracy was more inclusive than that of Jefferson. He supported equal rights for blacks, Catholics, and women before it was in vogue. His industrial vision matched that of Jefferson's agrarian one. McKinley was more representative of the average American and more responsive to the needs of average Americans. He lacked the intellectual scope of a Jefferson as well but excelled in the area of his focus. He never approached the mastery of writing and political thought of a Jefferson, but he was one of the first to apply statistics and scientific management to politics. Clearly, he is a president worth re-considering.

Chapter 1. Prologue

> A man's best gift to his country is his life's blood.
> — *William McKinley*

"Am I shot?" These were the simple words of the popular President after the second bullet entered. The blood on his hands answered the question before anyone could respond. As the President fell into the arms of a secret service agent, a black waiter quickly struck the assassin. Within moments, the assassin came under attack of both soldiers and police. As the agent placed McKinley in a chair, he grasped, "Let no one hurt him." William McKinley was a devout Christian in image and practice. His legacy had gone back to the 1870s, when, as Chair of the Ways and Means Committee, he initiated the era of tariffs for American industry. As the electric-powered ambulance rushed the still-conscious President to Exposition Hospital, he expressed several concerns. First, he worried about his wife and how she might take the news. Second, he did not want the assassin beaten or even lynched as the crowd wanted; and third, he expressed regret for the trouble the incident would cause the Pan-American Exposition, which was to highlight America's debut as a world power. McKinley had been looking forward to the exposition for years.

September 5, 1901 marked the final phase of a vision that had built an American industrial empire. The bulldog of protectionism had just completed a notable speech at the Buffalo Pan-American Exposition which most agree was the best of his long career. It heralded a significant change in America's view of its role in the world. The McKinley trade tariffs had brought an unheard of level of prosperity to industry in the last quarter of the 19th century. The problem now was the American market alone could not drive the industrial growth of the past 30 years. That growth was the result of one's man determination to protect, expand, and build a lasting legacy for domestic industry. From his youth, William McKinley had championed the belief of Henry Clay in industrial republicanism, which blended Jeffersonian creativity, Emerson's self-reliance, and Hamiltonian finance, with Washingtonian patriotism. American industry knew no rival and accepted no competitor under the McKinley Tariff. McKinley protectionism was unabashed Americanism. He viewed it more as an economic Monroe Doctrine than protectionism. It was a political alliance of big business and the workingman to secure America's industrial destiny. He believed the next world empire would not be one of militaristic strength but one of industrial might. It reflected a global, economic manifest destiny. To the cheers of the public that day in Buffalo, McKinley prepared to launch the final phase of industrial conquest — world markets.

McKinley's final public words were not much different than his great congressional speeches of years past. He took the grand platform that September Thursday to note the success of his belief in protectionism. McKinley roared with pride:

> My fellow citizens, trade statistics indicate that this country is in a state of unexampled prosperity . . . they show that we are utilizing our fields and forests and mines, that we are furnishing profitable employment to the millions of workingmen throughout the United States, bringing comfort and happiness to their homes and making it possible to lay by savings for old age and disability. . . . Our capacity to produce has developed so enormously and our products have so multiplied that the problem of more markets requires our urgent and immediate attention. . . . By sensible trade arrangements which will not interrupt our home production we shall extend the outlets for our increasing surplus. . . . Reciprocity is the natural outgrowth of our wonderful industrial development under the domestic policy now firmly established. . . . Reciprocity treaties are in harmony with the spirit of the times; measures of retaliation are not.

That day, McKinley defined government's role as a manager of trade, a promoter of industrial growth, an incubator of invention, and a facilitator of commerce. It was a view based on American exceptionalism: that America was a favored nation of Providence. In the speech, he proposed a rebuilding of the US merchant marine, which had been one of the few casualties of McKinley protectionism. He argued for the building of the Panama Canal (called the Isthmian Canal, as Panama was not a country at the time). He cited the need for a Pacific Cable for communications. He defined the concept of reciprocity in trade, saying, "By sensible trade arrangements which will not interrupt our home production we shall extend the outlets for our increasing surplus."[1] Reciprocity allowed

---

1 McKinley Pan-American Exposition Address, September 5, 1901, Buffalo, New York

an "America first" economic philosophy. McKinley's trade agreements were economic based. With McKinley's death, reciprocity became an international political tool which McKinley had hoped to avoid. The new breed of Republicans, old line Democrats, and Edwardian industrialists saw American manufacturing and business as a trading chip in international politics. America moved from the home economy focus of McKinley to an international political center focus, which trades jobs and international politics.

In 1901, Buffalo was the eighth largest city in the United States and had some of the largest office buildings in the world. Buffalo and Niagara Falls represented America's greatest industrial achievement, supplying the power that would light the country. Only three years earlier, in 1897, the world's greatest inventors had gathered at Buffalo's exclusive Ellicott Club to celebrate the yoking of Niagara Falls. German electrical engineer Professor Siemens estimated in 1888 that "the amount of water falling over Niagara is equal to 100,000,000 tons [of coal] an hour."[2] Sir William Siemens calculated that, "if steam boilers could be erected vast enough to exhaust daily the whole coal output of the earth, the steam generated would barely suffice to pump back again the water flowing over Niagara Falls." The power of waterfalls throughout the world remains preeminent in electrical generation, even today accounting for 25% of all power generated. The Pan-American Exposition was a celebration of American technology and industrial might. Its focus was the use of technology in everyday life. Ironically, the exposition hospital lacked electric lighting, and the X-ray machine on exhibition, which might have saved McKinley's life, was never used.

In his speech that day, McKinley sought to move the country forward into a more globalized market. America was about to begin an even more expansive role in the world's economy. This expansion would not be at the expense of the home industrial base but would spring from that very base. While he envisioned a new type of international trade, trade relations would be based on reciprocity, not "free" trade. He would not trade high paying jobs, which he believed were the right of America's democratic success, for cheap consumer goods. Those jobs had been paid for with American blood. This was clearly American industrial expansion without any apologies. He based his model on that of his friend and supporter, George Westinghouse, whose Pittsburgh workshops and workers supplied over ninety countries with railroad brakes and equipment. Such a model required the maintenance of a frail alliance of business and labor. It was a celebration of capitalism that realized that "the problem with capitalism is capitalists." McKinley had used his enormous popularity to hold this capitalistic alliance together in the face of the abuses of the capitalists. Yet it was also a simple philosophy based on the voters of his industrial hometown of Canton,

---

2 *Manufacturer and Builder*, November, 1888, Volume 20, Issue 11

Ohio. Simply put, the best thing for the country was high paying, long term jobs, and the only way to secure and create jobs was through the expansion of business. It was this "dinner-pail Republicanism" that was at the root of McKinley's popularity, America's industrial growth, and political success of the Republican party. His vision of the great capitalistic alliance of labor and owners monitored by government sank with his life signs.

The main opponents of his "dinner-pail Republicanism" were a rising majority of socialists, labor reformers, the muckraking press, an influx of politically-oriented immigrants, and neo-Luddites; however, the real problem was the capitalists themselves. The press, political reformers, and the socialists played to an undercurrent of discontent. McKinley's assassination in many ways came from the edge of that underground discontent. Leon Czolgosz, McKinley's assassin, was a socialist and an anarchist, but more importantly he expressed the emotion of a broader movement. In Czolgosz's own words, "what started the craze to kill was a lecture I heard some time ago by Emma Goldman."[3] Goldman was a Jewish émigré from Russia, a socialist and professed anarchist. Goldman's ex-lover had shot Henry Clay Frick after the 1892 Homestead Strike. Goldman, like Czolgosz, was an extremely frustrated person. Goldman was a nurse who felt society had prevented her from fulfilling her dream of being a doctor. In the speech Czolgosz heard in Cleveland on May 6, 1901, Goldman declared, "Men under the present state of society are mere products of circumstances. Under galling yoke of government, ecclesiasticism, and the bond of custom and prejudice; it is impossible for the individual to work out his own career as he could wish." This represented the antithesis of McKinley's view of America's industrial opportunity. Like Goldman, Leon Czolgosz fed off the setbacks of laborers in Detroit, Cleveland, and Chicago, and the abuses of the capitalists. The socialist movement found allies in the scandal-mongering press.

The capitalists, to a large degree, had profited by the use of cheap immigrant labor. Their abuses had given rise to the unions, but unions brought abuses of their own. McKinley had moved on both as needed to hold up his ideal of capitalism.

The 1870s were a time of labor unrest. In July of 1877, America's first general strike was called against the Pennsylvania Railroad and East Coast railroads over a 10% wage reduction. Two days of rioting in Pittsburgh alone left over twenty dead, hundreds wounded, and over $5 million in losses. The 1880s brought further unrest in the coalfields of Pennsylvania and the workhouses of Chicago. In 1893, the Homestead Strike at the Carnegie steel mills resulted in deaths and dire headlines. During it all, the extravagant life styles of the "robber barons" were making headlines as well. The great banking trusts of J. P. Morgan and August

---

3 Marshall Everett, *Complete Life of William McKinley*, (Marshall Everett, 1901), 70

Belmont seemed to have given the ownership of America's industrial assets to a handful of bankers.

McKinley united them in the need for a protective tariff, but he was never really personally close to them. McKinley needed them and labor needed them. In 1901, 65% of America's wealth was controlled by the trusts. They were feeding over ten million people and were responsible for the employment of most of America's industrial workers. Even with the relatively high wages of tariff protection, these trusts had pushed prices down through economies of scale and technology. The capitalists wanted protection as much as labor.

The immigrant Irish of the Northeast were reminded that free trade had ruined Ireland. All immigrants were reminded of the "great Satan" of free trade England. The Irish had heard the free traders of Britain promise much but deliver economic devastation. Immigrant workers well understood the relationship between free trade and jobs. It was better to endure abuse by the owners than the hunger pains of not working. Interestingly, cheap Chinese labor was pouring into the West coast with the approval of the Republicans. The simple fact, however, was that unions, such as the emerging Knights of Labor, focused mainly on the tariff. These European immigrants came to work, not to be sold out again by free traders. The abuses could be addressed later. The barbaric 12-hour day in the steel industry actually found labor union support because no one wanted a pay cut. Unions in the glass industry ignored child labor concerns in the pursuit of higher wages for skilled workers. Even labor disputes were exclusively over wages, not conditions. In fact, the fear mongers of the Republicans pointed to child labor and women workers in the dirty factories of England as a result of the British free traders.

Yet with all the unrest, America was prosperous. Immigrants who were jobless in Europe found work plentiful here. America's poor were well off compared to the poor of Europe and Asia. While Czolgosz and Goldman saw limited upward mobility, others read of the rags-to-riches dreams daily. Carnegie, Westinghouse, Schwab, Pullman, Edison, even McKinley had come from poor or modest backgrounds. Immigrants usually moved up the social ladder within a generation, which was unknown in Europe. Czolgosz's own family had made social progress within a generation. America's old money, such as the blueblood families of Adams and the Roosevelt families, amazed by the rise of new capitalists, looked down their noses at the newly rich. This mixed view was the nature of the era that allowed counter currents of discontent to flourish.

McKinley struggled to hold his alliance of business and labor together. By today's standards, it was an unusual alliance of labor and capitalists. He had fought for better wages for Ohio coal workers, warned the trusts of their abuse, and protected American manufacturing with tariffs. McKinley befriended the more progressive capitalists such as George Westinghouse. Westinghouse paid fairly and built family values among his employees. McKinley feared that if his manufacturing alliance of business and labor failed, the international movement of socialism would fill the void. The work alliance was holding and seemed to have a bright future based on the popularity of President McKinley. The alliance consumed the American government resources and focus, but there was no real international component of government to distract it in the late 19th century.

Anarchists such as Czolgosz did not represent the oppressed factory worker but an international political movement. Anarchists raged against the economic Praeto distribution of wealth in capitalist countries. Anarchists found allies in the world's socialist parties. Anarchists and socialists appeared whenever there were labor problems, but the American labor movement managed to remain above such political indoctrination. McKinley, as well as labor leaders such as Samuel Gompers, forged a unique and cooperative environment of labor resolution. It was a type of alliance that McKinley had tried so hard to foster. McKinley had grown up with ironworkers and knew their greatest fear was unemployment. He believed the American worker would never support the socialist platform if the factories kept working.

McKinley's view of American industrialism was an evolutionary view with deep roots. Even before the Continental Congress issued the Declaration of Independence, it passed a resolution for economic independence. John Adams urged in March 1776, "a society for the improvement of agriculture, arts, manufactures, and commerce, and to maintain a correspondence between such societies, that the rich and numerous natural advantages of this country, for supporting its inhabitants, may not be neglected."[4] Jefferson's agrarian society seemed to dominate after the revolution until Henry Clay developed the concept of American industrialism and capitalism called the "American System." It was recognition that independence was as much economic as political. In the 1820s, Clay became the apostle of protectionism. A growing group of Clay republicans continued to develop the philosophy of independence and national dominance through technology and industry. The Republican Convention of 1896 presented William McKinley, its presidential nominee, a well-deserved award. It was gavel carved from wood of Henry Clay's Homestead reading, "The Father of Protection." Like John Adams, New Englanders seemed to expound the philosophy of economic and technological freedom of McKinley. Writers like Emerson and Hawthorne found this new McKinley industrialism on a level with Jeffersonian ideals. These roots of technological innovation and economic freedom were at the heart of

---

4 Worthington Ford, editor, *Journals of the Continental Congress, 1744-1789*, (Washington D. C., 1906)

McKinley's dinner-pail industrialism. It was the Jeffersonian ideal applied to industrialism.

Historian John Kasson chronicled the movement into the 1840s:

> Republicanism developed into a dynamic ideology consonant with rapid technological innovation and expansion. The older moral imperatives of eighteenth-century republicanism were modified to suit a new age of industrial capitalism. As technological progress offered new stability for republican institutions, luxury lost its taint. For its part, the ideology of republicanism helped to provide a repetitive climate for technological adaptation and innovation. The promise of laborsaving devices strongly appealed to a nation concerned with establishing economic independence, safeguarding moral purity, and promising industry and thrift among her people. So too did the hope that increased production, improved transportation and communications would centralize a country that continued to fear regional fragmentation. Yet the union of technology and republicanism, while settling some issues, raised others. Particularly pressing was the question whether the new centers of American production, her manufacturing towns, could avoid the blight and degradation of their English counterparts and achieve a new standard as model republican communities. If not, then Jefferson's worst fears might stand confirmed.[5]

McKinley, the son of an Ohio iron furnace operator, knew about this type of capitalism first hand. His political base of Canton, Ohio was part of this Jeffersonian industrialism. From his earliest days in industrial Ohio, "he witnessed and felt the seasons of employment and idleness which come to the workers in mills and factories . . . his heart had been wrung by association with strong men suffering and seeking only work, and their sons no longer able to be at the district school."[6] McKinley's fight for protectionism had been the fight of the American worker, whose wages remained high against those in free trading Britain. McKinley believed that work was the key to the success of capitalism and America. It was a unifying vision that brought the capitalist and workingman together. When his funeral train left Washington for Canton, it passed the coalfields of Pennsylvania, West Virginia, and Ohio as well as the great mills of Braddock, Pittsburgh, and Youngtown, and Canton. This was McKinley country. McKinley's vision was the industrial version of Jefferson's agrarian society. The workers that lined the railroad tracks were McKinley Republicans, many just getting off their factory shifts. With the tears were concerns that free trade might again take their jobs. The days of "dinner-pail Republicanism" were over. American exceptionalism and industrial preeminence as a goal would go the way of his father's Poland, Ohio iron furnace, which today is in ruins. Still, McKinley's legacy was historically, if not practically, significant because of its unequaled success.

---

5 John Kasson, *Civilizing the Machine: Technology and Republican Values in America, 1776-1900*, (Grossman Publishers: New York, 1976), 50

6 Murat Halstead, *Life and Distinguished Services of William McKinley*, (H. L. Barber: 1901)

Maybe, just as important, was that it was a movement of Victorian industrialism that was heroic in nature. Writers such as Jules Verne, Mark Twain, Ralph Emerson, and many artists were part of the movement that glorified America's industry. The machines themselves were raised to art. Steam engines were made in Greek Revival design. Magazines like *Scientific American* and *Harpers* were filled with beautiful illustrations of machines. *Harpers Monthly* was one of the magazines subscribed to by the McKinley family at Poland, Ohio.

World Fairs were almost American religious pilgrimages, with almost 40% of the population having visited the 1893 Chicago World's Fair. McKinley had been active at the Chicago World's Fair as governor of Ohio. Finally, McKinley last speech would be at the Pan-American Exposition at Buffalo in 1901. The theme of his speech would be "World Fairs are the timekeepers of progress." The day before an assassin brought him down, McKinley stood before the opening fair crowd at Buffalo to hail the showcase of technology, "Comparison of ideas is always educational, and, as such, instructs the brain and hand of man. Friendly rivalry follows, which is the spur to industrial improvement, the inspiration to useful invention and to high endeavor in all departments of human activity. It exacts a study of wants, comforts, and even the whims of people and recognizes the efficacy of high quality and low prices to win their favor."

In many ways September 6, 1901, ended the heroic view of American industrialism. McKinley struggled for days at a private home in Buffalo, but the end came on September 14. September 14, 1901 was also the thirty-ninth anniversary of the Battle of South Mountain where he had distinguished himself for bravery in the Civil War. McKinley's last words were representative of his life: "Good-by, all; good-by. It is God's way. His will be done." He died a man of great faith and deep love for his country. He saw the best in people to a fault, often being let down. While a socialist bullet had ended his life, McKinley believed that America was a nation destined to lead the world with its capitalism. Unlike those who would follow, he never feared socialism would take hold here.

McKinley had a public viewing in Buffalo, and a workingman and his family were the first of thousands to view the body. They passed at sixty per minute, with the Buffalo working immigrant class making up the majority. The funeral train left on the morning of September 16 for Washington, and as the train approached the capital that evening, bonfires lit the way along the railroad tracks. His wife, Senator and campaign manager Mark Hanna, and the nation were visibly shaken. The crowds in Washington were almost unmanageable as thousands pressed to the Capitol to view the body. What reporters noted was the large proportion of women in the crowd at a time when women without the vote often paid little attention to presidents. McKinley would, however, be the first president to support women's suffrage. In 1872, when the Equal Rights Party nominated Ohio-born Victoria Woodhull for president, McKinley calmed local outcries by having a reception for her at his Canton home. As governor, McKinley helped get the right for women to vote in school board elections. McKinley was a handsome man who had the aura of future president J. F. Kennedy with women and the young.

On September 17 in the late evening, the body started its sad journey to Canton, Ohio. The funeral train was scheduled to arrive in Canton the next day at 10 a.m. It would follow the Pennsylvania Railroad tracks. In Maryland, the tracks were packed with people who had held a night vigil waiting to catch a glimpse of it. The train passed near the battlefields of South Mountain and Antietam, where McKinley had led a group of soldiers to get food to trapped Union forces. McKinley had loved to visit this battlefield to recall those honorable times and remember those who had fallen. A humble man, McKinley had stopped an appeal to give him the Congressional Medal of Honor in the 1880s for his efforts on the battlefield. Two years after this funeral train passed Antietam, a thirty-three foot monument was erected near Burnside Bridge to commemorate the heroism of the slain president.

Thousands waited in the dark at Baltimore for the special train that carried the body of McKinley, and President Roosevelt with the Cabinet. At Harrisburg the crowd was estimated at 20,000. Then the train turned into the Juanita Valley, where the Scots-Irish ancestors of McKinley operated iron furnaces. In the distance, the hills glowed with their orange pulsing skylights. The train moved over the mountains to the steel town of Johnston, which owed its livelihood to the McKinley tariffs. It was at Johnston that Cambria Iron had pioneered the use of steel in railroad rails and led America to dominance in the technology of steel production. The valley that day was filled with a thick sulfurous smoke that represented capacity production. Coal miner lanterns cut the thick smoke lighting up the valley. Civil War veterans again lined the tracks with steelworkers holding up dinner pails, which was the symbol of the McKinley campaigns. The crowds of women started to grow for the first president to push for women's suffrage.

In darkness, the train passed through the coalfields of western Pennsylvania, where thousands of miners came out of the shafts with their lanterns to pay tribute to a friend. The first large crowd was at Pitcairn, a major railroad center for the Pennsylvania Railroad in the Monongahela River Valley. Large groups of working women were there, waiting to see the train before they got their connection to the valley's Westinghouse plants. Westinghouse had pioneered the use of the working woman in industrial plants. Marshall Everett, a friend and writer, noted from the train: "In railroad cars at Pitcairn, hundreds of factory girls lined up. It was 8:35 a.m. when the train passed through Pitcairn, so most of the girls with their lunch boxes under their arms must have been quite late to work, all for the sake of a few seconds' look at the train." It is doubtful that their boss George Westinghouse minded their tardiness.

The funeral train passed through a town that McKinley hoped would be America's future, Wilmerding, Pennsylvania, which Westinghouse had developed. One of McKinley's closest supporters in industry was George Westinghouse. As the funeral train passed the large Westinghouse supported YMCA building in Wilmerding, many gathered to honor the former president of the Canton YMCA. Westinghouse and McKinley, who had been Chairman of the Ways and Means Committee in Congress, had worked together on railroad safety in the 1880s. Westinghouse had shown that capitalism could have a heart, and he had built a workingman's town for Westinghouse Air Brake and Westinghouse Electric. McKinley had often pointed to Westinghouse as the model industrial baron. Westinghouse respected the worker, but unlike the industrial barons of the time, he did not see himself as a distributor of wealth. Westinghouse gave his money to create jobs, work, and loans for family development. He believed the best philanthropy to be giving someone a job. Westinghouse built no large art museums or music halls, but workplaces that respected the worker and paid him fairly. His factories were not paternal industrial plantations but industrial democracy in the workplace. This was a town that would have convinced Jefferson that industry is not always harmful.

The beautiful town of worker homes and community centers stood in stark contrast to the next rail station, Carnegie's Braddock. The smoke of the Pittsburgh steel mills blocked the autumn sun at this point, but that smoke and sulfuric odor was itself symbolic of the great prosperity that McKinley had brought the valley. At the tunnel before the train entered Braddock a large group of brightly dressed young girls waved flags before the dark passage. Exiting the tunnel, the Pennsylvania Railroad passed the great slums of Braddock's First Ward at the gate of America's largest steel mill. This was the contrast that McKinley had struggled with. McKinley understood these ironworkers, having been one in his youth. Theirs was hot and dirty work, amid smoke and sulfurous fumes. The streets and rails were covered with thick mill dust as the many Bessemer steel converters had been running flat out through the night. Still, the workers in both towns lined the rails to honor the man who had kept wages high and the mills running at capacity. Thousands of these men had traveled by special train to Canton to shake hands with the candidate in 1896. Braddock, a town of poor immigrant steelworkers, had consistently supported McKinley in his presidential campaigns. Particularly notable was the huge salute of the Irish Catholic furnace crews as the funeral train passed the blast furnaces; they rarely gave tribute to Methodists, let alone a Mason.

Prior to Pittsburgh the train passed the village of Swissvale, the home of Union Switch and Signal. Union Switch and Signal was a special Westinghouse company that manufactured safety controls for railroad tracks. These controls came into use through the overview and legislation of Congressman McKinley, and they reduced rail accidents by almost 90%. Railroad safety had been a concern of McKinley throughout his congressional career. Across the Monongahela from Swissvale was United States Steel's Homestead plant, site of the bloody steel strike of 1892 which helped McKinley gain the White House. A few miles away was the home of McKinley's Attorney General, Philander Knox, who was on the train that day. Knox was traveling in the Cabinet car with President Teddy Roosevelt. McKinley had appointed Knox at the request of Andrew Carnegie and Henry Clay Frick.

Nearby also was the home of Henry Clay Frick, believed responsible for the Homestead Strike. Knox often played poker there with Frick, Carnegie, Westinghouse, and Andrew Mellon. Henry Clay Frick had been in charge of the Homestead Works at the time. Frick and McKinley were different men, but they shared a belief in capitalism and the American steel industry. Frick would lead a group of donors to build a memorial for McKinley in Niles, Ohio. McKinley's association with these men was often held up as evidence of his protection of big business, but this day it was steelworkers who paid honor to a man they considered their friend too. My grandfather Louis A. Skrabec, a steelworker, was in the crowd that day.

It may seem strange to the modern reader that these Democratic steel valleys of today were strongly Republican in 1901, but this was the result of the alliance McKinley had forged. McKinley had even won over the labor leadership of the Knights of Labor union and the Amalgamated Association of Iron and Steel Workers. Even the new Irish immigrants of these steel valleys, who hated the free trade policies of England (as well as anything British) were in many cases, McKinley supporters. These laborers and industrialists of the steel valleys had even formed a campaign fund for McKinley known as the "working-man's tariff club." Of course, these Pennsylvania valleys were still dominated by the Scotch-Irish to which McKinley belonged. The Scotch-Irish of these areas had belonged to the core of the western Pennsylvanian industrialists. No president until John F. Kennedy would command so much loyalty and would be missed so much in these steel valleys.

As the train approached the steel mills of Pittsburgh in late morning, thousands of steelworkers carrying their dinner pails lined the tracks. Again it was noted that about one hundred girls stood on railcars, making "a most picturesque appearance." The train passed in view of the Monongahela House where presidents from Lincoln to McKinley had stayed. Pittsburgh was an important port of call in this industrial era and McKinley had visited here often, and twice as President. At Pittsburgh's Second Avenue, the train passed the exact location where the railroad air brake had been tested successfully, saving the life of a peddler. McKinley would pass legislation over the years, which would make air brakes mandatory on American trains. Also in the crowd at the Pittsburgh station was M. M. Garland, who was president of the Amalgamated Association of Iron, Steel, and Tin Workers during the Homestead Strike. Garland had become a McKinley supporter and was working with him for labor peace. Garland, like Samuel Gompers, had come to realize that prosperity meant union membership as well as corporate profits. Union membership quadrupled during the McKinley administration.

The crowds were reported as massive from Braddock, Pennsylvania to the steel valleys of West Virginia. This stretch of track following the Ohio River had not seen such a turnout of humanity since Henry Clay passed through in 1848 as a presidential candidate. Thousands of steelworkers held their dinner pails high as the train passed, dinner pails being the symbol of his campaigns. This was a final tribute to McKinley, the President, Congressman, and party leader who had protected the steelworkers, the workingwomen of Westinghouse, and the area mills for so many years. The train entered McKinley's beloved Ohio around 10 a.m. Close to his boyhood home in northeast Ohio, the crowds were large even in these rural areas. Many trains were hauled to allow the funeral train to pass through industrial northeast Ohio, America's highest concentrations of tracks. A locomotive preceded the funeral train to assure traffic was cleared. The Mahoning Valley had been the bastion of support for protective tariffs since the days of Henry Clay. Here glassworkers joined steelworkers and miners to honor the slain president. The train moved past some of the coal mining districts where the young lawyer McKinley had helped with their struggle for better working conditions. It was a sunny autumn day and the crowds grew as the train approached Canton. Flags increased as veterans of the Civil War amassed along the tracks to honor "the major."

The train reached Canton around noon. At Canton, over 100,000 flooded the streets of this industrial town. Their industrial son had finally come home. The train approached in dead silence, no whistles or bells. After this solemn arrival at the Canton train station, the band played McKinley's favorite hymn, "Nearer, My God, to Thee." Hotels were packed to capacity with four to five per room. The town overflowed with veterans, politicians, and simple folk. This little industrial town in the center of Ohio best represented William McKinley. The casket came down the National Road (Route 30), which was the root of Canton's industrial growth. McKinley's idol, Henry Clay, had appropriated funds for the road in the 1820s from tariff revenues. This industrial burgh was where McKinley called home, running even his campaigns from his Canton porch. Now the world and the nation crowded into Canton to pay final respects to him. Admiral Dewey led the color guard down Market Street to the Courthouse for a public showing. Canton was filled with America's greatest leaders, industrialists, and bankers, but maybe the largest part of the crowd were veterans of the Civil War, including McKinley's 23rd Ohio.

Probably no greater assemblage of American government was ever held in an American city outside Washington. The day of the burial, the First Methodist Church of Canton overflowed in the streets. In the front rows were President Roosevelt, Roosevelt's cabinet, former President Grover Cleveland, future President Howard Taft, the Speaker of the House, 40 Senators, 120 Representatives, most of the US Supreme court, most of Ohio's state government, and an endless array of other state governments. America's top generals and admirals were there such as Admiral Dewey and General Miles. Civil War veterans from both sides flooded the city, camping in open spaces. The veterans worked as guards for crowd control as they had a few years earlier in McKinley's famous front porch campaigns.

Canton was draped in black. The courthouse where McKinley had started his career had a gold and black banner with his last words, "It is God's way; His will, not ours, be done." It was at this courthouse where McKinley defended miners against strike breaking owners. In that very court fight he would be opposed by his future friend, mine owner, and campaign manager Mark Hanna. The night before the funeral, gangs of miners lit the night with their lamps in Canton. Steelworkers had traveled from Pittsburgh as well to honor this "Napoleon of Protectionism."

The whole country honored McKinley on his burial day. Chicago factories declared a holiday as well as other industrial towns. New York City closed completely for the day. A national tribute was made by pausing the nation's work for five minutes as the body was laid to rest. Every train, factory, steel mill, mine, and activity stopped for five minutes. The nation's entire telegraph system was shut down for five minutes. Foreign capitals also paused to praise the American president. London, in particular, hailed the president that two years earlier had led American industry in overtaking that of Great Britain. London was filled with pictures of McKinley, and Westminster Abbey held a special service. In many ways McKinley represented the American version of Queen Victoria, who had died in early 1901. Like Victoria in the 1840s Britain, McKinley had ushered in America's industrial empire in the 1890s. One diplomat noted how the McKinley industrial era had changed things: "it is almost incredible that we should be sending cutlery to Sheffield, pig iron to Birmingham, silks to France, watchcases to Switzerland . . . or building sixty locomotives for British railroads."

The crowds and honors were a reflection of a man who had always been a bit naïve. He really believed labor and capital could live in harmony. He trusted too much at times, but he believed that all should benefit from being American. He shamelessly promoted American interests, believing in the supremacy of America's destiny and America's exceptionalism. He trusted that capitalists would behave honorably, and he was disappointed in their failures to live up to his Christian standards. He saw no future in socialism because it limited dreams. He also had that rare ability to forgive even his assassin as he agonized for days in pain. He had even won the support of the immigrant Irish Catholic workers. At his funeral in Canton, New York's Archbishop Corrigan of St. Patrick's was so moved he could not deliver the sermon; a local priest read the Archbishop's speech.

There were, of course, many eulogies in the Congress, but the one that McKinley would have liked best came from his friend Senator Chauncey Depew:

> . . . with Washington and Hamilton, with Webster and Clay, he came, not alone, as they did, by the cold deductions of reason, but also by observation and experience, to the conclusion that the solution of our industrial problems and the salvation of our productive industries could only be had by the policy of a Protective Tariff. As Union and Liberty had been the inspiration of his courage and sacrifices as a soldier, so now America for Americans became an active principle of his efforts as a citizen.

CHAPTER 2. LEGACY OF HENRY CLAY'S AMERICAN SYSTEM

> Legislation helpful to producers is beneficial to all.
> — *William McKinley*

The plaque and gavel to honor McKinley at the 1896 Republican Party meeting was made of wood from Henry Clay's estate; it was a great tribute to America's "father of protection." To understand William McKinley, you must pick up the flag of Henry Clay's protectionism and the "American System" as McKinley did. Clay's powerful economic policy had built a Republican framework in the 1820s, but its full application would await an apostle such as William McKinley. Henry Clay had constructed the foundation for a new model of American capitalism and protectionism. McKinley was like the apostle Paul, while not an original apostle, he would spread the gospel of American protectionism, Clay's "American System", and dinner-pail industrialization with a zeal not seen prior. McKinley was an unwavering advocate of protectionism as a core principle in Henry Clay's "American System." America has always been torn between two visions, that of Hamilton and Clay, and that of Jefferson and Jackson. These competing visions have to a large degree defined American history. Their tentacles can be seen in the national bank debate, the Civil War, the rise of robber barons, trust busting, progressivism, the formation of the Republican and Democratic parties, manifest destiny, and today's free trade debate. The root of the argument has changed little from the visions and arguments of Thomas Jefferson and Alexander Hamilton. Henry Clay would define the battle lines in the 1820s and 1830s. As Clay left the scene and Civil War had slowed the momentum for protectionism, a new standard bearer in William McKinley took up the flag, but the debate was as old as the nation itself.

McKinley's only writing project was his *The Tariff of Henry Clay and Since.* McKinley, more than any economist, understood the depth of Clay's American System. To fully grasp the roots of Clay's economic philosophy, one must first understand Thomas Jefferson's vision of the nation. Jefferson envisioned an agrarian society of farmers and merchants. In 1790, an estimated 90% of the American population was employed in agriculture. His vision demanded free trade to assure that American crops could move into foreign markets readily. Jefferson had grown up in a tobacco and cotton culture that depended on European purchases and their crops. While he believed in farm self-sufficiency, he feared the industrialization that he had seen in Europe. Hamilton on the other hand saw America's freedom rooted in its ability to achieve economic freedom through manufacturing and banking. Hamilton, the soldier, was well aware of the role of technology and manufacturing in the ability of a nation to win wars and believed that manufacturing was fundamental to America's freedom. Hamilton, as a young officer, found the colonial army constrained by lack of iron cannon and rifles because of the lack of American manufacture. Interestingly, McKinley would have the same experience in his regiment during the Civil War. Hamilton however remained a free trader like many of his federalist friends, believing that financial systems were the basis for industrialization. Actually, the Federalists were split on tariffs, some seeing no need for them because America lacked manufacturing, and others seeing tariffs as a source of federal revenue.

Both Jefferson and Hamilton were constrained by the agricultural nature and lack of manufacturing in America at the time, as well as by earlier colonial British constraints on industries such as iron making. These British prohibitions such as the British Iron Act of 1750 had infuriated Scots-Irish iron makers like James McKinley (William McKinley's grandfather) in western Pennsylvania. In particular, the Scots-Irish moved to the frontier to avoid regulatory laws. The Iron Act of 1750 allowed for all raw bars of smelted iron, known as pig iron, to be shipped to England duty-free, but outlawed the production of iron products such as kettles, skillets, stoves, forged iron for guns, and steel for the blacksmith shop. These frontiersmen remembered and vowed never to be economically restrained again by any government. Many of these same Scots-Irish would flee western Pennsylvania to Ohio, Kentucky, and Tennessee to avoid the federal tax on whiskey manufacture in 1794 and would become part of the political base of frontier politician Henry Clay. It would be a base that often disagreed with Clay wanting cheap imported goods.

If McKinley's economic roots can be traced to Henry Clay, then Clay's roots can be traced to Federalist and first Secretary of the Treasury, Alexander Hamilton. And like McKinley, Hamilton learned his economics as an army supply officer. Hamilton, while on Washington's staff, had struggled to get their soldiers clothing because of America's dependence on British goods. He also learned the hard lesson of inflated dollars as merchants rejected government notes. His experiences would be the foundation for Hamilton's classic in 1791, the *Report on Manufactures*, which "prophesied much of post-Civil War America."[7] It would augur both Henry Clay and McKinley's approach to government as it related to national industrial planning. Hamilton was the first to suggest a scientific approach to tariffs versus across the board revenue tariffs. First defense and national industries were to be protected, followed by targeted infant industries. He argued for lower tariffs on raw materials to help industry. Hamilton would win many disciples including Henry Clay.

Henry Clay was a Virginian lawyer who moved to Kentucky to launch a career. In 1810, he was elected to the United States Congress. Clay was a nationalist, patriot, republican, and federalist. In his junior years in the Senate, he advocated a strong national bank and a national road system. Often Clay favored the good of the nation over his own constituents. His oratory, compromising skills, and patriotism brought him quickly to the position of Speaker of the House. Clay not only fashioned the position of house speaker, but he formed the powerful standing committees such as the Ways and Means Committee, which would be the pedestal to launch the career of William McKinley years later. Clay also created a Committee on Manufactures to help stimulate American manufacturing. Clay appointed members for these powerful committees, and thus centralized legislative power under the position of Speaker. Clay used the power to create a national infrastructure for an industrial America. Clay's vision of an industrial empire took him from Jeffersonian Republicanism to Federalism and then to conservatism. Clay's arguments and the rise of American manufacturing won over many Federalists who believed in the destiny of the American republic as a world power.

The struggle and the delineation of these competing visions of agriculture and industry would evolve as the nation evolved. By the dawn of the 1800s, the nation had a developing manufacturing sector in New England. America was learning to produce guns, gunpowder, farming implements, and textiles. Even Jefferson marveled at the industrial growth and its contribution to the nation. Yankees had smuggled in new automated looms from England and American

7 Ron Chernow, *Alexander Hamilton*, (New York: Penguin Books, 2005), 374

textile manufacture moved to a new level. The acceptance of automation had given American textile manufacturers an advantage over the labor-intensive British industry. Its own anti-automation proponents known as Luddites had held England back. Furthermore, the War of 1812 had caused a surge in American textile production as part of the need for economic freedom as well as a boom in iron manufacture in the middle states. The McKinley family would ultimately purchase one of those infant iron furnaces of 1812 in Niles, Ohio in the 1850s. The War of 1812 and the economic warfare involved, which extended into the 1820s, proved Hamilton's view of the need for economic independence. The British attempted to destroy the American textile industry by dumping huge quantities of British textiles on American docks. Henry Brougham in Parliament declared, "It was well worthwhile to incur a loss upon the first exportation, in order, by the glut, to stifle in the cradle, those rising manufactures in the United States." The British were more successful in this type of war, bankrupting hundreds of American manufacturers. The Northeast put political pressure on Congress to save its manufacturing base.

Congress hesitated to act, torn by competing regional goals. The Southern cotton growers opposed any tariffs on British goods, believing Britain would retaliate with tariffs on cotton and tobacco. The major portion of the South's cotton and tobacco went to Great Britain for processing. Furthermore, even the Northeast representatives were torn between the textile manufacturers and the merchants, who favored free trade. The struggle in Congress in 1816 would produce a new champion in Henry Clay, Speaker of the House. The Congress appeared hopelessly deadlocked on the issue. Clay built an alliance for the tariffs based on nationalism versus regional politics. The debate took place in a temporary brick building (at the site of today's Supreme Court), known as the "Old Brick capitol". The city of Washington lay in ruins after the sacking by the British, and offered a stark reminder to Congress of the need for a strong defense. Clay found allies in southerners John Calhoun and President Madison, who would help tip the balance. Clay brought in the middle state representatives who had suffered from British dumping of iron products to suppress American industry. He astutely played on rising nationalism and anti-British sentiments to bring in enough southern votes to pass the tariff. The result was America's first tariff: the Tariff of 1816, which established duties of 25% on cotton and wool products and 30% on iron products. The Tariff of 1816 would help the financial security of the Pennsylvanian ironworker family of the future William McKinley.

With the tariff of 1816, Clay inaugurated the "American System" of focused, protective, and selective tariffs for the good of the nation. Henry Clay told Congress in 1820:

> In passing along the highway one frequently sees large and spacious buildings, with the glass broken out the windows, the shutters hanging in ruinous disorder, without any appearance of activity and enveloped in solitary gloom. Upon inquiry what they are, you are almost always informed that they were some cotton or other factory, which their proprietors could no longer keep in motion against overwhelming pressure of foreign competition.[8]

It was a story that could have been written today, and one that Clay wanted to change.

By doing this, Clay had broken not only with Jefferson's thinking but with his own Federalist leanings toward free trade. The Federalists were split because tariffs appeared to be a heresy. Federalists were free-trader Yankees, even though they favored helping national industries. The split would eventually lead to the Whig Party. Clay forged a new path for American capitalism that was nationalistic. It was a Magna Charta of American economic freedom. Clay realized that economic war was a reality in the world of the 1800s. Clay's vision was similar to Jefferson's, differing only in that industry was substituted for agriculture. Like Eisenhower in the 1950s, Clay envisioned a system of national transportation to support industrial growth. Clay molded a powerful new philosophy which blended Jeffersonian independence with economic manifest destiny. Clay went further to justify his "American System" by blending in a claim of American moral superiority with nationalistic capitalism. The momentum had turned in Clay's favor by 1824. The struggle, however, would not end, as skillful opponents arose such as Daniel Webster.

Congress in 1824 moved to debate even more extensive tariffs. Clay, the orator, would emerge as leader of this industrial movement. He thundered in Congress with an oratory reminiscent of Patrick Henry a generation earlier:

> Is there no remedy within the reach of the government? Are we doomed to behold our industry languish and decay yet more and more? But there is a remedy, and the remedy consists in modifying our foreign policy, and adopting a genuine American System. We must naturalize the arts in our country, and we must naturalize them by the only means, which the wisdom of nations has yet discovered to be effectual — by adequate protection against the otherwise overwhelming influence of foreigners. This can only be accomplished by the establishment of a tariff.[9]

Clay struggled against his oratorical match, Daniel Webster, and the entire Southern wing of the House of Representatives. Daniel Webster of New Hampshire opposed the tariff because it might hurt the New England shipping industry. Clay persisted, and on April 16 the Tariff of 1824 passed, 107 to 102. Ohio supported the tariff, not only in the Mahoning Valley but also in more western

---

8 Thomas Cochran and William Miller, *The Age of Enterprise*, (New York: Harper & Row, 1942), 12
9 Robert Remini, *Henry Clay: Statesman of the Union*, (New York: W. W. Norton & Co., 1991), 230

counties where an infant wool industry was emerging. President Monroe signed it in May. The Tariff of 1824 extended the general level of protection to 35% ad valorem (the percentage of value as represented by the invoice). The Tariff included cotton, wool, and iron products also extended it to the hemp producers of Clay's Kentucky.

Clay's politics started a change in what would become the core of McKinley's base — the Mahoning Valley, Niles, Youngstown, Canton, Pittsburgh, and Ohio's Western Reserve. These old frontier areas had a large Scots-Irish population who had opposed (with guns) the whiskey taxes of the Federalists. They tended to be frontier Jeffersonian, but the protection on wool and iron by Clay started to build base for a new type of Federalist. Industrialization was changing the area as well. National roads and canals favored the growth of these areas, which was fundamental to Federalist theory. This old Ohio frontier was also similar to Clay's Kentucky congressional district.

The victory of the 1824 tariff bill split the nation and cost Henry Clay the presidency in 1824. Clay would further develop his American System as Secretary of State for the new president John Q. Adams, but political opposition in the South was growing too, gathering behind Andrew Jackson and the Democrats.

The Jacksonians were positioning for a presidential run, and found success early by taking control of the Twentieth Congress in 1827. The Jacksonians of the Democratic Party had strength in the West and South. The result of the popularity of tariffs in the Eastern and Midwestern states and political division led to the "Tariff of Abominations." The Democrats actually allowed an unbalanced tariff to be passed by the National Republicans, turning the measure into future votes for the Democrats and ultimately lower tariffs. The bill extended the tariff on certain products from Ohio, Pennsylvania, Kentucky, and New York by increasing the duties on iron, spirits, hemp, and molasses. The wool products of New England, which Clay had initially used to justify the earlier tariffs, were basically ignored with a modest increase. Clay could only watch as the bill passed, assuring future Jackson votes in the powerful Northeast. President Adams signed it because its usefulness outweighed future political problems. The Tariff of Abominations would in retrospect give Jackson and the free trading Democrats the White House, set back the nationalistic tariff policy of Clay, and move the nation towards civil war. The Jacksonian movement strengthened the Democrats on the Ohio frontier because of the personal popularity of Andrew Jackson.

To focus solely on the political ramifications of Clay's American System, however, would also be to overlook the realization of Clay's (and ultimately McKinley's) dream of an Industrial Eden. It was a system where tariffs were focused to help new industries, and the revenues were used to build roads and canals. In the

Northeast, textile mills were growing; in Pennsylvania and Ohio, iron furnaces were being built; and the nation was moving from an underdeveloped country to an industrialized one in the first decades of the 1800s. The American system of industrialization was criticized by industrial critics such as Charles Dickens as utopian. The manufacturing methods and automation of industry was rapidly becoming the standard of efficiency for the world. Pioneering industrialists such as Francis Cabot Lowell started to develop uniquely American textile factories. While the work was still physically demanding, the factories were clean and offered schooling and training. Even old Jeffersonians were proud of the rise of American manufacturing supremacy.

Part of the superiority could be found in the American "factory system." The tariffs and government contracts produced high volumes never previously encountered, allowing a shift in many industries from a crafts system to the factory system. In 1812, Thomas Jefferson had contracted Eli Whitney to produce weapons with interchangeable parts; it was the first government contract. The Springfield Armory under Colonel Roswell Lee advanced the factory system in the 1820s with the application of labor specialization and automation. The real progress was not so much in the ability to produce standardized and large quantities of weapons, but the growth of the new industry of machine making to support such industries. The Tariff of 1824 had built a foundation for investment by stabilizing the market for industrial goods. In the 1830s, America was becoming a nation of mechanics — as exemplified by the appearance of mechanics' institutes, schools, magazines, and newspapers. The Franklin Institute of Philadelphia was founded in 1824 to promote the advance of mechanics and science.

The protective tariffs caused an industrial boom in New England's textile industry. The textile manufacturers were well protected and the industry grew; but what is more important, it birthed the machine industry. Utilizing the water power of the Connecticut River, the machinery industry expanded to support textile manufacture, arms manufacture, and farming equipment. The growth caused England's greatest machinists to immigrate to New England. They came with British machines, which were reverse engineered in New England and then enhanced into better machines. At the 1851 Crystal Palace Exhibition, the British were shocked and humbled by the American machine technology. The Connecticut Valley would become a bastion of tariff support for Clay and then McKinley.

The tariff created volume, and stabilization in the textile industry ushered in an era of invention and technology after 1812. An 1837 survey by the state legislature of Pennsylvania of the textile industry reported the amazing advance:

Ten years ago, it was generally supposed, that few improvements in machinery could take place. The machinery of that day is now useless; and another period of ten years may make the same difference; manufacturers are subject, in this particular, to a heavy tax. He who advances with the times, must incur the cost of continual improvement; he who lags behind, must lose in the cost of his production. The success of the American textile industry was a manufacturing miracle attracting the world's manufacturers, writers, and politicians.[10]

Henry Clay toured the textile industry several times in the 1830s to further promote his "American System." One of the mills was named after Henry Clay to honor his protective tariffs. Even Clay's enemy Andrew Jackson honored the textile industry with a personal tour. Clay was now able to address the hero of free trade and the Democrats — Adam Smith. Adam Smith's 1776 book *Wealth of Nations* had become the banner for free trade. Henry Clay now argued that free trade could reduce prices in the short run but at the expense of capital investment, invention, and automation. Furthermore, Clay saw capitalism as a national philosophy, not an attribute of free trade. Still, the farming majority saw it much differently, fearing international reprisals and higher prices for domestic goods.

Henry Clay, the lawyer, had actually read Smith's long and difficult narrative. Clay understood the weakness of the Scotsman's ideal of free trade. Smith had allowed for a number of exceptions in his free trade proposals such as defense industries. By doing so, Smith allowed exceptions for some of Britain's strongest industries. Clay saw industry itself as basic to America's defense. Clay believed in capitalism at the national level but felt political factors restricted the type of international capitalism suggested by Adam Smith. Furthermore, Clay was a true bigot, asserting that America was in some way superior and had a divine destiny. The survival of this form of economy and the society it engendered depended on the productivity of its laborers. To Clay, protectionism was critical to the American way of life. He further argued that Smith had based his thesis on the trade-based economy of Scotland, where industry was negligible. Clay's friend and amateur economist John Q. Adams agreed. Both of these men would champion the "American System" as a political alternative.

Another innovation of the 1820s was the development of utopian manufacturing communities. These movements came from Europe as part of the reaction to the miserable working conditions in factories. These manufacturing communities were essentially Jeffersonian in nature. They were self-sufficient communities, growing food and manufacturing implements. These manufacturing communities included the Shaker communities of Kentucky and New England, New Harmony of Indiana, Economy of Pennsylvania, Zoar of Ohio, and Oneida of New

---

10 Anthony Wallace, *Rockdale* (Lincoln: University of Nebraska Press, 1972), 186

York. Henry Clay had invested in the Shaker community near his home in Kentucky. Their success allowed them to sell their excess to surrounding communities as well as to invest in other American manufacturing. Before its closing in the 1870s, Economy Village in Pennsylvania was a major stockholder of the Pennsylvania Railroad. Clay never tired of touring these industrial communities. He was convinced that clean, comfortable living was compatible with manufacturing.

Clay's industrial vision was growing in 1828, but it lacked a national political base. The success of the American System was still a regional phenomenon, allowing Democrat Andrew Jackson to take the White House in 1828. The Jacksonians represented the Jeffersonian legacy of free trade and low tariffs, drawing support from the South and West. The Jacksonians' efforts to reduce tariffs were somewhat muted in Congress by Clay and his followers. Jackson's popularity won him re-election over a challenge by Henry Clay. The Tariff of Abominations in 1828 had caused the legislature of South Carolina to pass a Nullification Act. For the sake of the union, Henry Clay compromised with the Jacksonians to pass a slightly reduced tariff. The Jackson administration was a constant problem for protectionists such as Clay, yet the industrialism of the North and East represented a growing political base. The Jacksonians would bring down the National Bank system, but tariffs remained with only minor reductions.

The Jacksonians had much success through the 1830s and 1840s in defeating the creation of a national bank and holding the line on tariffs. Jackson's down-home popularity brought both political success and a social counter-revolution. A Pulitzer Prize-winning historian of the period defined the social core of Jackson's democrats: "The Jacksonians believed that there was a deep-rooted conflict in society between the 'producing' and 'non-producing' classes — the farmers and laborers, on the one hand, and the business community on the other."[11] Furthermore, the Jacksonians saw the working class as oppressed by the business class. It was American-style socialism, and as always, the clash of interests between one class and another could generate votes. Jackson's popularity as a war hero helped him win the presidency. In 1832, Jackson beat Clay in the presidential election by 4,707 votes in Ohio, but carried the eastern "Western Reserve" area of Ohio where McKinley's ancestors had moved in the 1830s.

Still, in the Congress of 1832, the Clay-based tariff was passed with the help of both Ohio senators and all the representatives' support. Ohio's growing manufacturing base, the need for more money, and its road and canal system had built support for the ideas of Clay, if not the man. The Tariff of 1832, in particular, helped a booming wool production industry in Ohio. Northeast Ohio, including

---

11 Arthur M. Schlesinger, *The Age of Jackson*, (New York: Konecky & Konecky, 1971

canal counties such as Mahoning, Stark, Portage, Summit, Medina, Belmont, and Columbiana, were rivaling New England in the production of wool. The wool and iron industries were leading the urbanization movement in Ohio as well as creating a new middle class of workers. Ohio's prosperity can be directly linked to Clay's American System, and in many ways Clay had stronger support in Ohio than in his home state of Kentucky. Columbiana and Mahoning counties were a stronghold of the Whigs, including the McKinley family. These "Western Reserve" Whigs would become the foundation of the Republican Party in Ohio.

The counter-revolution of Clay and Webster resulted in an alliance between labor and capital under protectionism, which would be embodied in the formation of the Whig party. Clay believed the laborer to be part of American capitalism. This fundamental premise of an alliance of labor and capital and the strength of that alliance would define the success of the new Whig party as well as the Republican Party for the next 60 years. To counter the folk hero image of Andrew Jackson, the Whigs elected Davy Crockett of Tennessee to Congress. They would also attract future leaders such as Abe Lincoln and a young William McKinley in the 1850s.

As slavery and regional differences took center stage in the 1840s and 1850s, Clay refined and supported his American System. The American System was built on four pillars:

1. Tariff protection for industrialization development versus income
2. Tariff rates to be based on the need of American industries and national interests
3. Tariff revenues to be applied for the development of national infrastructure
4. A strong central bank to assure capital for investment.[12]

Clay firmly believed the role of government was to promote, monitor, and maintain industrial growth.

In particular, Clay and his Whigs believed in the old Federalist idea of a strong transportation network of roads and canals to foster manufacturing. Clay's tariffs helped supply money for the Erie Canal in the 1820s. By the 1830s, the Ohio Canal system connected the Western Reserve" to the Erie Canal and Western Pennsylvania. This allowed iron, iron ore, coal, wool, and other products to flow into or from international markets. The price of shipping a ton of iron product to the east dropped from $125 to $25 a ton. It was a boom for eastern and southern Ohio, but generally the taxes found a lot of opposition outside the manufacturing areas. Columbiana County and the Mahoning Valley prospered from the canal.

12 Clay to Senator Johnston of Louisiana, July 23, 1831, in Clay, *Papers*, vol. VIII, 375

Cast iron pig bars and iron products found large markets in New York and New England. The low sulfur nature of Ohio-produced iron made it extremely popular in Eastern markets because of its toughness. Glass products, which could not be shipped by wagon over the mountains without major breakage, could move by canal. The canal system would give way to the railroads in the 1880s, but Governor McKinley made one last unsuccessful effort to revive it in the 1890s.

In this respect, his policy was consistent with his Federalist roots and became the foundation of the Whig Party in the 1840s. Henry Clay's program was, at its core, an American system. Clay felt that America had to come first in government policy. It was patriotic, not economic, at its core. He believed that America would be the light of the world — but not its master. He firmly believed that if the government asked Americans to fight and die to protect the economic/social set up, then the government owed them job protection. In trade negotiations, he maintained that American workers were the first priority.

In 1844, Clay ran for president, gaining the Whig Party nomination through the strong support of Ohio's "Western Reverse Whigs" in the iron-producing northeast Ohio. Puritan New Englanders had settled the "Western Reserve" until the 1830s. The Western Reserve would also be the cradle of Republicanism and McKinley's area of strength. While Clay carried Ohio, he lost nationally to James Polk. In 1844, the Whigs took control of the legislature of the United States. Both McKinley's grandfather and father were Whigs, and as Pennsylvania and Ohio residents were major supporters of Clay.

Clay's hypothesis would be proven over and over again as the nation's tariff rates varied up and down. Economists and historians have ignored the evidence since free trade economics came in vogue after World War II. The 1840s, 1880s, and 1890s are decades that appear to be designed experiments on the efficiency of tariffs in promoting growth, invention, and jobs. In the 1840s, railroad rails accounted for one third of the demand for iron, and the manufacture of this iron tells a vivid story of the impact of tariffs. In the 1832 Tariff, Congress exempted railroad iron from the tariff, concluding that American rails lacked the quality, technology, and cost to compete with the rails of Britain. Almost all railroad iron was imported from Britain. Britain had the rolling mill technology to produce the T or H rail, while America lacked this ability to roll these shapes. Britain's coal-produced iron was also superior in quality to that produced by wood fires. The American iron industry was driven by low tech heating, using hardwood because of its easy availability, while Britain had adopted coal, gaining quality and efficiency. In the 1840s, the American iron industry was consuming more forest acreage than Brazil today. Interestingly, Brazil still uses wood to make iron because of the availability of rain forest wood.

Henry Clay was one of the few in Congress that had not given up on America's ability to produce railroad iron. The Whigs and Clay took over both Houses of Congress in 1840, setting up the tariff of 1842 which specifically included railroad iron as well as restoring the overall tariff levels of 1832. It would be Clay's last tariff bill, as he resigned prior to its actual passage. As a result of the high tariff, the investment in iron rolling technology and coal furnace technology boomed. By 1844 mills such as Mt. Savage in Maryland were rolling the first T iron rails. Furthermore, that year a number of iron furnaces such as those built by the Phoenix Company were making coal-smelted pig iron.[13] In 1847, Congress reduced the tariff, allowing Britain to flood the rail market with cheap iron to keep their furnaces running. By 1850, of the fifteen rail companies that had started in America due to the Tariff of 1842, only two were still in production. In the early 1850s Britain took iron production away from America to support its needs in the Crimean War. American market prices rose due to a shortage, bringing American producers back into the market.

Thanks to the Tariff of 1842, an American iron rail industry was developed in time for the railroad boom of the 1870s which saw the rise of Carnegie Steel. Until the 1870s, British iron rails had ruled because of their price and quality. The 1842 tariff allowed Americans to make the necessary investments and develop the technology to improve quality. Clay realized that without protection or some form of subsidy, strategic American industries would never develop. In the 1870s and 1880s, the continued Republican tariffs allowed the infant American steel industry to flourish with the world's largest and most technologically advanced rail mills at Johnston and Braddock, Pennsylvania. By 1898 American steel ruled the world and employed tens of thousands of workers, and American steel rails were being shipped to China and Europe. During this period of protectionism, the miracle of steel technology emerged from iron production, American furnace sizes dwarfed their European counterparts, American steel quality was uncontested, and the America steel industry overtook all other industrialized nations. Henry Clay's vision for iron and manufacturing would be fully realized during the McKinley administration.

Clay would live to see the world hail his "American System" at the Great Exhibition of 1851. Queen Victoria and Prince Albert had designed the World Exhibition to be a coronation of Britain's industrial supremacy, but it was the upstart Americans who captured the crowds in the Crystal Palace. In particular, the heavily protected textile, ordnance, and woodworking mills showed advanced machinery that challenged Britain's claim to be the world's premier

13 Thomas Cochran, *Frontiers of Change*, (New York: Oxford University Press, 1981), 106

manufacturer. Prince Albert formed a Committee on the Manufacturing of the United States.

How had the world's best example of Adam Smith's free trade principles been trumped by the world's greatest protectionists? According to Adam Smith, protectionism would suppress innovation and invention. What had happened was that the stabilized manufacturing market attracted capital investment and that stimulated innovation. The committee found that American manufacturing aggressively pursued experimentation and invention. What's more, the free trade environment in England had reduced investment in the manufacturing of machinery. Furthermore, since the 1820s, there had been a steady immigration of mechanics to the United States. Clay, not Smith, had correctly predicted that the application of free trade principles would alter Britain from a great manufacturing nation to a nation of merchants. The same trend can be seen today in the United States.

Clay found support and hope in the textile factories of Lowell, Massachusetts. One of the deep fears of the Jeffersonians was that American cities would become the "Satanic mills" of England. The great textile mills of Lowell were much different places. They were relatively positive and healthy working environments in the 1830s. Ventilation and light were abundant. The communities offered education for the working men and women as well. The workers earned enough, with the aid of company-supported housing, to save money. Clay would often send critics to Lowell to see the "American System." Things were not as utopian as advertised, but it was a dramatic improvement over British cities such as Manchester. Lowell would even win over Daniel Webster to protectionism, and when he became president, Andrew Jackson faced hundreds of banners declaring "Protection for American Industries." This is the model that H. J. Heinz, George Westinghouse, and George Pullman would hope to emulate decades later.

Clay found little presidential support in his lifetime, but his visits to manufacturing areas such as Pittsburgh, New England, the Mahoning Valley, and Cincinnati produced the largest crowds ever seen in American politics. Mills, factories, furnaces, mines, and streets (and many children such as Henry Clay Frick of Pennsylvania) were named after him.

After his death in 1852, a young Abraham Lincoln took up the cause of the American System, and it remained the cornerstone of Republican administrations throughout the last half of the 19th century thanks to William McKinley. Lincoln used tariffs to raise money for the war, which was a basic use of tariffs as proposed by the federalists. Lincoln's economic advisor, Henry C. Carey was a huge supporter of Clay's American System. Carey saw the free trade of the British as a great error, stating in his 1851 book *The Harmony of Interests*:

> The whole basis of their [England's] system is conversion and exchange, and not production, yet neither makes any addition to the amount of things to be exchanged. It is the great boast of their system that the exchangers are so numerous and the producers so few, and the proportion which the former bear to the latter the more rapid is supposed to be the advance towards perfect prosperity. Converters and exchangers, however, must live, and they must live out the labor of others: and if three, five, or ten persons are to live on the product of one, it must follow that all will obtain but a small allowance of necessaries or comforts of life, as is seen to be the case.

These words certainly ring true today to those of protectionism. Carey became a key political ally of Clay, forming the Pennsylvania Society for the Encouragement of Manufacture, as well as the American Industry League. Carey was a prolific writer in support of tariffs throughout his career.

Carey requires some note because he was the most influential economist of the 1850s, 1860s, and 1870s. He was for easy money and strong tariff support, ideas supported by both Clay and McKinley. He understood the nature of the money supply as a stimulus, and supported the printing of greenback dollars. Today, of course, he would be considered an inflationist; but he argued that while inflation hurt the bankers, it helped the manufacturers. He correctly identified the "enemy" as the Eastern banking concerns as banking monopolists who favored importing and trade. Carey argued that these bankers were actually hostile to American industrial enterprise. Carey also predicted the banker's takeover of the railroad industry to control trade. His writings foreshadowed the rise and dominance of J. P. Morgan in the McKinley era. Carey was the major influence on Lincoln's tariff policy that would become the policy of the Republican Party for many decades. Carey's disciples in the Congress such as "Pig Iron" Kelley and Thaddeus Stevens carried the protectionist banner in the time period between Clay and McKinley.

Clay's struggle to fulfill what he called the industrial destiny of America consumed a lifetime. He built a philosophy and even a party to support his American System, but the realization of his dream eluded him. Congressman McKinley would take up the fight for Clay's American System. He would suffer setbacks and defeats in his almost single-minded effort, but America would reap the benefits. Clay and his American System inspired two presidents who idolized him, Lincoln and McKinley. In a keynote address in 1912 at Cleveland's Chamber of Commerce Hall before then-President Taft, Senator Chauncey DePew said: "That was the service of McKinley in his 20 years of grueling combat for the American System. He put value into every rod of real estate — he reinforced the good right arm of every honest man — he made it possible for the American brain to conquer the obstacles of nature — and create a great workshop on the American continent. In so doing he prodigiously increased the scope and influence of American moral and spiritual ideals — and caused the nation to leap forward with accelerated pace in its march toward human happiness. When the Dingley bill was passed in 1897, McKinley's great service for industry was completed, and the nation took its rightful place of influence and power among the mighty workmen of man."

Chapter 3. The Formative Years in an Industrial Family

> If there is a lesson in my life or death, let it be taught to those who
> still live and have the destiny of their country in their keeping.
>
> — *William McKinley*

William McKinley came from a long line of ironmasters, blacksmiths, and manufacturers. Two of his great grandfathers served in the Revolutionary War and a grandfather in the War of 1812. On his father's side, William was one of the industrious Scotch-Irish or Scots-Irish who were also known as the "Ulster Scots," Scottish Highlanders (Protestants) who had been enticed to Northern Ireland in the 1600s to colonize Ireland for the British. Finding little religious and economic freedom in Ireland, they immigrated to America. They were Presbyterians who were often persecuted by the British because of their strict Calvinism and commitment to the Scottish Kirk. This group would become the early industrialists of America. James McKinley, William's great-great grandfather, came to a Scotch-Irish settlement in the South as a blacksmith and ironmonger. On his mother's side, his descendants included Dutch blacksmiths who fled Europe with William Penn; they established an iron furnace around Doylestown, Pennsylvania, which produced cannon balls for the Revolutionary War. His great grandfather, David McKinley, moved to western Pennsylvania with a group of Scotch-Irish to start an iron making business. Western Pennsylvania was the frontier at the time, allowing the McKinleys to produce iron without the interference of the British Iron Act of 1750, which prohibited the colonies from producing iron products. George Washington's brother Lawrence also had a frontier iron furnace near western Pennsylvania. This area was rich in low-grade iron ore and hardwood fuel.

McKinley's great grandfather, David McKinley, joined the many Scots-Irish iron-making settlements (which they called iron plantations) in Westmoreland County, Pennsylvania, east of Pittsburgh, after service in the Revolutionary War. Like most of Westmoreland County, David McKinley was a Jefferson Democrat. McKinley had participated in the Whiskey Rebellion of the 1790s. This area experienced a boom in 1812, as armaments were needed for renewed war with Britain. The British had suppressed iron making for centuries in America. The Scots-Irish responded as they always did to a lucrative opportunity, opening new furnaces in Pennsylvania and eastern Ohio. Immediately after the American victory in that war, the British began dumping cheap iron and textiles on the American market. While the British lost the military war, they imparted a crushing economic blow to American industry from 1813 to 1824. The flood of British goods resulted in the first recession in America, known as the Panic of 1819. Particularly hard hit was the western Pennsylvania iron industry. Baltimore editor Hezekiah Niles (the namesake of Niles, Ohio) teamed up with Pennsylvanian, Matthew Carey to pursue Henry Clay, Speaker of the House, to bring action in Congress. The result was the Tariff of 1824, which was America's first protective tariff.

Both lines of McKinley's descendants were drawn to the new iron ore deposits of the Mahoning Valley near Youngstown. This ore was known as "kidney ore," and while low grade, it would provide the historical roots of the Youngstown steel industry. The brown colored kidney shaped stones can still be seen in the valleys around Youngstown. The McKinleys came to New Lisbon, Ohio to open an iron business. Furnace operations in the Mahoning Valley had started before the War of 1812. This kidney or bog ore, while low grade according to today's standards, was superior to the ores of western Pennsylvania and thus pulled iron producers to the area. James Heaton began operating a furnace and forge on Yellow Creek near Poland, Ohio. Heaton was one of the first Americans to produce rolled iron bar, a product that would reign in the area for a hundred years. Gideon Hughes had also built a charcoal furnace at New Lisbon and partnered with the president's grandfather, James McKinley.

McKinley's father, William Sr., was born in New Lisbon in 1807. The McKinleys produced cannonball in the War of 1812 and cast iron products in the peace. William Sr. moved to nearby Niles in the 1830s. The president's parents, Nancy Allison and William McKinley, Sr., married in Niles, Ohio. William Sr. was a manager and part owner of an iron furnace and rolling mill known as Rebecca Furnace. The family and the region depended on the tariffs that Henry Clay provided in order to keep their furnaces profitable. The better technology, economies of scale, and government support had given the British iron industry major advantages. The furnaces of America still used wood for fuel while the British industry had converted to coal. Coal produced iron more economically and with higher quality. The struggling infant iron industry needed stability to experiment with coal as a fuel to make the necessary furnace adjustments. The Niles-Youngstown area had coal seams and that would further advance experimentation. The Clay tariffs were just starting to generate the capital needed for such research and development in the 1840s.

The charcoal iron furnace industry of the early 1800s depended on iron ore, limestone, and most important, hardwood or hardwood charcoal for fuel. Also, a source of waterpower was needed to power the bellows to raise the heat. All necessary elements came together in the Mahoning Valley and Hocking Hills area of Ohio. The first furnace in the Mahoning Valley was on Yellow Creek in 1802. The operation of a furnace was hard work. The Scots-Irish were known to mix heavy drinking with iron making, but the McKinley's' conversion to Methodism kept them sober managers (much like the ironmaster in Dickens's *Bleak House).* The investment capital and know-how came to Ohio from two sources, the English of Connecticut and the German and Scots-Irish of western Pennsylvania.

Niles, Ohio also had a secondary boom in 1830s as a very rich layer of black iron ore was discovered at Mineral Ridge. Niles soon became not only a smelting town, but it grew its rolling mills for iron and steel. The Mahoning Valley was probably far ahead of Pittsburgh as an iron center in the 1840s due to the ore deposits of the valley and its canal system linking it to Cleveland. Many were comparing the Mahoning Valley's manufacture of iron products to America's earliest manufacturing center in the Connecticut Valley. In 1853, the first shipments of rich Lake Superior ore arrived in the Mahoning Valley via Cleveland and the northeast Ohio canal system. The canal system was the national priority of Henry Clay, and a key cause of the area's industrial development. The McKinleys had a series of small furnaces in the Mahoning Valley from the early 1800s. McKinley's father and Niles would struggle through America's first depression known as the Panic of 1837. Money for investment dried up and demand for iron products dropped dramatically. This depression and period of bank failures would make Niles a center for Henry Clay's Whig party. The Ohio canal system helped the area out of the depression by giving access to new product markets.

In the early 1840s, the Mahoning Valley iron makers made a breakthrough in blast furnace technology by using the newly found coal deposits. These coal deposits were found near Niles on Mineral Ridge. The technology saved the Mahoning Valley industry from extinction due to the lumbering out of the hardwood forest. It also created a new mining industry in the area. Niles, Youngstown, and

Columbiana County all prospered with the use of coal in blast furnaces. The area also started to pioneer rolling mills producing bar stock and plate. Additionally, the mills started to produce nails, which were badly needed on the Western frontier. The Eastern markets grew with canals since wagon train shipment of iron over the mountains was difficult and costly. Blast furnace iron made by coal or coke was cleaner and stronger, giving the Mahoning Valley an edge in the world market.

It was in Niles that William McKinley, the future president, was born on January 29, 1843, into a large family of seven children (an additional brother and sister were born after him). It was the same year that Karl Marx and Friedrich Engels met and started the socialist movement, which would be a factor in President McKinley's assassination. Henry Clay's Whig party was in control with Whig president John Tyler in the White House. The McKinley families were Whigs and abolitionists. The Whig Party stood for abolition, a federalist approach to government, a strong banking system, and growth of American industry. But their rise to power occurred with their support of protective tariffs, a national bank to supply investment capital, and a strong network of roads and canals to support commerce. The Mahoning Valley of Ohio was a Whig (and future Republican) stronghold. McKinley was born in Niles in a large two-story house that would fit into a middle-class suburb today.

When McKinley was eleven, his family moved to the nearby and upscale village of Poland, Ohio on Yellow Creek. Poland's Old Stone Tavern was an important stagecoach stop between Pittsburgh and Cleveland. Poland at the time was experiencing an industrial boom due to the discovery of bituminous coal that could be used in the area's iron furnaces. McKinley's parents had selected Poland because of its academy and strong educational system. William's father had always been a promoter of education, having served for years on the school board of Niles, Ohio. More importantly for William, he was born into a family that had a passion for learning and education. The academy the McKinleys attended was part of Poland Union Seminary owned by the Methodist Church. An academy was a type of high school offering study of religion as well as the basic subjects. Like the Methodist Church, the academy was strongly antislavery. Poland's political leanings reflected antislavery enthusiasm by giving Lincoln 78% of its votes in the election of 1860. The area was also an important station on the Underground Railroad. McKinley's political views were developed early in this Republican and former Whig stronghold. His family fully reflected the areas politics.

The nine children with parents would gather every evening for reading sessions. Their modest library included the novels of Charles Dickens, Gibson's *De-*

cline and Fall, G. A. Henty's tales of Scotland's William Wallace, and *Uncle Tom's Cabin*. McKinley often noted the powerful impact the book *Uncle Tom's Cabin* had on him, drawing him to the abolition policies of Lincoln's Republican party. Young McKinley became a lover of Walter Scott and Robert Burns, like so many of the young Scots-Irish of the time including industrialists Andrew Carnegie and Andrew Mellon. Young McKinley's favorite novels were *Robinson Crusoe* and *Swiss Family Robinson*. The central book for the family was, however, the Bible, which was read every night. For a small town in Ohio, the McKinley family subscribed to a number of major periodicals such as *Harpers Monthly, Atlantic Monthly*, and the *New York Weekly Tribune*. *Harpers Monthly*, in particular, presented a heroic view of American manufacturing and science, as well as an antislavery view. Reading late into the night would be a lifelong habit of William McKinley.

When McKinley entered the academy, he loved Latin, Greek, poetry, and mathematics. He had a particular love of poetry, especially that of Byron, Burns, and Longfellow. His mother, a strong influence throughout his life, hoped he would be drawn to a religious career in the Methodist Church. There is some evidence that he gave such a religious career some thought. He enjoyed Sunday school and summer church camps. McKinley's favorite extra-curricular activity was Everett Literary and Debating Society of Poland. One of his earliest debates included those on protectionism and Henry Clay's American System. He loved studying and seemed to have a healthy balance of physical activity and study, even though he was described in his youth as "pale and slight in build."

He participated in athletics and enjoyed dancing, but he also took to working summers in his father's foundry and forge. He was fond of a game called "Old Sow", which was a cross between field hockey and golf. His mother noted his fondness for "bow and arrows", kite flying, and marbles.[14] He enjoyed a pick-up game of baseball. Fishing was too slow paced for this active youth, but he enjoyed skating in the winter and swimming in the summer. The skates he used were made by one of the many blacksmiths' shops that manufactured products for the valley. One of his boyhood friends, Joseph Butler, who would become a steel master, steel historian, and Director of the American Iron and Steel Institute, was involved with him in a near-drowning incident. Butler would remain a lifetime friend and industrial consultant. Through Butler, McKinley had direct ties to American industry often overlooked by later biographers, who saw Mark Hanna as McKinley's industry contact. Butler was one of a key group of friends and industrialists who McKinley talked to informally over the years.

---

14 H. Wayne Morgan, *William McKinley and His America*, (Syracuse: Syracuse University, 1963), 10

McKinley worked various part-time jobs including those in the rolling mills and forges. His friend and biographer, Marshall Everett, reminisced after McKinley's death:

> And it was proof of still another virtue on the lad's part that he preferred, of all the industries that came to his hand, the heavy labor of the forge and foundry. Those years of healthful life, when native powers were developed by bodily industry, when regular hours, plain but abundant food, and long hours of restful sleep were adding to brain and brawn, when the wise mother was guiding him so gently in morals and manners — in those years the character of a future President, the statesman, the soldier, and American patriot, was formed.[15]

This American Spartan, combining academic study with industrial working experience, was the ideal man to defend American manufacturing. He would be America's first middle class president, and he certainly was our first president to labor in a factory. He could argue on Adam Smith's theories, and show empathy to the workers.

The Mahoning Valley, being a manufacturing area, knew well the ups and downs of economic cycles. The early 1850s saw an industrial expansion as coal and iron production expanded. An illuminating energy crisis arose with the diminishing supplies of whale oil pushing prices high. Mahoning Valley had several pioneering companies develop a technique to produce illuminating oil from coal. The canals allowed rich lake ores to flow into the valley as well as high quality coal from Pennsylvania. Whig control in the late 1840s and early 1850s favored iron tariffs for the area and industrial prosperity. The area would, in return, further expand the iron smelting technology via Lake Superior ores, which would fuel the steel industry for over a century and a half. The area's furnace owners' Whig support became known as the "Pig Iron Aristocracy." The "Pig Iron Aristocracy" was known for its ironclad control of area politics and included old friends like Joe Butler and James Ward. They were accused by the Democrats of handing out Republican ballots to their workers and buying votes. When the Democrats took back the Whitehouse in 1853, the iron industry lost favor, and many suggested they were being punished through tariff reductions.

McKinley's father remained working at the furnace and forge in Niles, usually staying overnight and riding to Poland on weekends. One of the overlooked points of McKinley biographers was the loss of his father's furnace operation during the recession of 1857. A flood of cheap British iron, reduction of iron tariffs, and banking credit problems created a pullback in the Mahoning Valley. Furthermore, the Panic of 1857 was a worldwide industrial depression that lowered iron demand and prices. The British lowered iron prices to export more to

---

15 Marshall Everett, *Complete Life of William McKinley*, (Marshall Everett: 1902), 124

America. America could not compete with the British economies of scale, and the Mahoning Valley had to bank its furnaces. The American iron industry was made up of hundreds of privately owned furnaces, which could not get the raw material price breaks or the operating efficiencies of the huge British companies. In good economic times, American furnaces could garnish a market in surplus demand, but in downturns, the American iron industry was not competitive. The up and down cycles prevented long term investment, so the Americans had a built-in disadvantage. Protected industries felt secure enough to make long-term investment even in tough times. McKinley's father re-invested in the iron industry, but had to travel weekly to Michigan. The middle class McKinley family experiences first hand the struggle of economic hard times and mill closings. There is no question that this impacted the young McKinley's views on economic policy. His belief in a full dinner pail was rooted in the economic cycles impact on his own family. They knew first hand the worries over feeding a family when a mill closes, and the strain on the breadwinner to find work. McKinley understood that the biggest fear of the mill worker of the period was not low wages or poor working conditions but unemployment. This was an insight that few politicians shared, and few presidents in our history have had this type of personal experiences with economic downturns.

The McKinley family was an artifact of the industrial revolution which saw the rise of a new middle class. Clearly the McKinley family, going back several generations from the president, was part of this new emerging middle class. In the 1700s, the middle class of the mercantile system were the traders and shop owners. The new middle class of the Industrial Revolution included foremen, managers, small factory owners, and investors, and evolved from the merger of capitalism and democracy. This middle class was uniquely dependent on the strength of the domestic economy. These middle class families wanted growth in the economy, protected industries, strong defense, upward mobility, and support for family values. Inflation was not a major concern if it came with industrial prosperity. Unlike the old middle class of traders and shop owners, they wanted protection for their source of income: domestic industries. Generally they were anti-immigration and wanted easy money. In terms of the debates of the 1800s, they wanted bimetallism for more growth versus the gold standard of the rich to protect against inflation. McKinley's middle class roots explain some of his ambivalence towards the gold standard supported by the rich capitalists of the Republican Party of his time. This new class cared little for socialism, which appeared as a philosophy in the 1840s, but they were sympathetic for the condition of the poor. Another characteristic was their fierce patriotism and belief in the manifest destiny of America.

Another facet of McKinley's upbringing was his deep religious values, which he shared with most of the workers and middle class. The Scots-Irish McKinleys had deep Presbyterian roots and a strong work ethic. German sociologist Max Weber believed that this "protestant work ethic" was the underpinning of capitalism. McKinley certainly exemplified the linkage of religion, capitalism, and the protestant work ethic. McKinley's parents switched to Methodism when they moved to Niles. In fact, they were charter members of the Niles Methodist Church. While the roots of McKinley's view of capitalism can be seen in his Methodism and he was a devout Christian, he respected all faiths. His biographers noted that he was not a "shouting Methodist." Methodists of the time were going through a major revival by active evangelism and had become America's most popular creed. Many Ohio Presbyterians and Pennsylvanian Scots-Irish converted because of a lack of Presbyterian churches. McKinley, however, was true to his ancestors who had crossed the ocean with William Penn. Later in Canton, McKinley stressed the non-denominational nature of his favorite charity, the YMCA. Many biographers have noted:

> His devout Methodism did not lead him to concern himself with dogma or denominational differences. The loving kindness of God was McKinley's religion, and the source of his inner serenity. . . . He made many friends among Canton's large Roman Catholic population of German and Irish extraction. In a day of sharp sectarianism, McKinley was devoid of bigotry possessing as a grace of his nature that is unconscious of its own virtue.[16]

Christianity was fundamental to McKinley, and it affected how he viewed everything. Like his ancestors, he believed in religious tolerance. While the Mahoning Valley and northeast Ohio had been strongly Methodist and Presbyterians, Canton was a religious melting pot, not only of Protestants and Catholics but Amish, Mennonite, German Reformed, and Quakers who required this type of tolerance. It is true also that while McKinley linked strong religious values with the rise of capitalism, he departed from the Weberian thesis that it was the result of a few Protestant denominations. This tolerance for all faiths was a critical factor in McKinley's ability to build a labor-management alliance since the labor-management lines often reflected religious lines. Roman Catholics were by far more representative of America's working class.

McKinley's religious beliefs were reflected in his strong abolitionist view. McKinley's mother was an active Methodist and church member. Both parents, as charter members of the Poland Methodist Church, were active in fund raising. Mother McKinley tried in every way to encourage young William to join the ministry. While his mother was dominant in his intellectual formation, his father passed on some key life principles as well. William Sr. became a radical on

---

16 Leech, Margaret, *In the Days of McKinley*, (New York: Harper Brothers,1959), 12

the need to free the slaves, but he went much farther, demanding civil rights for them, too. William McKinley Sr. believed that blacks should have full rights and equal opportunity. This would be a passion for President McKinley as well.

Mother McKinley, as she was known, was the dominant force in his life. She was a strong and somewhat overbearing mother, who did most of the character building of the children. She had to deal with the long absences of William Sr. and family financial problems in the late 1850s. In 1860, Mother McKinley applied her modest savings to get young William into Allegheny College in Meadville, Pennsylvania. McKinley struggled to make ends meet at college. His cousin, friend, and roommate, William McKinley Osborn, went with him to college. At the end of the first year, the money strains became overwhelming and McKinley left college and returned to Poland.[17] He had hoped to return the next year, but his father's finances continued to be problematic due to the continuing recession, the Panic of 1857. Young McKinley was badly needed to help support the family.

He worked for a while in the post office before taking a job as a teacher in a nearby school district for $25 a month.[18] Teaching at the time was a common transitional job for young men. He was only seventeen but was well versed in most subjects and an excellent speaker. He had to walk three miles to the schoolhouse and three miles back each day. In the summer, he returned to work in the post office. As the Civil War approached, the young man was torn between family obligations, the ministry, probably some fear, and his patriotism. In June of 1861, the Sparrow Tavern set up a recruiting station where McKinley and his cousin Osborn enlisted.

In a 1906 address, William Day, Supreme Court Justice and McKinley friend, noted the impact of this interval in McKinley's life: "Brought into early contact through the business of his father, who was an iron-master, with men who would toil in shop and factory, he early conceived a strong sympathy for them, and he became an ardent advocate of every measure which he believed would lead to the betterment of their condition and give them a greater share of the comforts of living."[19] McKinley knew the desire of the middle class to work at a steady job and its importance to families.

He would later note: "The labor of the country constitutes its strength and its wealth; and the better that labor is conditioned, the higher its rewards, the wider its opportunities, and the greater its comforts and refinements, the more sacred

---

17 John Johnson to William McKinley, September 5, 1900, William McKinley Papers, Library of Congress

18 Alexander McClure and Charles Morris, *The Authentic Life of William McKinley*, 1901

19 McKinley Memorial Addresses, (Cleveland: Tippecanoe Club Company, 1913), 181

will be our homes, the more capable will be our children and the nobler will be the destiny that awaits us." Recent biographers and historians have failed to realize the true nature of McKinley's conviction on protecting American industry. For McKinley, protectionism was personal, not just simply economic theory.

Chapter 4. Major McKinley and War Logistics

> With patriotism in our hearts and with the flag of our country in
> the hands of our children, there is no danger of anarchy and there
> will be no danger to the union.
>
> — *William McKinley*

McKinley often felt the years during the Civil War were his best years. He was extremely proud of working his way to the rank of major, where sons of the upper class often started their careers. As America's last president to be a Civil War veteran, he well understood the sacrifices the government had demanded of its citizens. McKinley maintained that his Civil War years were the happiest of his life, and they therefore represent an insight into the nature of the man. The experience had made him extremely patriotic, believing that any soldier had a right to all of America's opportunities. He was a civil rights leader stating that "his black allies" of the war deserved nothing less. He passionately believed that the giving of lives to support the American government obligated the American government to protect American jobs against foreign competition. He believed, like Henry Clay, in American capitalism, not international capitalism. He believed the American government existed for the economic freedom of its citizens and held no foreign obligations.

McKinley's simple, hard-working approach to success can be summarized in his advice to nephew Lieutenant James McKinley during the Spanish American War: "Be attentive to all your duties. Do everything the best you know and if you are in doubt ask some superior officer the best way to do it. Be careful about your writing. See that your words are spelled correctly. Better have a little pocket dictionary with you. It mars an official paper or letter to have a word misspelled."[20] This was almost a statement of McKinley's philosophy of life. Another deep belief of McKinley's was the Whig commitment to freedom from slavery.

The Whigs of the "Pig Iron Aristocracy" helped carry Ohio's iron and coal districts for the Republican Abraham Lincoln. Lincoln easily carried Ohio because of his support for tariffs and abolition. When the news came to Ohio via telegraph on April 12, 1861 that Fort Sumter had been fired on, Ohio quickly rallied with a call to arms. Poland, like most of Ohio, had many patriotic parades and rallies. Interestingly, a month before, the Everett Literacy and Debating Society of Poland had argued whether to stay at Fort Sumter or leave the fort. McKinley was on the losing side of the debate, which supported staying and fighting. Young McKinley, as noted, did not rush to enlist because he had many things to weigh in the decision. Meantime, the Valley was experiencing a demand for iron and bar for war needs. This war could finally relieve the economic problems of the Panic of 1857. As in the War of 1812, the Mahoning Valley would be a key manufacturing contributor to the victory. On a personal level, it would allow McKinley's father to find local work in the iron industry.

McKinley's decision to enlist waited until June and the mustering of the Poland Guards. The decision would be typical of McKinley. He discussed it and thought it over for weeks. McKinley and his cousin, William McKinley Osborn, joined the Poland Guards, a little late, in Columbus, Ohio. Pay for a recruit was $13 a month with a signing bonus of $400. Later in 1863, men could avoid the draft by paying substitutes $300. The Poland Guards joined nine other volunteer units forming the 23rd Ohio Volunteer Infantry, the Poland Guards becoming Company E. William S. Rosecrans was named first colonel and Rutherford B. Hayes was named first major. The regiment was mustered at Camp Jackson, a few miles west of Columbus on the National Road. His company saw McKinley as somewhat bookish, with his copy of Bryon's poems and his dairy. He was selected to be a correspondent to Poland's hometown newspaper the *Mahoning Register*.

The regiment was extremely religious and held many camp gatherings. McKinley's letters to his sister Anna reflect a deep personal sense of religion. The company of Poland Guards, in particular, stood out with two daily religious exercises. McKinley often wrote about the religious meeting, which he clearly enjoyed. The company became known as the "psalm singers of the Western Re-

---

20 William McKinley to James F. McKinley, April 13, 1899, roll 18, William McKinley Papers, Library of Congress

serve." McKinley was a bit of a straight arrow, he did not drink or swear, but did start smoking cigars. As a volunteer unit, they found regular army supplies lacking. The men wanted uniforms badly — McKinley noted that everyone was anxious to wear colorful uniforms, which young men (and women) were always attached to. They were issued only underwear.

McKinley learned an early lesson on the need for strong manufacturing as a national defense priority. Uniform shortages were an inconvenience, but the lack of muskets was another story. When the muskets did arrive, they were smooth bores of 1812 design and manufactured in the 1820s. These young men felt they deserved the very best weapons, but, in general, the Union Armories had mostly 1840 vintage armaments. Five of the regiment's ten companies, including McKinley's, refused to use the muskets. Emotions ran high as a small rebellion and standoff ensued. McKinley recalled, years later: "None of us knew how to use any kind of a musket at the time, but we thought we knew our rights and we were all conscious of the importance [of having viable weapons]." This musket rebellion was not unique to the 23rd Ohio, but was being repeated across the nation as it had in Alexander Hamilton's unit in the Revolutionary War.

The rifled Springfield musket had been well advertised in the 1850s as a triumph of American manufacturing. The Springfield rifle had even been adopted by the US military for general use, but in 1861 there were only enough of them to arm 10% of the regiments.[21] Lincoln was directly involved in the shortage, but the problem went throughout the supply chain. Even the special iron needed for barrels was in short supply and would have to be imported from Europe. America at best produced 15,000 rifles from 1861 to 1862. More than half the Union regiments were supplied with foreign rifles. Lincoln also made a political decision to deliver the new American rifles to border state regiments to keep them in line. Orders for over a million rifles went out to Europe, half of which were never delivered, and the balance were of poor quality. In later years J. P. Morgan was implicated in arms sales fraud and that may have been part of the coolness between McKinley and him during the presidential years. McKinley would come to forgive the Confederates, but he never forgave those in the North that profited from the war, or those in the North who failed to support it — known as "copperheads."

For the 23rd Ohio, Commander Rutherford Hayes settled the rifle controversy, just in time for the regiment's departure for western Virginia. They were being shipped to western Virginia to prevent Confederate raids and protect the Baltimore & Ohio rail tracks. McKinley and Company E were stationed at the small town of Weston. The 23rd were involved in some guerilla actions and a

---

21 Robert V. Bruce, *Lincoln and the Tools of War*, (Chicago: University of Illinois Press, 1989)

few minor battles before settling at Fayetteville in November for winter encampment. McKinley adapted slowly. It also appears Mother McKinley visited him in western Virginia to lift his spirits. As a private McKinley performed the basic duties of camp life with care and attention to every detail. McKinley reminisced as Governor: "I always look back with pleasure upon those fourteen months in which I served in the ranks. They taught me a great deal. I was but a school-boy when I went into the array, and that first year was a formative period in my life, during which I learned much of men and of affairs."

In the spring, McKinley was promoted to commissary sergeant. As commissary sergeant, he learned the need for logistics and manufactured goods to enable an army to function well. He saw first hand how the limited canning capacity and tinplate production in the United States limited supplies to the Union Army. McKinley took to the clerical as well as the logistical requirements of the work. Supply management and logistics were changed with the invention of the tin can. In the early 1800s, Napoleon had offered a reward for a better method of preserving food for his army. Nicholas Appert won the award in 1810 and contributed to freeing his army from daily foraging for food. The United States lacked the tinplate and the tinsmiths to follow suit, being totally dependent on England. Still, the Union was is better shape than the Confederates who had to forage for food.

The wealthy classes entered the army at the officer rank of major, but the lower classes had the opportunity to work their way up the ranks.

In the Battle of Antietam, McKinley earned a battlefield promotion to lieutenant. Antietam, September 17, 1862, would be remembered as the war's bloodiest day. With part of the regiment beaten down, fatigued, and lacking food, McKinley packed wagons of supplies and moved to the front lines to relieve his comrades. The Union army suffered through the night with the casualties stacking up at Burnside's Bridge. McKinley continued to get supplies to the front throughout the battle. He not only earned a promotion, but two years after his assassination, a memorial was erected to honor him at Antietam.

General Hayes wrote the following on the request for promotion: "That battle began at daylight . . . without breakfast, without coffee, they went to fight, and it continued until after the sun had set. Early in the afternoon, naturally enough, with the exertion required of the men, they were famished and thirsty, and to some extent broken in spirit. The commissary department of the brigade was under Sergeant McKinley's administration and personal supervision. From his hands every man in the regiment was served hot coffee and warm meats — a thing that had never occurred under similar circumstances in any other army in the world." From that point on, Hayes followed the progress of and helped his young officer.

McKinley viewed his promotion to the officer ranks as a turning point in his life. He reminisced in an 1888 letter to Hayes: "Let me tell you General, that the proudest and happiest moment of my life was in 1862 when I was sent from the regiment on recruiting service with other sergeants, and upon arriving at Columbus found that you had my commission to 2nd lieutenant, and that it had been issued upon your personal recommendation, for what as a boy, I had done at Antietam."[22]

McKinley also admired Hayes, and he became a major influence on McKinley's political formation. Hayes was a lawyer from Cincinnati with a wealthy family background. He had graduated from Kenyon College in 1842 and Harvard Law School in 1845. Hayes was a Whig, Republican, and abolitionist. As a lawyer in Cincinnati, he had defended runway slaves. Ultimately Hayes would become President in the election of 1877. While Hayes opposed most formal religion, his wife Lucy was a strict Methodist who, as first lady, banned alcohol from all state functions. Hayes carried an extensive library in camp and McKinley was well schooled by reading from it in his free time. Hayes's wife Lucy helped school McKinley in social graces.

In October 1862, the 23rd was ordered to Pennsylvania to protect against possible cavalry raids on the iron valleys of Pittsburgh and possibly even Mahoning Valley. Pittsburgh had started to ship out cannons in case of a raid by Morgan. Through the spring of 1863, there were rumors of Confederate cavalry near these manufacturing centers. Most of these never proved out, but Hayes did cut off an attempted raid by Jim Morgan into Ohio. The southeastern counties of Ohio were the major producer of pig iron during the war. This "Hanging Rock Iron District" was a 30-mile belt in the counties of Scioto, Lawrence, and Gallia on the Kentucky border. Some of the largest Union blast furnaces were in this strategic area. Even the British had found this high quality Ohio ore superior to their own, and had used large amounts of it to produce armaments for the Crimean War (1854-1856). The 23rd was one of many regiments used to defend against planned Confederate raids in this strategic area. This area would be part of the "pig iron aristocracy" that supported McKinley's presidential runs.

One of the battles to cut off Confederate Morgan in the Hanging Rock area was the battle of Buffington's Island. Confederate General had entered Ohio near Gallipolis about 30 miles from some of the Union's largest blast furnaces in the summer of 1863. Furthermore, McKinley had used Gallipolis as a depot. The 23rd

---

22 McKinley to Hayes, July 2, 1888, Hayes Papers, Hayes Memorial Library

Ohio, the 13th West Virginia, Union gunboats, and Union regulars amassed to chase Morgan's cavalry. At Buffington Island this combined force killed over 800 and captured 2,300 Confederate raiders (208 by the Ohio 23rd).[23] Still over 300 of Morgan's cavalry moved north towards the Mahoning Valley area. Every able-bodied man in the valley took up arms and marched south. Panic struck the area, with banks moving money to Cleveland. Finally Morgan was forced to surrender at West Point, Columbiana County about 25 miles from Poland (it was the farthest point north the Confederate army reached in Ohio).

In 1863, General Rutherford B. Hayes had taken a real interest in McKinley's career. Hayes promoted him to Brigade Quartermaster and also to his staff as an adjutant officer. McKinley was now in a position that was normally held for those of wealthy or important families. He would meet many of America's future leaders from the country's best families. The year 1863 would be a defining period for young McKinley, who re-enlisted. The gubernatorial election of 1863 would crystallize his support for the Republican Party. His family roots were already deep with Whigs and Republicans who supported protectionism and abolition. The Democratic Party in Ohio nominated Clement Vallandigham, a peace candidate who some considered a traitor. Vallandigham was the Scots-Irish son of a Presbyterian minister from the lower Mahoning valley and was a friend of the McKinley family. Ohio was war torn and weary. John Brough was the candidate for the Unionist Party, which was composed of old Whigs and Republicans. Victories at Gettysburg and Vicksburg helped cement Unionist support by September.

The soldiers were fiercely anti-Vallandigham, as were General Hayes and the 23rd. McKinley's regiment fully endorsed Brough, as did Hayes's brigade, but some coercion was suspected. Certainly both Hayes and McKinley were passionate Unionists and might well have applied at least gentle pressure. For most in the military, Vallandigham was an abomination. The 23rd wrote letters home to keep Vallandigham and his "Copperheads" out of office. Copperheads were Democrats who wanted to call for peace and end the war. McKinley had supported Lincoln through the darkest hours. McKinley, who was known for his ability to forgive others, never really could forgive the Copperheads. McKinley had called the war "the most sacred cause in history". Brough won the election, carrying the Ohio soldiers 41,492 votes to 2,288 votes for Vallandigham. Brough carried the state by 187,492 votes.[24] It would be McKinley who awoke General Hayes on October 13 with the good news. Abraham Lincoln believed that the Ohio vote for Brough "saved the Union."

---

23 William H. Armstrong, *Major McKinley*, (Kent: Kent State University Press, 2000), 55
24 Eugene Roseboom, *The Civil War:1850-1873*, (Columbus: The Ohio Historical Society, 1944), 421

In the spring of 1864, Hayes's brigade got orders to move south towards Virginia with General John Crook's division. This was in response to the move of Confederate General Early into the Shenandoah Valley. Hayes's division took the lead in entering Winchester, Virginia. Crook's division moved deep into Virginia, destroying a branch of the famous Tredegar Iron Works near Lexington. Eventually the Confederates forced an organized retreat by Crook. Freed slave families followed the retreating army. McKinley helped these refugees, and they in turn shared their food with his hungry regiment. A veteran later remembered: "Once I saw him help a poor contraband who had his wife and three children with him, and several heavy bundles of household goods, probably everything the poor fellow had in the world. McKinley helped carry one of the children along the road for at least a mile, and helped the woman over more than one ditch."[25] This, of course, is a powerful image of William McKinley's humanity. McKinley would, throughout his life, refer to blacks as "our black allies." He defended the need to fully establish their civil rights beyond mere freedom from bondage.

On July 24, 1864, McKinley and the 23rd were involved in the Battle of Kernstown. Early Confederate outnumbered Crook's division, forcing a retreat to Winchester. One regiment of Hayes's was lost and cut off from the main body. Hayes sent McKinley to find them and bring them back. Hayes fully believed that McKinley would never return from the mission. Another veteran related the following story:

> None of us expected to see him again, as we watched him push his horse through the open fields, over fences, through ditches, while a well-directed fire from the enemy was poured upon him, with shells exploding around, about and over him. Once he was completely enveloped in the smoke of an exploding shell, and we thought he had gone down; but no, he was saved for better work for his country in future years. Out firmly seated, and as erect as a hussar. Now he had passed under cover from the enemy's fire, and a sense of relief came to us all.[26]

McKinley's heroism would result in a promotion to Captain, which was signed by Abraham Lincoln.

McKinley's leadership, cool head, and bravery won him a position on General Crook's staff. McKinley received a promotion to Major on Crook's recommendation for "gallant and meritorious service during the campaign in West Virginia and the Shenandoah Valley" in March 1865. Not being regular army, this was a promotion in name only without pay or a change in his permanent rank. This, however, was an honor that McKinley cherished for the rest of his life. As did

---

25 William Armstrong, 66

26 *The Life of William McKinley*, (New York: P. F. Collier & Sons, 1901)

many who had earned their rank on the battlefield, he preferred the title of "major" to even president.

A hospital scene involving a Union surgeon's compassion for a wounded Confederate soldier moved McKinley at Winchester. He found the two to be brother Masons. He later observed the surgeon passing out money to crippled Confederate soldiers to help them start over. This revelation of fraternity and friendship between "enemies" convinced him to become a Mason. He entered Hiram Lodge No. 21 at Winchester, Virginia, on May 3, 1865. Later he was elected to the Canton Lodge and took a particular interest in the Knights Templar. McKinley remained a member throughout his life, but little is recorded of this. McKinley would visit various lodges as he traveled. He always spoke of the fraternity and brotherhood. He was known to take a group after the meetings to local taverns and restaurants to discuss politics into the early morning.

McKinley considered a career in the military, filling out a formal application for a captain in the First Army Corps. General Hancock received his application and a board of examination recommended him. At the last minute, under the advice of his father and mother, he turned down the position. While McKinley moved away from a military career, he maintained that his five years in the army were the best years of his life. He was proud of his accomplishments but personally he was becoming interested in politics, for which a law degree might offer a better advantage.

The key to understanding McKinley is in his Civil War experience. He spent his formative years between 17 and 22 in the army. He was at some of America's bloodiest battles, such as Antietam, where more casualties occurred in one hour than in the entire Spanish-American War. Starting as a private (at 18) and rising to major, McKinley experienced more front-line duty than any other president.[27] McKinley, though fiercely proud of his service, never talked of the glories of war. In fact, as a war president, he hesitated to involve the country. In his 1897 Inaugural Address, McKinley affirmed: "We need no wars of conquest, we must avoid the temptation of territorial aggression. War should never be entered upon until every agency of peace has failed; peace is preferable to war in almost every contingency." Later, as war approached, he declared: "I have seen war; I have seen the dead pile up, and I don't want to see another." Still, when the decision for war was needed, McKinley faced it and made the tough decision. In doing so, he lost the financial support of his biggest contributor, Andrew Carnegie.

He was active in veteran's organizations such as the Grand Army of the Republic and insisted that veterans deserved the best opportunities the nation had

27 James Cash, *Unsung Heroes,* (Wilmington: Orange Frazer Press, 1998)

to offer. He was personally disturbed when black veterans were given anything less. While he struggled with forgiving the Copperheads, he tried later in his career to embrace Confederate soldiers. As president, he appointed more Confederate officers than those who had gone before him. Many of these appointments were highly publicized, such as those given to the sons of Generals James Longstreet, George Pickett, and J.E.B. Stuart.

Chapter 5. Canton Lawyer

When McKinley returned to Poland after being mustered out of the army, the citizens of Poland organized a celebration and picnic to honor the 23rd, 60th, and 105th regiments. Over five hundred people gathered at nearby Kirtland's Grove. The lead speaker was Judge Charles Glidden; Major McKinley and a few other veterans were also asked to speak, and he distinguished himself with patriotic ardor.

He did not share his mother's dream that he become a minister. His father felt a military career would be a mistake and may have steered him toward a future in law and ultimately politics. His sister Anna, who had remained close to McKinley throughout the war, seems to have suggested law as a career. While Poland was a mere village of 400, it had a first class lawyer in Judge Charles Glidden. In the summer of 1865, McKinley entered the law office of Glidden in nearby Youngstown. McKinley borrowed the money to go to law school from his mother and sister. In September, McKinley went to Albany Law School to study. He was remembered there for studying into the early hours of the morning, and McKinley graduated in nine months (not uncommon in those times).

His new mentor, Rutherford B. Hayes, cajoled him too late to go into business: "With your business capacity and experience, I would have preferred railroading or some commercial business. A man in any of our Western towns with half your wit ought to be independent at forty in business. As a lawyer, a man sacrifices independence to ambition, which is a bad bargain at best. However, you have decided for the present your profession, so I must."[28] In hindsight, McKinley's

---

28 Hayes to McKinley, November 6, 1866; *Dairy, V,* Hayes Memorial Library

debating skills, love of study, and calm demeanor made him a natural for the law. It appears that McKinley had been looking at politics early on. He recalled later in life: "I have never been in doubt since I was old enough to think intelligently that I would someday be made president of the United States." Governor Harris of Ohio reminisced in 1907 about McKinley's mastery of the handshake: "He never allowed anyone to get the 'drop' on him. He always got hold of the other fellow's hand first, and with such a high reach as to prevent gripping or squeezing." In late 1867, McKinley passed the bar exam and faced a decision on where to practice law. McKinley's political ambitions are often overlooked because they do not fit the notion that he was a wandering soul until found by Mark Hanna. What was different is McKinley viewed the political ladder as step-by-step process, like that of rank and promotion in the military.

Poland was far too small and too close to Youngstown to support a new lawyer. Canton, in the neighboring county of Stark, offered more potential. In addition, his sisters Anna and Helen were schoolteachers in Canton. The sisters had established a social network there which could help start up his legal business. He also had a cousin, Mrs. William Miller, married to a reaper factory manager in nearby Massillon. William Miller worked for the manufacturing firm of Russell and Company, firmly tied to the new emerging industrial middle class. Canton was also gaining a reputation for industrial and agricultural growth. Also Canton was the county seat, and McKinley's friend Judge Glidden had some business in the area. Politics was not foremost in his mind, since Stark tended to be a Democratic area, and McKinley's beliefs were clearly with the Republicans of the time.

When McKinley arrived in Canton in 1867, it was a town of 7,000 inhabitants in the farming county of Stark, total population around 50,000. The economy was based on a mix of manufacturing enterprises such as paper mills, woolen factories, and blacksmith fabricating shops. Stark County was basically agricultural, but it was also a center for the manufacture of agricultural implements. The Cornelius Aultman Company was the largest manufacturer of reapers and mowers in the world, and with nearby Russell Company in Massillon, the area was the world center of reaper manufacture. Albert Ball had started manufacturing the "Hussey Reaper" and "Ohio Mover" at the Canton plant in 1851. The area was also part of the Ohio Canal system with extensions in nearby Massillon and north through Portage County. While Canton and Stark County were only 60 miles from Niles, it was a completely different political world. Stark County was traditionally mixed between old line Whigs and Republicans as well as a majority of Democrats. The county had gone Democrat against Lincoln in 1859, but had rejected the Democratic Copperhead governor of 1863. Politically, it proved out to be a poor move with tough congressional fights and an easy mark for state gerrymandering.

The Democrats in the district were German immigrants from Pennsylvania, loyal to both the union and the Democratic Party. There were also Scotch-Irish and English immigrants from the east that tended to be Republicans (formerly Whigs and Unionists). But even the Democrats of Stark County were mostly Union Democrats, not Copperheads. These old Copperhead counties would be problematic to McKinley throughout his congressional career. Copperheads tended to have strongholds in the old Irish canal building communities of Ohio and the east. The Irish remembered how they had gotten off the boat in New York to be sworn in as citizens, then moved to the recruitment line to be mustered into the Union Army. Often they were congratulated on becoming citizens of the United States, then told, "now, go fight for your country." There was no doubt the Irish bore more than their share of the fighting. The canal counties around Stark were Copperhead strongholds. There was also a significant group of Irish that had come in the canal building days and became permanent settlers of the surrounding areas. For most of McKinley's early career, Stark County was considered Democratic, and a difficult home base. It also lacked the protectionist base of the Niles-Youngstown iron and steel district.

The farming culture of the local Germans was isolationist. These Germans, sometimes called "Dunkers," had little interest in developing villages, tending to be Jeffersonian agrarians who were strongly anti-Federalist and later anti-Whig. They were also often religious separatists unrelated to mainstream German Lutherans and Catholics, but significant portions of the 1840s German immigrants were Roman Catholic. They were opposed to tariffs because they raised the prices of basic goods they needed for farming. They also were active in general trade in goods along the rivers and canals, which again tariffs harmed. Another root of Democratic support was a dislike for Federalist ideas such as taxes on the whiskey and beer they made. Whiskey was actually one of the main exports moving by canal to the Ohio River and then to New Orleans for shipment to the East Coast. On the other hand, the English settlers in the town of Canton had prospered when the Tariff of 1828 allowed domestic wool factories to prosper. The townspeople clearly tended to be Whig and then Republican by the 1860s. The old struggle of the Jeffersonians and the Clay Federalists in Stark County continued under various party names for decades into the 1900s, and that struggle would be the center of McKinley campaigns for his whole career.

McKinley opened a small office in downtown Canton covering routine cases in probate court. McKinley came to know the powerful industrial Aultman family through the Methodist Church. Both McKinley and Aultman were active in the church's Sunday school. McKinley's real breakthrough came with his partnership with Canton's George Belden. Anna was a friend of Judge Belden's sister, and Judge Glidden had written a letter of introduction. Judge Belden, at first sight, might seem a strange bedfellow. Belden was a fierce Democrat, but a Union Democrat, not a Copperhead. McKinley was a proud Republican, but they found common ground in Masonry. Judge Belden not only made McKinley his partner but also introduced him to the Canton Lodge. McKinley seems to have made some early political speeches in North Canton to support his old commander, Rutherford Hayes, for governor. McKinley also quickly adapted to the community, becoming active in the Methodist Church and the YMCA. He gained a reputation as a speaker almost immediately with his support for women's suffrage in a YMCA-supported debate. McKinley was elected president of the Canton YMCA in June of 1868. He also became good friends with industrialist and YMCA supporter Cornelius Aultman.

In July of 1868, McKinley was elected Secretary of the local Republican Party based on his speaking ability. He was also active in the 1869 campaign of Ulysses Grant. Grant was extremely popular, and McKinley traveled the county speaking in his support. McKinley was rapidly becoming a recognizable personality in Stark County. He was involved in a subtle debate that was going on in the Ohio Republican Party. Ohio was on the forefront of the American transition from an agricultural to an industrial economy, and no county better exemplified that transition than Stark County. Farmers wanted cheap imported goods and opposed tariffs, while industrial areas wanted full protection for industry. While Grant supported high tariffs, some Ohio Republican leaders, such as Rutherford Hayes, James Garfield, and Jacob Cox were moving away from a high tariff position. The pressure was coming from anti-tariff Democrats, who had made deep inroads into the farming communities as well as with recent Irish immigrants. McKinley, however, remained a supporter of protective tariffs.

In 1867, Stark County had gone against Republican Rutherford Hayes's successful run for governor. Normally Democratic Stark County was carried for Grant by 297 votes in 1869. McKinley shared in this great Republican victory. That same year, his law partner Judge Belden died, leaving McKinley as sole proprietor. McKinley's old friend General Hayes had moved rapidly from being congressman from Cincinnati to Governor of Ohio. Yet Hayes's support as a congressman for higher tariffs had been questioned by many northeast Ohio Republicans. The normally Republican Ohio Wool Growers Association had not endorsed Hayes. This had cost Hayes votes in the industrial counties. While McKinley would support Hayes throughout his political career, he would develop his own alliance and beliefs around the middle class. McKinley, unlike

Hayes, was not from a privileged class. His friends and family were all tied into the industrial health of the nation.

A key year was 1869. McKinley's sisters and brothers purchased a home in Canton for Mother McKinley at Shorb and Tuscarawas streets. His father was still managing an iron furnace operation in Michigan. McKinley would also live there until he married. It was also in 1869 that McKinley ran for his first political office, that of Prosecuting Attorney. He won the election in this Democratic region by building a cross party lines alliance. Another strength was the support of war veterans. McKinley won with votes of 5,001 to 4,866 votes for his opponent William Lynch. His salary of $1,000 a year as Prosecuting Attorney was typical of a middle class salary of the time, but far from the upper class income of his future father-in-law James Saxton at $53,000 a year. The leading industrialist, Cornelius Aultman, had an income of over $100,000, while his sister was paid $600 per year as a school principal. His one term lasted only two years as the angered Democrats mounted a major effort to defeat him in 1871. In 1869, McKinley began dating Miss Ida Saxton from a prominent Canton family.

Ida Saxton's father was a wealthy banker and alderman of the Presbyterian Church. Her grandfather was the owner and founder of the Canton paper, the *Repository*. Her family had also invested in local banking and industry. Ida was educated at a boarding school in Cleveland and at Pennsylvania's Brook Hall Seminary. She had taken vacations to Europe, yet she insisted on working at a bank so that she might learn to be independent. The banking job was also a statement of her support for women rights, a belief she shared with her father, who said, "I have seen enough girls left stranded by sudden losses of means. I don't intend that this shall ever happen to my daughter." Women's rights comprised one of the middle class issues that McKinley supported. Ida was known for her nervousness and possessiveness. McKinley, for his part, was an extremely good match and demonstrated love and loyalty throughout his life. They were married at the Presbyterian Church in 1871.

McKinley's run for re-election in 1871 was a difficult one. Lest anyone think that McKinley built alliances for political advantage alone, the 1871 election was another example of his ability to put moral stands ahead of politics. Ida had gotten McKinley interested in the temperance movement. As the prosecuting attorney, he went against the large German and Irish population that opposed government control of personal drinking habits. He started to gain a local reputation as a temperance reformer, winning a number of prosecutions. One of the most interesting would be involved in his eventual destiny. He prosecuted the illegal sale of liquor to students of nearby Mount Union College (Alliance, Ohio). One of his student witnesses was a Philander Knox of Pennsylvania, who would later become attorney general in his second administration. His successes led to a number of ordinances limiting the sales of liquor. The Germans took their revenge in the 1871 election, with William Lynch winning this time by 5228 votes to 5085 votes for McKinley. Still, McKinley had built strong ties with local industrialists such as Cornelius Aultman, who also supported the temperance movement. Temperance, women's rights, civil rights, loyalty to the Union, and protectionism were areas that McKinley never compromised on regardless of support in his districts.

In May of 1871, McKinley's younger brother joined him in the law firm, but the first years of his political defeat seemed to cause a withdrawal from his previous activity. He resigned as Republican Party Chair and as president of the YMCA. It is not clear why he did this, though it might have been at the request of his wife. They had their first child, a daughter, Katie, a few months after the defeat, in late 1872, and McKinley might have decided against a political life. There is evidence he was becoming involved in his father-in-law's businesses.

The Panic of 1873 hit the nation and Canton hard. The panic lasted five years, with 30% unemployment and another 40% working for less than seven months a year. Nationwide 3 million would lose their jobs and daily wages fell 25%, while Canton was hit equally hard. Railroad workers suffered a 35% decrease in wages. Wages for Ohio coal miners dropped by half during the panic. The nation and Canton noticed an increase of "tramps" on city streets. Nationally, a quarter of the nation's 360 railroads failed as well as 20,000 other businesses. The Panic started as a bank crisis, and within a few days the stock market closed for the first time in its history. Looking back, Andrew Carnegie found the Panic of 1873 to be the hardest on capitalists: "So many of my friends needed money, that they begged me to repay them. I did so and bought out five or six of them. That gave me my leading interest in this steel business." The fact is, Carnegie was one of the few to profit from the 1873 Panic because he kept investing, against the trend. Still, many see the recession of the 1870s as an equivalent to that of the 1930s.

McKinley had seen how recessions and panics had hurt his family, but now he would see the full impact on the economy firsthand. The Canton bankers held a special meeting in October of 1873 to slow withdrawals. Currency tightened in Canton, and local manufacturers were paying employees in scrip, or loan notes, to keep going. The year 1874 was probably the worst of the panic for Ohio, with 11,442 of Ohio's 22,650 employees working less than fifty weeks.[29] Even worse, money was deflating, with the value of the silver dollar (in gold standard terms) worth $1.00 in 1873, 99 cents in 1874, 96 cents in 1875, 89 cents in 1876, and 92

---

29 *Annual Report of the Bureau of Labor Statistics*, (Columbus, 1878)

cents in 1877.[30] McKinley saw first hand how these "panics" or recessions affected the whole community of Canton and surrounding areas. Farmers were impacted by tight money. Tight money meant they could not borrow for planting and equipment needs or had to accept high interest loans against their mortgages. As equipment purchases of the farmers tapered off, the reaper and farm equipment manufacturers laid off employees, adding to the downward spiral.

One of Canton's largest manufacturers, Diebold & Kienzle, suspended operations and approached bankruptcy. A few years later, McKinley would put together a reorganization plan to keep Diebold in Canton. McKinley was thrown directly into the crisis, taking over as president of his father-in-law's Stark County Bank in October of 1873. Stark County Bank was one of six in Canton in 1873 of which several failed. His small bank was similar to thousands of small banks that went under during the panic. The McKinleys also had inherited a city lot from his wife's family early in the year, and McKinley found himself short of the necessary money to develop it. He was also recruited by the YMCA to help them manage mounting debt. This congressional district contained the core of the Ohio iron and steel industry, which was particularly hard hit. The new iron foundry business, which the Civil War created, went into a deep decline, as machinery parts were not being purchased. For the first time, beggars appeared on the streets of smaller industrial towns like Canton. McKinley's banking experience gave him an aggregate view of the economy that he had not seen before.

The Panic of 1873, like the Panic of 1857, was a hard time that cut across political lines. Temperance and suffrage would take a back seat when there were families to feed. This panic even pressed the farmers, who were now dependent on selling their goods to urban centers. Railroads not only failed by the hundreds, but traffic was drastically reduced, hurting transportation centers such as Canton. The canals started to lose business due to lack of farm traffic. Canton had been benefiting from the great railroad expansion of the early 1870s, but the panic cut railroad expansion until the late 1870s. The agrarian society of Jefferson no longer existed. It was a lesson that few politicians had experienced. McKinley saw the interconnectivity of the economy, where others saw segments such as farmers, businessmen, laborers, merchants, and capitalists. The very assumptions of Adam Smith's view of a simplistic economy were being challenged. He knew the fear of a bank run firsthand.

These times favored the rise of socialism, which promised more of a fair shake for the working classes. The Panic of 1873 delineated the huge class differences of the Gilded Age (1873 was the year Mark Twain published *The Gilded Age*). Even

---

30 Charles Olcott, *The Life of William McKinley*, (Boston: Houghton-Mifflin, 1916), 203

in the small town of Canton, the contrast was highlighted by the mansion being built by industrialist Cornelius Aultman. In the large cities, the difference were even more striking and could be seen within just a few blocks. McKinley, like most Americans, spent his life looking up at these mansions. He understood how the unemployed father could be filled with anger passing these industrial palaces. In the 1870s, socialists and various anarchists, coming from or inspired by similar movements in Europe, were starting to organize in cities like Chicago. German immigrants in Chicago had a 5,000-person parade to call for aid for the unemployed in December of 1873. While most upper class politicians feared socialism, McKinley understood its appeal. Labor unions had reached a peak of twenty-five nationals in 1873, but by the end of the panic only nine survived. Union membership declined from 300,000 to about 50,000, sending a message even to union leaders of the importance of a strong economy. McKinley would transform these experiences in an adroit political understanding and an aggregate view of economics.

The farmers were hit particularly hard during the Panic of 1873 because of its international roots. This was one of the first international recessions. Europe's problems resulted in reduced exports of cotton and food crops. Farmers suffered not only from reduced market, but inability to get money for planting needs. Loans of any amount had dried up by the end of 1873. Corn prices dropped from $.59 a bushel to $.22 a bushel and wheat fell from $1.07 a bushel to $.89 a bushel. The international market collapse also hurt manufacturing, which had experienced a boom supplying war torn Europe. Only half of Ohio's iron furnaces operated at any level between 1873 and 1877. Many of these furnaces would never be fired again. Lack of European trade greatly affected transportation companies in the United States such as the railroads and canals.

Personally, 1873 was not much better for McKinley. His second daughter Ida was born but died within five months. Mrs. McKinley slipped into a mental depression, which seems to have developed into other medical problems. Mrs. McKinley started to have attacks of epilepsy. Katie, their surviving daughter, would die of typhoid fever in 1875, further aggravating Mrs. McKinley's health problems. Many biographers consider she was a nervous invalid for the balance of her life.

The Panic of 1873's heavy impact on the lives of Ohioans and Americans resulted in some grassroot political movements. In Ohio the Peoples Party was formed of liberal Republicans and main line Democrats in Ohio. The Peoples Party held that the corruption of the Grant Administration had caused the 1873 depression. In the East, silver and paper money advocates formed the independent Greenback Party. The Greenback Party aggressively supported policies favorable to manufacturing and farming. The "Greenback" was paper money not backed by either silver or gold, and it was believed responsible for monetary expansion. Their 1876 candidate Peter Cooper was a nationally-known iron manufacturer.

The Panic of 1873 would cause social upheavals such as the Railroad Strike of 1877, but closer to Canton there was trouble in the coal mining industry. Trouble reached the breaking point at the Warmington Mine south of Canton in the Tuscarawas Valley in 1876. The wages of the miners per ton of coal dug had been reduced throughout the years of panic from $1.00 a ton to $.65 a ton. The miners struck to stop the wage decline, and the company called in strikebreakers. It was a scenario that was occurring across the nation. Initially, the miners had public support as well as strong support from Democratic politicians. The mine owners were also from the Cleveland area; one of them was Marcus Alonzo Hanna, who would become McKinley's friend and manager. The mines had remained profitable through the cutting of the miners' wages.

The appearance of the "scabs" or strike breakers resulted in violence. In this particular case, some mine supervisors were severely beaten and almost killed. The violence escalated, with mines being set on fire. Governor Hayes was forced to send in troops. Hayes hesitated siding with the cause of the miners, but the violence brought cries for troops from Massillon and Canton. Furthermore, Ohio and, even more so, Stark County had a delicate balance of Democrats and Republicans. Hayes recognized the political issue, but he had no choice. Public opinion in the urban areas shifted away from the miners as the violence spread towards the towns of Massillon and Canton. A number of the miners were arrested for disorderly conduct. It was a case none of Canton's law firms wanted. Republicans, in particular, considered it political suicide.

William McKinley took the side of the arrested miners without a fee. McKinley now faced Democratic prosecutor Lynch, but McKinley's Republican base was against him. To make matters worst, McKinley had just been selected as a potential congressional candidate. The *Repository* protected McKinley by not using his name as the miners' attorney. One biographer suggested that even the court records had been adjusted to hide McKinley's name, but word got out. McKinley was brilliant in not defending the violence, but stressing the mine working conditions and wage cuts that inspired it. He highlighted the miners working conditions and long hours. Miners typically worked over eight hours amid dangerous conditions. Miners faced one of the highest injury and death rates for the time. In 1873, over 250 miners were killed and over 700 miners were injured in Ohio.[31] The company, on the other hand, maintained its profits in bad

---

31 Thomas Baker, "Growth and Progress of the Coal Mining Industry," *Ohio Labor Statistics*, 1901, 291-5

times by wage reduction. In fairness, some of the owners such as Mark Hanna had been a bit fairer, or at least claim they were not directly involved in the poor conditions.

McKinley was only partially successful with the case, but the results would give him two very powerful political allies. Of the five miners, one received a three-year sentence, and the others got only thirty days and a shared fine of $30. McKinley, however, won the support of the Ohio coal miners, which would be key to his political future. That miner support translated nationally to coal mining districts. He also impressed one of the case opponents, Mark Hanna. Hanna would be a loyal friend and political advisor throughout McKinley's career, but they started out on oppose sides of the court. Hanna, like McKinley, came to believe that workers and management must resolve differences fairly and peacefully. Years later President McKinley would often send Mark Hanna to cajole and pressure capitalists into better treatment of their workforce. Both men came to realize that political victory would lie in the strength of the alliance of labor and capital. Interestingly, one of the opposing lawyers, William R. Day would also become a key factor in McKinley's presidential future.

In 1875 prior to the trial of the miners, McKinley had entered into politics again, supporting his old commander Hayes for a second term as governor. Hayes would need the help, his temperance support was in deep trouble with the Germans. Furthermore, the Anti-Catholic School stand had him in trouble with the Germans and Irish. Farmers wanted silver and paper money to stimulate monetary growth and make loans easier to get, but Hayes held to the Eastern Republican line of the gold standard. He was weak on tariffs, which did nothing for him in McKinley's industrial district. McKinley, always the loyal soldier, stood with his old boss. Hayes would win by 5,549 votes out of 590,077 cast, which was an ominously thin margin in a heartland state.

By May 1876, McKinley was in the thick of things, campaigning for the October state elections and also for the upcoming presidential election in November 1877. In August, McKinley accepted the congressional nomination for the Republicans. Mahoning and Columbiana counties were key to his nomination victory. McKinley immediately signed up for a number of debates with his opponent Democratic L. Lamborn. McKinley's strength was debate versus the pure stump speech. The debates centered on the full Republican ticket, which featured Hayes for President in November. He handily won the debates and had strong support in the manufacturing, iron, and mining districts. Perhaps the most remembered event was the presentation of a carnation during the debates at Alliance, Ohio. McKinley would adopt the carnation as a lucky piece. Alliance would go on to become the Carnation City, and the carnation the state flower of Ohio. Ohio politicians of the Gilded Age were full-time campaigners with Federal offices filled in even-numbered years, and state offices in odd-numbered years. McKinley actually was a natural campaigner and well suited for a career in politics.

The elections were a tough battle for the young McKinley, but he stuck to tariffs and help for veterans, issues that cut party lines. McKinley stood for strong protectionist tariffs even though Hayes favored lower rates for revenue only. Hayes, for his part, soft pedaled the tariff issue and down played his anti-Catholic sentiment. While the Hayes Republicans tended to be nativist, anti-immigrant, and anti-Catholic, McKinley opposed all three tendencies. Hayes saw tariff as a losing issue outside the eastern and southern industrial counties. He was also being pressured by a national "Liberal Republican" movement, which was strong in his base of Cincinnati. The liberal Republicans stood for tariff reform (lowering). Both McKinley and Hayes soft-pedaled their stance on temperance because of the heavy German vote. Hayes followed the national Republican line on the gold standard, which had gone into effect in 1873, but would allow greenbacks. McKinley was a bimetallist, wanting both gold and silver coinage. The Westerners and farmers tended to favor free silver, while the Eastern bankers favored gold. McKinley saw problems with both extremes, but kept his stand low-key, preferring to use protection versus currency for economy adjustments. McKinley used the term "sound money" to ride the middle ground. McKinley put American jobs ahead of everything, including the warning of inflation. The gold versus silver issue was just starting to build in 1876, but it would be a major issue in McKinley's two future runs for the presidency.

McKinley sensed a split even among businessmen. The old money and Eastern bankers wanted gold as a hedge against inflation. The manufacturing community and industrial middle class wanted some split that would allow for monetary expansion. This was a confusing election for most Ohioans, who were experiencing their first industrial and internationally based recession. Many were unclear about how monetary issues, such as gold, silver, or greenbacks, affected the economy. However, the existence of the Greenback Party's manufacturing and farming support were getting their view out for loose money. The point was that printing greenbacks would expand the money supply, expand industry, make mortgages easier to get, and cause inflation as well. These underlying economic factors allowed for politicians to spin the issues to their advantage. Democrats added silver and greenback support quickly to their platform. McKinley fought for middle ground with a "sound money" policy. Politicians played farmers different ways with the fear of inflation or the shortage of loans in deflation. One group that both McKinley and Hayes could count on was the Civil War

Veterans, which stood with the Republicans nationally, having never forgotten the Copperhead Democrats' lack of support for the war. Stark County alone had well over 1,000 veterans who tended to vote Republican. In addition, McKinley's congressional district was home to the veterans of Hayes and McKinley's 23rd Ohio.

The Greenback Party represented an unsuccessful effort to tie labor, farmers, and capitalists together. Its national candidate was industrialist Peter Cooper. Greenbacks would offer the same type of money expansion that could be derived from silver coinage, so it was popular with farmers. Cooper was well known in the iron, railroad, and engineering industries, but the Greenback movement remained one of the farmers. Farmers had a pragmatic understanding of currency issues, while laborers did not. Cooper only took 81,000 votes nationally, mostly from Midwest farmers. His votes in industrial cities were extremely poor, with Chicago only casting 251 and Pittsburgh 93 for Cooper. The alliance of farmers and labor was one that McKinley thought possible and was the basis of McKinley's "sound money" approach. McKinley knew he wanted available money and economic expansion, but he, like most of the middle class, was unsure of how that related to the gold, silver, and greenback mix. He therefore broke philosophically with the old Radicals of the Republican Party on the gold standard and talked of sound money.

While McKinley wavered on the gold issue, he never wavered on tariff protection, which gave him strength in the iron districts of Columbiana County and Mahoning County. The congressional election was a tough fight in this split district, but McKinley was victorious. He beat Lamborn by 3,300 votes, but carried Stark County by only 352 votes (6,050 to 5,698). The industrial counties of Columbiana and Mahoning gave him a victory margin of 1,000 votes each. It is important to note that McKinley won against a Democratic majority in Stark. Hayes won the presidency in a highly disputed election settled by the Supreme Court. McKinley at age thirty-four embarked for Washington and a new career.

Chapter 6. Congressman McKinley

McKinley came to Congress in 1877. He was given a piece of advice by his old commanding officer and now President, Rutherford B. Hayes: "To achieve success and fame, you must pursue a special line. You must not make a speech on every motion offered or bill introduced. Confine yourself to one particular thing. Become a specialist. Take up some branch of legislation and master that. Why not take up the subject of the tariff? That being a subject that will not be settled for years to come, it offers a great field of study for years to come."[32] Hayes was well aware that it was almost pre-ordained that this would be McKinley's field of study. This purported advice may well be a bit of Republican revisionist history, since Hayes was never a strong supporter of protectionist tariffs. Another mentor, William "Pig Iron" Kelly of Pennsylvania, then Chair of Ways and Means, would point him in the same direction. Pig Iron Kelly had taken on the mantle of protectionism from the now gone Henry Clay. Within a year, McKinley would be known as "Kelly's Lieutenant," and an apostle of Henry Clay. McKinley studied tariffs and duties like no one before him.

McKinley did make tariff his specialty, and in doing so he fought both Democrats and Republicans. Often, like Henry Clay, his constituents in his congressional district deserted him. Three Republican presidents opposed him as well. His closet friends often opposed him. Democrats forcibly tried to remove him through gerrymandering because of his tariff views. The wealthy Eastern Republican bankers opposed him. He was made fun of for being simple-minded. Colleges saw him as simple minded in his economics as well. He could compromise

---

32 McKinley Memorial Addresses, 94

on almost anything except tariffs. He generally faced an anti-tariff Democratic majority in the House of Representatives. In the end, his tariff policy would even cost him his congressional seat. While he had financial campaign support from business, he barely managed to break even personally. Capitalism had not really benefited him personally. His investments turned out no better, if not worse, than those of the average middle-class investor. He proved a poor businessman himself and had no real aptitude for it. His law firm income barely put him in the middle-class. He entered the Congress with $10,000 in assets and left for his first administration in the White House bankrupt. He was as far as you could get from the robber barons that many called his "cronies."

As a freshman, McKinley was in the Forty-fifth Congress. The Democrats controlled the House 153 members to 140 members for the Republicans, but the Speaker was a protectionist Democrat, Samuel Randall of Pennsylvania. The Republicans controlled the Senate with 39 members to 36 Democrats and one independent. A weakened Hayes controlled the White House due to a Supreme Court decision. The national debate was the silver versus gold issue. McKinley was immediately on the hot seat. Hayes and the Party supported gold, but McKinley favored silver. The first bill he faced was the "Bland Bill" of Richard "Silver Dick" Bland of Missouri. The Republicans and their floor leader James Garfield of Ohio opposed the pro-silver bill. McKinley stood alone in his party as a freshman to vote for silver because he believed it was good for manufacturing. Hayes used the veto but the house overrode it, with McKinley voting to override. Many overlook this early courage to go against even his party for American manufacturing. Too often McKinley has been characterized as a puppet of his party, when, in fact, his conviction was always to support American manufacturing. How many freshmen congressmen would go against their party on a major bill in their first vote? This was not only a mark of courage but also a measure of his commitment to manufacturing. The Canton Repository noted in 1877: "Major McKinley voted for the re-monetization of silver the other day, like a man who has the courage of his convictions." On the day McKinley was shot, he was carrying a well-worn silver nugget in his trousers as a remembrance of his sound money stand over his lifelong career.

Another important event of McKinley's freshman year was a tariff bill. In 1877, the Eastern and Southern Democrats wanted to reduce tariffs from protectionist levels to revenue only levels. Recall that the main revenue of the United States prior to the income taxes of the 20th century were tariffs. The Democrats had run on a revenue-only approach, and Hayes even mildly supported at least a reduction. The House Republicans were mixed, lacking leadership on protectionism. New York Congressman Fernando Wood brought a bill to the floor to reduce the tariff. Word got out, and the steelworkers of Ohio brought a petition to William McKinley. There was some popular support for the lower prices that free trade would supposedly bring, and free trade had the support of academics and theorists. The Republicans had a supporter in "Pig Iron" Kelly of Pennsylvania, but he was considered self-serving and lacked national credibility. The Democrats controlled the House and without Republican leadership, the bill was expected to pass.

When the freshman congressman took the floor for his first speech, he represented a split district more representative of the assembled body. He rose with the petition of Ohio laborers in hand and roared: "Reduce the tariff and labor will be the first to suffer. Home competition will always bring prices to a fair and reasonable level and prevent extortion and robbery. Success, or even apparent success, in any business or enterprise, will incite others to engage in like enterprises, and then follows healthful strife, the life of business, which inevitably results in cheapening the article produced." He argued forcibly that lower prices mean nothing to the unemployed. He espoused a national type of capitalism reminiscent of Henry Clay and Alexander Hamilton, whom McKinley had studied endlessly in preparing his first speech. He argued that free trade between the states was all that was needed and that it would afford national security. The freshman congressman sparked the leadership needed to defeat the Wood Bill in the Democrat House.

Academics of the time turned against the shameless nationalism of McKinley, but McKinley argued that protection might not be "favored in colleges, but it is taught in the school of experience, in the workshop, where honest day's labor, and where the capital seeks the development of national wealth." He completely rejected the fashionable theories of Adam Smith in favor of the simplistic nationalism of Henry Clay. With the defeat of the Wood Bill, McKinley took the leadership and united his party around protectionism. McKinley was the best-versed on the whole subject, studying long into the night routinely. His success made him a major target for the Democrats.

The Hayes Administration faced some tough times with labor on a national level. The railroads were becoming known for their monopolistic practices and had found resistance from organizations such as the Grange. The rate schedules had drawn criticism from many segments of the population, including businesses. The Pennsylvania Railroad was in a direct battle with Standard Oil in Cleveland. It was trying to force Rockefeller to refine more oil in Pittsburgh because it was to the railroad's advantage. McKinley had spoken against these practices, but the real problem would be a building employee problem. In mid-July 1877 the Pennsylvania Railroad and the Baltimore & Ohio, still struggling at the end of the Panic of 1873, decided to cut the wages of the brakemen and firemen by ten percent. In addition, the companies announced their intention to run "double-headers." A double header meant two locomotives and 34 freight cars versus one locomotive and 17 cars. A double-header effectively cut the workforce in half while doubling the work of the remaining employees.

The struggle reached the crisis point on July 17, 1877 at Martinsburg, West Virginia, where a protest strike started at the Baltimore & Ohio railroad hub. State militia was called in and one of the strikers was shot. At Baltimore's Camden Yards, the strike closed down what was then the nation's hub. Troops again confronted the workers and ten men were killed. On July 21, a full riot broke out in Pittsburgh as citizens joined the strikers in destroying 1383 freight cars, 104 locomotives, and 66 passenger cars. Freight was looted as a real riot progressed. Union Depot was burned down. The Pittsburgh militia refused to shoot at the locals so Philadelphia troops were sent in. The mobs surrounded the troops and over 25 people were killed and hundreds wounded. Hayes had to augment the National Guard with Federal Troops. The nation's sympathy was with the striking workmen.

Chicago at the time was suffering from a major heat wave, and that, combined with its large number of socialists, made it ripe for riots. Riots did break out as crowds took to the streets shouting, "Pittsburgh, Pittsburgh, Pittsburgh!" The socialists took advantage of the riots to make a statement against capitalism. Striking lumbermen and butchers joined in. Hayes sent in troops and the headlines called it a "reign of terror." In the end, 30 men and boys died, most of whom were Irish. Priests walked the streets in Pittsburgh and Chicago, giving last rites to the wounded lying on the streets. The railroad strike hurt the Republicans nationally with labor, immigrants, and the Irish.

The same year, Irish gangs in California were attacking Chinese immigrants. Chinese immigrants had been encouraged to flood the West Coast to work for the railroads. The Chinese displaced mostly Irish laborers. In San Francisco, the Irish were killing Chinese on the streets. Congress passed a law to ban Chinese immigration. American businessmen not only wanted cheap labor but saw China as a great opportunity for market expansion. Hayes vetoed the ban, which helped turn what few Irish republicans existed to the Democratic Party. The Republican Party was now becoming the party of Big Business and the Eastern bankers. McKinley, however, was part of a labor-focused wing of Republicans closer to Clay's Whig party.

The Democrats controlled the Ohio Legislature and had the ability to re-draw the districts. By gerrymandering they put Stark County in the 16th district with rural Ashland, Portage, and Wayne. By doing so, they took away from McKinley his strength in the heavy industrial counties of Columbiana and Mahoning. Columbiana, in particular, was considered a Republican stronghold with roots going back to Henry Clay. On paper these counties had a Democratic majority of 1300 votes. The Democrats were gaining with labor and Irish during the late 1870s. The Democrats seemed sure of McKinley's defeat in 1878; but to make defeat a reality, they nominated Aquila Wiley. Wiley had an outstanding military record which would help mute McKinley's advantage with veterans. Now factory workers and manufacturers in Stark County rallied behind McKinley. It was an uphill fight, but McKinley won with 15,489 votes to 14,255. His silver vote had helped him with the farmers enough to diffuse large Democratic majorities in Ashland and Wayne counties. Furthermore, McKinley had survived a rising national Democratic movement in the election. The setback only strengthened the resolve to defeat McKinley, whose popularity was rising on a national level with his tariff stand.

His second term was less dramatic, but he was appointed to the powerful Ways and Means Committee after the presidential election of Garfield. He introduced some anti-liquor legislation, which again probably cost him some votes back home. He did start to build a closer relationship with the farmer's Grange by supporting bills on railroad regulations. McKinley also took an interest in railroad safety, which was becoming a problem in Ohio. More importantly, McKinley's view on the American System was gaining support within his own party. McKinley, like Henry Clay before him, loved to tour factories and mills. He was building a national following as well. Manufacturers were starting to help support his political career beyond his district base. For his part, McKinley loved to speak to anybody that would listen about the role of protectionism. He had won over two more Republicans, James Garfield of Ohio and James Blaine of Maine. His passion for protectionism was now becoming part of the national Republican strategy. His growing popularity with labor nationally and the farming vote inroads put him high on the Democratic list to be defeated.

The year 1880 brought another challenge to McKinley's seat and additional duties in supporting his friend James Garfield's run for the presidency. This time the Republicans gained the state legislature and returned Stark County to its affiliation with Mahoning and Columbiana. It was the first time his district would be a solid Republican one. With some security for holding his seat in Congress, he was elected chairman of the Republican state convention. On a national level, McKinley supported the strong protectionist James Blaine as the Republican candidate. Ohioan James Garfield placed John Sherman's name for the Republican nomination. John Sherman had been Hayes's Secretary of Treasury. Hayes chose not to run for a second term and lent his support to Sherman. Sherman also had the strong support of Cleveland industrialist Mark Hanna. McKinley saw Sherman as weak on protection and a strict gold standard supporter, a judgment that proved wrong in the long run. The National Republican Convention became split and deadlocked, and on the thirty-fourth ballot James Garfield took the nomination as a compromise candidate. Garfield was middle of the road on protectionism, but McKinley, the party loyalist, came in line for the election.

Senator John Sherman had risen through the ranks but didn't go far enough on protectionism for McKinley. Sherman was backed by Mark Hanna and tended to favor business over the more balanced approach of McKinley in favor of labor. In 1878, he told a struggling coal dealer in the Mahoning Valley to go west to find a better future. McKinley found telling Ohioans to move west shameful. Sherman had been a Senator since 1861, and he remained a dominant force in Ohio politics into the 1890s.

The gold issue would always be a problem for McKinley within his own party. Most of the Republican Party stood with the Eastern bankers for the gold standard. The gold standard tightened the money supply and this particularly hurt the farmers. Farmers needed mortgages. The use of silver could help bring down interest rates. The Grange supported the most liberal money standard known as "free silver," that is, silver exchange not based on gold. Generally, the Democratic Party had supported the farmers and the silver issue. McKinley was in the middle with his bimetallism, which was the right approach for mixed farming and industrial states such as Ohio. McKinley's district included a lot of farmers, which often were the determining factor in the local elections. Without some farming votes, no Republican could win in most Ohio congressional districts.

The economic theory behind the gold-silver question was never fully defined. The amount of gold and silver fluctuated with gold and silver strikes in the West. McKinley was not interested in the theory, but the effect. He remained a bimetallist, watching closely what might be best for both laborer and business. McKinley always preferred to talk "sound money" versus gold or silver. It was a very polarized issue. Eastern bankers tended to assert the necessity of gold for international trade and domestic stability. Most other countries supported the gold standard and this was an essential underpinning to trade. Western farmers, rightly or wrongly, believed silver was the answer for debt and reducing interest rates. Gold and silver confused the underlying issue, which was the money supply and interest rate.

The farmers formed a politically strong organization in the Grange in 1867. The Grange functioned as a cooperative able to reduce prices on manufactured products through volume buying. They formed cooperative mills and grain elevators, and even formed banks and insurance companies. Their real focus, however, became the abuses of the railroads. The Grange would be a political force throughout McKinley's career. Often he found their support for his railroad reform and bimetallism, but often his protective tariff stands cost him significant farm votes in a district that he could ill afford any block opposition. McKinley was always ready to speak at the Grange to explain his stands. The Grange played a key social and educational role throughout the McKinley era. McKinley would eventually incorporate their educational methodology into his national political campaigns.

The farmers had united with labor in 1878 to form the Greenback-Labor Party at Toledo, Ohio. This again was an effort to unite labor and the farmers into a political block. In the congressional elections of 1878, the Greenback-Labor Party won over a million votes for its candidates, but more than half of these were in the Midwest. In 1880, the party put together a platform endorsing free silver coinage, women's suffrage, regulation of railroads, and restrictions on Chinese immigration. They nominated James Weaver as their candidate for president. It was a fractional group but one large enough to affect the presidential elections. Its platform favored the radical wing of the Democrat party and took votes away from the Democratic candidate. It also slowed the socialist movement as the Socialist Labor Party endorsed Weaver for president.

McKinley stumped the state for Garfield, who was running against General Winfield Scott Hancock, the hero of Gettysburg. Hancock opposed any tariff, and McKinley became worried should Hancock win. Nationally it was another close fight with Garfield winning by only 7,018 votes. The Greenback-Labor Party produced 308,578 votes for James Weaver. Garfield carried the industrial cities and the big states, however, and won in the Electoral College by 214 to 155. McKinley fared better, beating his Democratic opponent 20,221 votes against 16,660. McKinley was also instrumental in Garfield's selection of James Blaine as Secretary of State. The Democratic strength was building nationally with their Catholic, farming, and labor alliance. The Republican platform was pro-gold, anti-immigration, and, with the exception of a few like McKinley, Kelly, and Blaine, neutral on tariffs. More specifically, most Republicans supported revenue-only tariffs, not protective tariffs. Seeing his own party split on protective tariffs, McKinley started to work on his concept of reciprocity in tariff applications. Blaine had originally pioneered reciprocity and McKinley hesitated but later fully embraced it. This concept of reciprocity would evolve with McKinley and would later be featured in his second administration.

The most important effect of the Garfield election resulted in McKinley replacing Garfield on the Ways and Means Committee. McKinley already had the support of the Committee's chair, "Pig Iron" Kelly. The upward trend of the

Democrats disrupted many in the Republican Party. Scandals in the Republican administrations from Grant on were taking their toll. The assassination of Garfield, ten weeks into his presidency, caused further problems. The Republican Party was badly split on the worthiness of Chester Arthur, the man who replaced Garfield. Vice presidents at the time often represented minority party ideas and were put on the ticket to "balance" it. Arthur suffered from Bright's disease and his future was in doubt. He posed a real threat to McKinley when he proposed a reduction in the tariffs. The growing government surplus from tariffs was actually considered a problem! Tariff reformers were gaining strength in both parties as prosperity returned.

McKinley had built a tariff fortress in the House, but Arthur threatened to scale the House walls. Arthur wanted tariffs reduced. In December of 1881, Arthur appointed a bipartisan committee to study the tariff issue and make recommendations to Congress. McKinley, like Henry Clay before him, started to tour factories in the industrial districts. Tariffs were a national issue, and McKinley had to gain support nationally. In many ways, this was the start of his quest for the presidency. He was the nation's "Napoleon of Protectionism." Unfortunately, his national work on tariffs hurt him in his own split congressional district, and his district would be his Achilles' Heel. Democrats saw the chance to win over enough liberal Republicans to possibly defeat McKinley. The Arthur Commission started a nationwide tour to study the tariff, which gave them some breathing room.

McKinley was moving into the area of railroad safety and rate controls as tariff opposition temporally subsided. Here again he was in opposition with the business wing of his party. It was during this time that he met George Westinghouse. Westinghouse didn't fit the robber baron label of the time. Westinghouse had invented and was manufacturing the air brake and other railroad safety devices. McKinley asked him to testify on the need for railroad safety. Westinghouse came from Pittsburgh in his special Pullman car to pick up McKinley and go to Washington. The men shared a deep Christian faith and an interest in the YMCA, and the belief that labor and capital should cooperate for the success of the nation. They would become railroad safety crusaders and friends over the years.

Like all of McKinley's living arrangements, his Washington residence was meager. McKinley had little resources to buy or rent a home in Washington; furthermore, he and his wife were absent from the social scene. McKinley rented two rooms at the Ebbitt House. Their quarters consisted of a bedroom and a workroom; they used the parlor downstairs for social meetings. It was cramped and difficult living, and the couple looked forward to summers in Canton. McKinley had the hometown paper delivered and preferred it to the Washington papers. There was almost no socializing, given Ida's health and the couple's financial status. Their main assets were mortgaged property back in Canton, and McKinley was often short of cash between paychecks. Ida's condition remained poor, and her medical bills were a clear burden on the congressman's salary. McKinley sent notes to Ida while he was at work in Congress, but generally she passed the time in solitude. During the Hayes and Garfield Administrations they were often invited to the White House. The Hayeses in particular lived a sober, cloistered existence, and welcomed the quiet visits of the McKinleys. They cherished their out-of-session periods back in Canton where they lived at the Saxton house and could be seen daily sitting on the veranda talking and greeting passers-by.

McKinley faced a major challenge in 1882. Initially, things looked bright as state Republicans returned Stark County to its old district with Mahoning and Columbiana, but the threat came first from within his own party. Tradition at the time held that a congressman should step down after two terms; in addition, Ohio congressional districts rotated candidates among the counties in the districts. The Republican chairman of Columbiana County challenged McKinley to step down and let a candidate from Columbiana take the nomination. The county was also Sherman territory and McKinley had supported James Blaine of Maine over Ohio's John Sherman. Sherman represented the liberal low tariff wing of the Republican Party. The battle against tradition dragged on into the fall elections of 1882. The Democrats, seeing the division in the Republican Party and having control of the House, felt the time was right for tariff reduction. Arthur was very unpopular at the time, and the election trend was Democratic. As a result, McKinley won the election by only eight votes. A large part of this was McKinley's anti-liquor stand based on his moral beliefs. It cost him heavily with the Germans and Irish that dominated his district, and he had nothing to gain politically from it. The Republican-controlled state legislature certified McKinley, but his opponent Jonathan Wallace took the contest to Washington where the Democrats were in control. A Committee was formed to look at the election results as McKinley took his seat in Congress and on the Ways and Means Committee.

In early 1882, McKinley realized that the national tide was turning against protective tariffs. The National Democratic Party mounted a focused effort to turn out McKinley. McKinley needed the Democrats to avoid a tariff reduction. He adroitly moved for a House Committee to study the tariff question, feeling any hard look had to be favorable. McKinley stated: "I have no fear of an intelligent and business-like examination and revision of the tariff by competent civilians who shall be known as Americans and favorable to the American system."

He also needed to pacify Arthur's personal view for lower tariffs and a Democratic majority. It was a compromise position, since there were also high tariff hardliners. McKinley gave a 35-page speech which supported high tariffs, yet helped build support for a commission. The committee heard over 600 witnesses as the tariff issue took center stage. The McKinley speech was well received and Pittsburgh iron manufacturers paid to have it printed and distributed. Lest some think that McKinley's stand against some of his own party was a result of a form of kickback by industry, it should be noted that McKinley was having financial problems and refused help from even his friends at the time.[33] A Commission was formed to study and report.

Amazingly, the results of the Commission were extremely liberal, suggesting a reduction in tariffs. Major reductions were called for on wool, iron, and steel, which were the major products of McKinley's district. The Committee report was approved by both houses, even though McKinley tried and failed at a filibuster in the House. In the debate, McKinley made one of his most famous retorts. McKinley rose on the floor on January 27, 1883 to denounce the report. He drew heavily on his belief that free trade ultimately hurt the laborer by baiting initially with lower prices. He stated: "I speak for the workingmen of my district, the workingmen of Ohio, and of the Country," as Democratic congressman Springer yelled out, "They did not speak for you very largely in the last election." McKinley calmly but forcibly replied: "Ah, my friend, my fidelity to my constituents is not measured by the support they give me. I have convictions upon this subject which I would not surrender or refrain from advocating if a ten thousand majority had been entered against me last October." McKinley faced powerful Republicans like John Sherman of Ohio, weakening in the support for protective tariffs. Not even his enemies doubted his belief in the good of high tariffs.

With the conference report accepted, the Democrats moved for a bill with a 20 percent across-the-board reduction. Known as the Morrison Bill, it probably overplayed this Democratic hand by extending the reduction across the full list of protected products. The across-the-board approach allowed McKinley to build support with Democrats in manufacturing districts. McKinley's speech against the bill cut to the heart of the matter:

> It has friends today that it never had in the past. Its adherents are no longer confined to the North and the East, but are found in the South and in the West. The idea travels with industry and is the associate of enterprise and thrift. It encourages the development of skill, labor, and inventive genius as part of the great productive forces. Its advocacy is no longer limited to the manufacturer, but it has friends the most devoted among the farmers, woolgrowers, the laborers, and the producers of land. It is strong in the

---

33 Morgan, 73

country as in the manufacturing towns or cities; and while it is not taught generally in our colleges, and our young men fresh from universities join with the free-trade thought of the country, practical business and everyday experience later teach them that there are other sources of knowledge besides books, that demonstration is better than theory, and that actual results outweigh an idle philosophy. But while it is not favored in colleges, it is taught in the schools of experience, in the workshop, where honest men perform an honest day's labor, and where capital seeks the development of national wealth. It is, in my judgment, fixed in the national policy, and no party is strong enough to overthrow it.

In the end McKinley prevailed with a 156-151 vote in the House, and he succeeded in bringing over 41 Democrats. The victory brought McKinley onto the national scene with the support of industrial district newspapers.

McKinley's leadership and speaking ability had become a significant problem for the Democrats, and his success in defeating the Morrison Tariff Bill was short lived. A few weeks later, the House Elections Board recommended that McKinley be unseated. The strongly Democratic House delivered a 158-108 decision to unseat McKinley. He accepted the decision and Jonathan Wallace took the seat on May 27, 1884. McKinley returned to a hero's welcome in Canton, but it was a low point in many ways. McKinley declared: "Before I went to Congress I had $10,000 and a practice worth $10,000 a year. Now I have neither." The local crowds hailed him as the "Napoleon of Protection." By now McKinley had a national following throughout the industrial regions.

McKinley was out in one respect, but was made Chairman of the Ohio Republican Convention within weeks. In addition, McKinley went to the National Convention as a delegate, where he was promptly made Chairman of the Resolutions Committee responsible for the national platform. Industrial and urban districts in the United States saw McKinley as a martyr to protectionism and started to follow his career. McKinley worked hard on the platform, which stood for high tariffs with a scientific look at reform, railroad reform, bimetallism, curbs on Chinese immigration, and the eight-hour work day. The platform was a labor platform on all counts. The convention was a wild one in which fistfights were common. McKinley opposed his own Ohio delegation, which supported John Sherman, by voting for James Blaine. As always, McKinley support depended on the tariff issue, and John Sherman, though an Ohioan, was weak on tariffs in McKinley's view. Blaine won the nomination, and McKinley's platform gave the Republican Party a labor plank to stand on. It was an amazing platform that addressed most of the problems of the emerging middle class, middle class, laborers, and farmers.

The addition of a call for the eight-hour day was particularly friendly to labor. McKinley, however, had always maintained that management was part of the labor problem and often spoke for better management. This platform was, however, representative of McKinley's middle class following. The eight-hour day was visionary, but it seemed doubtful that a Republican Party could fully endorse it. In most manufacturing, the twelve-hour day was standard. McKinley believed in the eight-hour day and actually pointed to the work of plant manager Bill Jones of Carnegie Steel. Bill Jones had implemented the eight-hour day in the early 1880s over the objections of his boss, Andrew Carnegie. To everyone's surprise the Braddock plant rose to become the world's most productive. Another Pittsburgher and friend, George Westinghouse, had also shown productivity increases with an eight-hour day. Also, the Republican Party still had the substantial support of the trade union leadership because of its strong protectionism stand. McKinley had triumphed over the Eastern bankers with a bimetallism plank. J. P. Morgan was particularly upset with the Republicans who were going away from the gold standard.

McKinley's platform was probably too liberal for the Republican candidate to embrace, but it reflected where McKinley was. The Farmers Grange particularly applauded McKinley's support of railroad reform. As a congressman, McKinley had often introduced bills for the Grange. Such bills were in opposition to the big money wing of the Republican Party represented by the likes of J. P. Morgan. The same wing opposed his support for bimetallism. McKinley's work on the platform was reflective of the overall population. It was a tough presidential election because scandals haunted the Republicans. James Blaine had a suspect record, having been named in some scandals. That, coupled with his support of railroads and the gold standard, caused many Republicans such as George Westinghouse to vote Democratic. These Republicans were known as "Mugwumps." McKinley could certainly relate to most of the Mugwump Republicans but, as always, tariffs were the issue and Blaine, while not strong on tariffs, was better than the anti-protectionist Democrats.

The Democrats nominated a conservative, Grover Cleveland. Cleveland was a middle-of-the-road Democrat with business support from the likes of Charles Goodyear and George Westinghouse. He actually counted the "prince of capitalism," J. P. Morgan, as a close friend. They frequently lunched together in downtown New York. The Democratic Party avoided the gold issue, while Cleveland supported the gold standard privately. In many ways Grover Cleveland looked more like a Republican than Blaine. Cleveland ran on a reform platform pointing to the endless scandals and abuses in the business community. In particular, Cleveland had the strong support of the Grange. The farmers and their Grange were particularly upset with railroad abuses and high tariffs. The Republican Platform addressed the issue, but the Republicans lacked the record. Cleveland also stood against the anti-Catholic and immigration stand of many Republicans. It was even believed that Blaine could win Irish Catholic support since his mother was an Irish Catholic and his sister a Mother Superior at a convent. In the end, James Blaine carried Ohio by 30,000 votes but lost the national vote. The separation was less than 100,000 votes, but it was enough to elect the first Democratic president in twenty-eight years.

McKinley's Congressional District was gerrymandered in 1884 to include the counties of Stark, Summit, Wayne, and Medina counties, which tended to go Democratic in elections. McKinley's loss of the seat suggested this effort to take it back would be easily defeated, especially as the national trend was once again Democratic. McKinley reversed the trend and carried the district by 2,000 votes. The return to Washington was a great personal victory and established him nationally as a leader. In many ways this was his greatest victory since Cleveland carried Ohio and his district. McKinley's stand and victory against the Morrison Tariff Bill had strengthened his industrial base.

McKinley and Ida returned to their somewhat monastic routine in Washington. In the House, he once again faced a substantial Democratic majority, and could expect Cleveland to push for tariff reforms. McKinley rose early and shaved while reading the newspaper and letters (as a soldier, he had learned to shave without a mirror). They breakfasted at the Ebbitt House after McKinley had done a few hours of work. Ida always wore black dresses, even for breakfast. McKinley was carefully dressed and always wore a Prince Albert coat with a red carnation. In good weather, he walked to the Capitol and in bad took the horse car. He arrived promptly at his seat every morning. He used the telephone or sent notes to his wife throughout the day. They would dine at the Ebbitt House in the evening. McKinley would have a smoke after dinner in the parlor with other residents or would take a short walk, knowing Ida couldn't abide cigar smoke. As a congressman he was noted as a heavy smoker, and he also took up chewing tobacco. Often the McKinleys would pass the evening reading the bible or playing a game of cribbage. When the Hayeses were in the White House, they used to play euchre together. Ida remained in solitude with the Hayeses gone. While McKinley had emerged on the national scene and campaigned in the east for Blaine, he stayed close to Washington. He hired a maid to stay with Ida when he was gone, which strained his budget.

Expenses were somewhat overwhelming at times. Ida had very expensive tastes, having come from a wealthy family. McKinley had some rental income besides his congressman's salary. He also might have received some money from the law firm in Canton, which his brother maintained. Ida's medical and care expenses were surely a great burden. There is evidence that he even considered another line of work because of the financial strain.[34] Ida did improve or at least the nervous condition became more manageable in the late 1880s. Also, upon the death of Ida's father in 1887, she received a generous inheritance. Over the years, this inheritance would be eroded.

In 1885 McKinley made one of his famous protection speeches in Petersburg, Virginia. In the speech, he responded to the rural Jeffersonians who talked of factories bringing cholera: "I tell you, manufactories do not bring cholera — they bring coin, coin: coin for the poor man, coin for the rich, coin for everybody that will work; comfort and contentment for all deserving people. And if you vote for increasing manufactories, my fellow citizens, you will vote for the best interests of your own State, and you will be making iron, and steel, and pottery, and all leading products." McKinley was not just a great orator; he was a student of economics. He often studied journals and statistics into the early morning. He built a small library on trade and economics and few were as well versed even at the best universities. He was always well prepared for even minor debates. Democrats feared him because he had the ability to persuade opponents, and it was a necessary skill since he mostly faced a strong Democratic majority throughout his career.

The spring of 1886 shocked America with the famous Haymarket riot in Chicago. The Haymarket riot was different because this was more of a populist movement than a general strike. Prosperity had brought labor tension to America's industrial centers. The socialists focused the average people's dissatisfaction on the wealthy. In Cincinnati, there were May Day parades for the eight-hour day with plenty of red flags. In Chicago, labor problems at McCormack Reaper Company and the Pullman Company mixed with parades for the eight-hour day. Anarchists and socialists rallied as well. The riot turned to a bloodbath when President Cleveland sent in Federal Troops. It was later speculated that Leon Czolgosz was at the riots, but it seems unlikely. The trial and hanging of the Chicago anarchists, charged with instigating the Haymarket Riot, did impact his belief in class warfare. It would also impact a young Theodore Roosevelt, who saw America heading toward class warfare. Roosevelt was typical of the country's old money at the time.

McKinley did not fear socialism or anarchism. He believed they could only prosper if capitalism and democracy failed, and he would see that they did not fail. His solutions were not military or anti-union measures. He believed that fair wages, industrial growth, better work conditions, and mobility to the middle class were the answers. In his defense of the Ohio coal miners, he had learned

---

34 Margaret Leech, *In the Days of McKinley*, (New York: Harper & Brothers, 1959), 22

how poor working conditions could lead to labor discontent. He had often talked to his friend George Westinghouse on the importance of being fair as an employer. Westinghouse believed the best thing a capitalist could do was to give workers good pay and working conditions. He was, of course, well aware that a winner-take-all attitude was the Achilles' Heel of capitalism. He opposed the paternal capitalism of Andrew Carnegie, preferring better wages to community welfare. The steel valleys of Ohio and Pennsylvania had avoided the labor problems of the 1880s with some very enlightened middle managers such as Bill Jones at Edgar Thomson Works. The Democrats and Cleveland had lost some labor support with the introduction of troops, but even McKinley supported the strict rule of law in such cases. Thanks to McKinley, the Republican platform had put them in the forefront of the eight-hour day issue. The eight-hour day, support for fair wages, the rule of law, and tariff protection made McKinley Republicans popular with conservative labor unions such as the Knights of Labor.

In 1886, Congress prepared for new battles on tariffs as Grover Cleveland was determined to reduce them. Cleveland had the tacit support of the Eastern bankers who saw more profits in global and free trade. J. P. Morgan could help with the political support of the Eastern bosses. McKinley prepared by lining up his support in the unions and manufacturers in Ohio, Illinois, and Pennsylvania. He had strong support from union leaders, which gave the Democrats pause at the local level. In early 1886, William Morrison of Illinois drafted a bill for tariff reduction. At the time, Morrison was Chair of the Ways and Means Committee. McKinley once again built a floor alliance with the protectionist Democrats and defeated it. The Democratic Party remained split, while the Republicans remained united on protective tariffs. Grover Cleveland, however, continued to push for tariff reductions against the McKinley House alliance.

The Congress was also split on the need to regulate the railroads, which were increasingly coming under public pressure for reform. The issue really cut party lines, which slowed legislative reform. The root was an obvious and glaring inconsistency between higher short haul rates and low long-term rates. Eastern merchants, farmers, and manufacturers were the losers, while Western farmer-businessmen had a huge advantage. The low rail rates from the West to the East had, in large part, made American wheat dominant in the world market. It was even more complicated by rebates to big rail users such as Rockefeller's Standard Oil and Carnegie Steel. Big money Republicans such as J. P. Morgan headed the railroad trusts, and opposed railroad legislation. Railroad practices hurt the smaller manufacturers of McKinley's district. McKinley supported the passage of the Interstate Commerce Act, which regulated such practices. It was yet another example of McKinley breaking from the big business Republican wing.

The 1886 election went well for McKinley who carried the district by 2,559 votes. The 1887 annual presidential address to Congress focused on one topic-tariff reduction. The Congress was again Democratic, and Cleveland was confident of victory. The government had a surplus, so the Democrats argued tariff revenue was unnecessary. The battle was building, and McKinley was building statistics and rallying industry and labor leaders. This time McKinley's opposition was Roger Mills of Texas, who was now chairman of the Ways and Means Committee. Mills was representative of the Southern Democrats who opposed tariffs because of their negative impact on the cotton industry. Cleveland had the support of the Eastern Republican bosses and Eastern Democrats. There was still a protectionist wing of the Democratic Party, but Cleveland was applying pressure for a party vote. McKinley's effort to kill it in committee failed as the Democrats moved it to the floor.

This time McKinley met the full force of the Democratic administration to break the McKinley House alliance of Republicans and Democrats. Cleveland lobbied the protectionist Democrats using special favors. Cleveland used the government rules to have the Democrats load the bill with pork barrel amendments. Mills lined up America's best academic minds to testify for free trade. McKinley looked for middle ground, but Cleveland wasn't interested. The Eastern protectionist Democrats weakened on their opposition. The floor debate started on April 17, 1888, but McKinley didn't rise to speak until May 18 as he sized up the turning tide. The Republicans added amendments and moderated the reduction level. McKinley had an every effective grass roots operation even beyond Ohio. In Pittsburgh, McKinley was becoming a national figure. He had the necessary popular support, but Cleveland had bet the House. When McKinley did speak, he spoke to the people more than to Congress: "I would rather have my political economy founded upon the every-day experience of the puddler [union steel maker] or a potter than the learning of the professor, or the farmer and factory hand than the college faculty." McKinley realized the fight was lost on the floor but extended the debate. In early summer, the Mills Bill passed in the House, but the Senate tied it up until the fall elections.

McKinley had lost his first big floor battle on tariffs, but gained the people's support nationally. He, however, did make some enemies with the bosses of the east and the big Republican bankers such as J. P. Morgan. The floor fight was well covered nationally, making tariff the key issue in the 1888 presidential elections, and McKinley was now a national figure. Grover Cleveland's popularity was hurt with his push to end protective tariffs. The election issue would now center on tariffs. Even a weakened Cleveland had the Democratic nomination assured, but the Republican nomination was up for grabs. McKinley supported

Ohio's native son John Sherman, but James Blaine had big money support. There was also an array of others; even McKinley's name was coming up. Blaine who was vacationing at Andrew Carnegie's castle refused to run. John Sherman withdrew as well. The nomination was wide open. McKinley was even being considered as a dark horse. He declined consideration, knowing he was not ready and not sure he wanted to. The Republicans did have one divisive issue that of the gold standard again. The Republican money favored gold, and McKinley's history of bimetallism ruled him out, but they needed to defeat the pending Mills Bill in Congress. Benjamin Harrison of Indiana offered the compromise of being strong on tariffs and the gold standard.

The Congressional election of 1888 was as important as the presidential election to the Republicans. McKinley needed help in the House, and the Democrats had to be unseated. The Republicans targeted three free traders: William Ralls Morrison of East St. Louis, John Carlisle of Kentucky (and Speaker of the House), and Frank Hurd of Toledo. Morrison had been a target of Republican gerrymandering for years, but all had been unsuccessful. The year 1888 was different in that Republicans had labor support, in particular the Knights of Labor. Strangely, the Knights might publicly support a candidate, but its members would secretly campaign for another. Local Knight Chapters often went against national endorsements to support high-tariff Republicans. The Master Workman of the Knights, Terrence Powderly, is believed to have issued a directive to defeat Morrison.[35]

Another Republican operative was John Jarrett. He had been a leader of the Knights and a Pittsburgh Lodge member. He had served as President of the Amalgamated Association of Iron and Steel Workers. He had become invested in the iron and steel industry over the years, although the sources of his investments and money are not clear. He was sent to East St. Louis to oppose Morrison with a bag of money. Officially, he represented the Workingman's Tariff Club, which some believed was a front for the owners' American Iron and Steel Association. Jarrett was also active in Carlisle's Kentucky district. In Toledo the Knights and the various glass worker unions united to target Hurd. Republican money poured into labor unions as well, such as the Window Glass Workers. The glass industry of northwest Ohio had been a huge benefactor of the McKinley tariffs. In the end, the Knights took down Morrison, Carlisle, and Hurd in stunning upsets. In particular, with the defeat of the anti-tariff Speaker Carlisle, labor sent a strong message of its support for the McKinley tariffs.

---

35 Mark Summers, *Party Games*, (Chapel Hill: University of North Carolina Press, 2004), 217

Jarrett's money often went to the production of flyers that addressed the link between free trade and jobs. The 1888 election was known as the "election of education," targeted at labor. "John Bull baiting" could be tied into the tariff issue and helped gain Irish laborer support. Jarrett was skillful in reminding the Irish that free trade had been used by the British to destroy Ireland. To assure success Republican candidates spoke of "independence" for Ireland. The deflection of the Irish and the Knights even helped shake the Tammany Hall Democratic machine in New York. With the exception of McKinley, few politicians realized that the Irish vote could become a Republican strength. It was a goal that McKinley never fully achieved, but he did break up the Irish Catholic vote in some industrial cities.

The presidential election for the fourth time in a row was close. While tariffs were the main issues, a number of political tricks may have given the Republicans the victory. A solicited letter from the British Minster supporting Cleveland hurt Cleveland with the Eastern Irish vote. The Union Labor Party, an attempted combination of farmers and laborers, probably took up to 150,000 votes from the Democrats. Cleveland actually won the popular vote by 90,000 votes but lost the Electoral College by losing the big states such as New York. Harrison received 233 electoral votes to Cleveland's 168. It was the second time in twelve years that the Democrats won the popular vote but lost the presidency. The Democrats, in particular, had shown strength in farming districts and states. McKinley won in 1888 by his largest majority of 4,100 votes, which also reflected his new national reputation. McKinley had won the votes of the Knights, defeating their own Democratic candidate. One Democratic observer noted that the Ohio Knights were: "some of the biggest flatheads to be found. It would require a club as big as a telegraph pole to knock sense in some of their thick skulls." But really the issue for labor was tariffs, not robber barons or oppressive capitalists. Labor pulled their votes from third parties such as the Labor Party and Greenback Party to give Republicans the victory. The Republicans nationally had a slight advantage in the House and Senate.

McKinley observed the first signs of a new realignment of the Republican Party. Labor votes and labor leadership support could become part of a Republican strategy. Tariffs were clearly an issue that could unify labor and capital. The pending battle over the tariff issue in Congress had rallied and built a new alliance. The problem in the Republican Party remained the Eastern bankers and their financial support. The bankers demanded that Republican candidates support the gold standard. This support for gold had driven the farmers firmly into the Democratic Party, and this loomed as a major problem for McKinley in his heavy farming congressional district. The new realignment, however, had made McKinley a national leader and that was where his future lay.

CHAPTER 7. THE NAPOLEON OF PROTECTION — THE MCKINLEY TARIFF BILL OF 1890

> Half-heartedness never won a battle.
> — *William McKinley*

The Fifty-first Congress assembled with the idea of pursuing tariff increases, but the assumed "mandate" was not really reflected by the close election. McKinley, however, with Harrison, planned to finally push an extensive and scientific tariff. He was better prepared after years of defensively battling bills to reduce tariffs. McKinley also had fifteen years of House experience, no small feat in those times. The real risk of McKinley's push on tariffs would be the farmers in his home congressional district. He understood the opposition of the farmers but felt he could educate them on the long-term benefits of domestic manufacture to reduce prices. It would be a tough battle since farmers tended to think in annual cycles and needs, but he was prepared to make compromises such as a tariff on wheat. McKinley was not alone in his thinking; businessmen such as Mark Hanna saw it as the perfect time to make the case.

McKinley started the session with an unusual bid to become Speaker of the House. He had been a loyal soldier and warhorse for the party, and he seemed a prime candidate. McKinley wanted it badly, but as always, he decided to run a quiet, behind-the-scenes campaign. His opponent for the speakership was Thomas Reed of Maine. They offered a study in contrasts. Reed was tough and sarcastic; McKinley, easygoing and likable. Reed was a parliamentarian and vote counter, while McKinley was a diplomat and orator. Reed was highly educated and fluent in French, while McKinley was self-educated for the most part. Reed was a major political boss in the east, with a New England machine behind him. Reed engaged two managers, Henry Cabot Lodge and Theodore Roosevelt, to help in the political battle. McKinley ran a good campaign against the trend for Reed. Thomas Reed's support for the high tariffs was not clear; it was even suspected he favored a reduction. In the final weeks, Mark Hanna came to Ebbitt House to lend his political managerial support. Hanna represented many business interests, which could count on McKinley's unwavering support. Hanna was not, as many biographers claim, behind McKinley's decision to run for the Speakership. In the end, McKinley lost, 85 votes to 38 votes. While Reed had little respect for McKinley, he had held his fire in the campaign. Reed looked at McKinley as an overzealous patriot with limited knowledge (and education) on the issues. McKinley, for his part, made the vote unanimous with a motion for Reed, and then became the loyal soldier, a role he knew so well.

Years later, McKinley would suggest it was for the best that he lost the Speakership. Due to sickness, "Pig Iron" Kelly left as Chair of the Ways and Means Committee and McKinley was selected to replace him. Actually, the Ways and Means Committee would be the right place to launch his tariff legislation. Despite Reed's lack of respect for McKinley, he drew on his experience in rules and assigned him to the Rules Committee. Reed and McKinley would make a great team, and the fifty-first Congress would be one of the most productive. The rivalry would again surface years later.

The Tariff Bill of 1890 was the signature legislation of William McKinley's career, and it would give him national support — and a local defeat. What at first was called his Waterloo would actually forge the sword of victory. The Fifty-first Congress of 1888 formed with what was believed to be a mandate for tariff reform. The Republicans controlled the White House and both branches of the legislature. Providence seemed to have favored McKinley, and McKinley's power was peaking. The tariff issue, now pre-eminent, was what McKinley had studied most of his political life. Although the new president, Benjamin Harrison, was in favor of high tariffs, he was not a personal friend. McKinley drew on old friends such as ex-president Hayes and showed true brilliance in his compromises and teamwork, not only in the House but also with the Senate and White House. He was dealing with a mix in both parties. The tariff bill included many innovations which especially helped American farmers. The bill completed the evolutionary steps of revenue generation to the protection and development of American industry. The bill aimed to generate and develop new industries, which had been the dream of Alexander Hamilton and the Federalists. No bill preceding it had been directed at a policy to build industries such as tinplate and sugar.

The American tinplate industry became the poster child for this new approach of tariff legislation. America's demand for tinplate was enormous with the tin can market for food in 1889 at $29,000,000 alone, with the oil industry providing an even greater demand for large tin cans (refined kerosene being sold in tin cans). In 1889, there wasn't a single tinplate mill in the country. Because of its large tin deposit at Cornwall, England had a world monopoly on tinplate. Working with steel makers, McKinley believed that with a tariff of around 50%, a domestic industry could be developed. Manufacturers from Wheeling, West Virginia; Youngstown, Ohio; and Pittsburgh, Pennsylvania were highly supportive. Old friends and rolling mill owners in Niles lobbied McKinley on the industrial potential. The Democrats fiercely objected to this type of industry building by tariff reform, arguing that it would mean years of high price tinplate before any results could be seen. America would also have to import or develop a new technology. In addition, new mines of tin would have to be developed. Finally, Democrats argued it favored a small group of manufacturers at the cost of all the rest of the country. This approach to use tariffs to promote specific industries was novel at the time but had roots back to Henry Clay.

The tin amendment had the point of the attack. The bill did provide an escape clause if American manufacturers failed to make the necessary investments. If American manufacturers could not maintain a third of the market demand, then tin plate would become duty-free again. If success were not obtained by 1896, the tinplate tariff would be eliminated. Manufacturers, however, did respond, providing millions for investment. They imported thousands of skilled tinplate workers to develop the technology as well. By 1895, there were sixty-nine American tin mills. Unfortunately, the investment could not come fast enough to avoid the initial political backlash to McKinley.

McKinley's Bill of 1890 was extremely well researched and used science and statistics to apply the tariff rates. McKinley developed pamphlets with outstanding graphics to make his points. His presentations showed business skills not usually seen in politicians of the time. McKinley argued that the revenue tariff approach was the real problem. His statistics were convincing: "Before 1820 nearly all our imports were dutiable; scarcely any were free; while in 1824 the proportion of free imports was less than 6 percent; in 1830, about 7 percent.... The percent of free imports from 1873 to 1883 was about 30 percent, and under the tariff revision of 1883 it averaged 33 percent."[36] For his 1890 bill it would be 50%. The difference was that the focus was on the nation's needs, not revenue producing, which for years had been the only major source of government income.

---

36 William McKinley, "The Value of Protection," *The North American Review*, June 1890, Volume 150, Issue 403, pages 747-48

Although the McKinley plan was the result of years of study, and no one knew more about tariffs than McKinley, he would have to make political compromises to get it passed. He pored nightly over the tariff schedules, and surveyed his colleagues on industry needs.

McKinley argued that protective tariffs had not restricted exports, and again the numbers supported him: "We sell to Europe $449,000,000 worth of products and buy $208,000,000 worth. We sell to North America to the value of $9,645,000 and buy $5,182,000. We sell to South America $13,810,000 and buy $9,088,000." McKinley was not alone in his evaluation. In 1882, Bismarck had hailed the protective tariffs of America: "Because it is my deliberate judgment that the prosperity of America is mainly due to its system of protective laws." The McKinley tariffs were focused on building the economy, not restricting trade. They were applied in a manner that did not produce trade wars. Still, McKinley was clear that his tariffs were nationalistic: "The free-trader wants the world to enjoy with our citizens equal benefits of trade in the United States. The Republican protectionist would give the first chances to our people and would so levy duties upon the products of other nations as to discriminate in favor of our own." McKinley's extensive study had truly brought scientific management into tariff rates, but Congress preferred politics to science.

The McKinley Bill was hard fought in Congress with the Republican majority being slight. Democrats had brought in a cohort of college professors to suggest that McKinley's view was too simple and that, after all, the consensus among economists was that free trade was necessity. McKinley argued that it was the worker, not the professor, who best understood "free trade." In McKinley's Ways and Means Committee there were 1,400 pages of testimony alone. Committee review started in January and went into April. After each day, McKinley held a type of war room review of schedules and problems in the parlor of Ebbitt House. McKinley loved the detail that many avoided. He was battling Harrison and James Blaine from the White House as well. Blaine wanted a type of political reciprocity for South America and Blaine was against tariffs on sugar for the same reason. Blaine represented a growing wing of Republican trade expansionists. McKinley's objection was not with economic reciprocity, but political reciprocity. Blaine wanted to propose "free trade" in the American hemisphere, and he had Harrison's support. Rebuked by the Committee, Blaine went on to argue removal of South American sugar from the tariff list on the floor and later in the Senate. McKinley would oppose political reciprocity for his whole career, seeing it as defeating the reason for protective tariffs — to take care of the United States first. McKinley had little interest in international movements. He was willing to compromise domestically and added tariffs on farm products to help the Western states and farmers. This helped the wheat growers against cheap imports from Canada and Europe.

The battle in the Ways and Means Committee ended with a simple call by McKinley:

> With me this position is a deep conviction, not theory. I believe in it and thus warmly advocate it because enveloped in it are my country's highest development and greatest prosperity; out of it come the greatest gains to the people, the greatest comforts to the masses, the widest encouragement for manly aspirations, with the largest rewards, dignifying and elevating our citizenship, upon which the safety and purity and permanency of our political system depend. [37]

The bill then moved out of Committee, bearing the name of the chair — William McKinley.

The groundwork for floor success had been set in the first days of the Fifty-first Congress. McKinley had teamed up with Speaker Thomas Reed for a critical rule change. Democratic and Republican minorities in the past had perfected the invisible or "disappearing" quorum, thereby blocking a vote on an important issue. The trick was achieved by not answering the roll call, then arguing a lack of quorum for the vote. The fight over the rule change to count all present caused a small riot on the floor and in the galleries. This easy filibuster technique had become entrenched over the years. McKinley realized that the rule would be a major weapon of the Democrats in the upcoming tariff battle. McKinley made key speeches on the rule change and worked the floor to hold all Republican votes. It came down to a strict party vote, with Reed carrying the rule change proposal. Without this rule change, it is doubtful that McKinley's tariff bill would have made it through before the 1890 elections.

As the Tariff Bill came to the House, McKinley had earned the title "Napoleon of Protection" by marshaling his forces on several fronts. He had to balance the growing call from the White House for trade expansion within his own party. He realized that he needed to address the concerns of the farmers if he were to get some Democratic support. He also wanted a scientific look at the duty-free list and the amount of tariff, which had grown as politically complex as today's tax system. There was also a major problem in the management and administration of the tariffs. McKinley wanted to use the tariff to build this nation. He wanted to create employment, protect infant industries, but also target a group of embryonic industries for growth. Clearly, the Tariff Bill of 1890 takes the hardest look at the tariff schedule since the birth of the republic. It included years of study by McKinley as well as a large dose of political horse-trading.

---

37 Morgan, 131

As expected, McKinley marshaled the bill through the Ways and Means Committee. The bill included a tariff on sugar, which Secretary of State, James Blaine, opposed. McKinley allowed for a sugar duty in order to gain the support of the Southern Democrats, who were normally free traders but controlled by the domestic Sugar Trust. Blaine, however, was already dealing with the Senate to correct this. Blaine and Harrison wanted reciprocity amendments in the bill, in particular on sugar, so that the Harrison administration could make political arrangements with South America. McKinley opposed them, not on principle, but because they complicated the bill. The reciprocity amendments of Blaine gave the president powers to use tariffs for economic and political retaliation. McKinley would ultimately hammer out a compromise with Speaker Reed and the White House. It was necessary to hold the Republicans together for passage. With the Reed rules, the House debate was restricted to four days. In the end, the bill passed the House on strict party lines — 164 to 142. McKinley would state that the bill was "protective in every paragraph and American in every line and word."

Blaine continued to work on the sugar tariff in the Senate. Besides the Congress, Blaine was working on a possible treaty with Hawaii, which exported over 99.9% of its sugar to the United States. Blaine wanted political reciprocity in exchange for duty free sugar from Hawaii. These political agreements would include exclusive use of Pearl Harbor for US naval operations. Many saw this as a positive, but it was these types of political favors for economic favors that McKinley feared. Blaine saw similar "opportunities" in Cuba, Haiti, San Domingo, and South America. Blaine, who had served in the Garfield and Harrison administrations, looked also to China and Korea as markets. Blaine represented a growing group of businessman, politicians, and manufacturers who were economic expansionists. McKinley, at least initially, saw little value in this approach. Political reciprocity was a slippery slope fraught with the potential for abuse. The Harrison-Blaine strategy seemed to offer new markets to farmers and manufacturers but offered little to the labor side of the McKinley alliance. Furthermore, free trade and the Harrison-Blaine strategy of political reciprocity would augur the downfall of the house of American labor, and McKinley's vision of industrial America was anchored on that alliance.

Still, it cannot be overlooked that the McKinley view was always designed to help the domestic industries that hired Americans; he had little interest in international relations. Many historians argue that McKinley was part of an empire or imperialist movement of the late 1800s to expand the American nation. In particular, Walter LaFeber in his work *The New Empire* noted an emerging strategy for Pan-Americanism, a type of economic expansion into South America.

James Blaine of the Harrison Administration was the author of the strategy, but McKinley's bill consistently did not aid any type of Pan-Americanism. Blaine was on the forefront of American manufacturers looking to new foreign markets. McKinley was slow to come to the benefits of Pan-Americanism, but he did come to see reciprocity as a means of maintaining fair trade. Blaine had hoped to forge an alliance with farmers and industrialists through a series of government controlled trade agreements. In the McKinley Tariff Bill, McKinley remained fully nationalistic, however, driving the tariffs of wool to new highs to protect American farmers. He would not negotiate on wool, but would ultimately give in to Blaine on sugar and reciprocity. For his part, Blaine used the Senate to force McKinley where possible.

The Senate, however, would be the main challenge. McKinley had been working closely with the Senate leadership to help, but the Senate held it up. The "Silver Senate" had a slight Republican edge, but six of them were from the newly created Western states. These Silver Senators demanded free silver in return for the tariffs. In addition, the Democrats were demanding anti-trust protection if these tariffs were passed. Two bills of Ohioan John Sherman played a role in the ultimate passage of the McKinley Tariff. First was the Sherman Anti-Trust Bill. This bill's passage required help in the House where there was opposition. McKinley and Sherman worked out the needed compromise to achieve a balance for the consumer. More recently, Robert Bork has argued that the passage of the Sherman Anti-Trust Bill was a pure vote getting political compromise to give Republicans a defense for helping the trusts via tariffs.[38] McKinley would surely agree, but it was the tariffs that McKinley felt tipped the scales in favor of the American voter.

The Sherman Anti-Trust law, passed in July 1890, has been noted by many as cover for the tariff bill. Many called it the "Swiss Cheese Act" because of its many loopholes. The bill, however, had bipartisan support and seemed a natural, considering the level of public support. The Anti-Trust Bill is generally seen as ineffective. The Harrison Administration brought seven suits under the bill, and future administrations, for instance Cleveland's, brought eight, and McKinley's three. The increase in industrial combinations did increase over the next fifteen years, but under a new formation of the holding company versus the trust. Others argue that the Sherman Anti-Trust was an anti-union bill. In fact, some of its initial uses were against unions, but there is little evidence of its formation of an anti-union measure. McKinley voted for the Anti-Trust Bill, and he strongly supported unions.

---

38 Robert Bork, "Legislative Intent and the Policy of the Sherman Act," *Journal of Law and Economics*, October 1996, 7-48

The more difficult of the summer "compromise" bills was the Sherman Silver Purchase Act. The gold issue was dominant after the Civil War resolved the slavery issue. The issue of gold versus silver, while as hot politically, was not as clear cut as the slavery issue. Its history, however, enjoys the same twists and turns as the early slavery issue. In the Coinage Act of 1837, the United States had a bimetallic policy. The policy allowed unlimited coinage of gold and silver with the restriction that the ratio of 16 units of silver for every 1 unit of gold (thus the 16 to 1), or in other words 1 unit of gold was worth 16 units of silver. Silver became undervalued in the ensuing years. In the marketplace, it took 32 units (grains) of silver to equal 1 unit (grain) of gold. This difference meant everyone wanted gold coins and certificates, as they were more valuable. This hurt the silver mines in the West and to a degree reduced the money supply. The farmers, with higher mortgage rates, suffered from a reduced money supply.

The next political twist in the story came in the Coinage Act of 1873. The Panic of 1873 was successfully blamed by the bankers on silver coinage. Silver caused inflation, which is always the enemy of the rich. The Coinage Act of 1873 put the country on the gold standard. The "free silver" supporters knew it as the "crime of 73." The farmers wanted silver because the currency increase would reduce mortgage rates. Another group had a psychological problem with gold. Irish immigrants had always blamed the miseries of the Irish farmer on the British gold standard. Many observers are confused by whole silver–gold debate of the Gilded Age. Confusion abounded in the Gilded Age between the average American and middle class voter. Voters could easily be manipulated by politicians, who themselves didn't understand the issue, but did the vote count. The issue came up in every election with continuing intensity until 1900. It wasn't until 1894 that free silver advocates realized they needed to educate the population. William Harvey published a little book called *Coin's Financial School*. It was to be for the silver–gold debate what *Uncle Tom's Cabin* had been for the slavery issue. Harvey's book quickly became a best seller, reflecting the voters' degree of confusion and their desire to understand the issue. The success of the book, in part, led to the strengthening of the Populist Party.

Still, in 1890, prior to Harvey's book, silver had strong support by the farmers, Western states, small businesses, many manufacturers, and the Irish. Some congressmen saw an opportunity to use silver as a wedge. The chant by Senate Democrats and Western Republican Senators was "No silver, No tariffs." McKinley was now personally torn. The Senate was holding up his tariff bill as they debated free silver. McKinley was a bimetallist, even though there was a great deal of support for free silver in his district. He had opposed free silver often on the House floor, but now the tariff bill was clearly blocked. President

Harrison threatened to veto any free silver bill, and the silver Republicans and Democrats didn't have the votes to override a veto. The result was the passage of the compromise Sherman Silver Purchase Act, which took the country off the gold standard. The Sherman Silver Purchase Act returned the country to the 16 to 1 bimetal standard. McKinley supported the compromise, so the Senate could move on to the tariff bill. Mark Hanna was outraged as were most of the Republican big money supporters. With the silver bill and anti-trust bills passed in July of 1890, the Senate moved ahead on the tariff bill. The McKinley Tariff Bill went to conference review in September; the conference committee faced rate reviews of 4,000 items and 450 amendments. The members worn out by the long House and Senate debate passed it in 17 days, and the President signed it in October.

McKinley had battled throughout the conference's bill formation. He argued: "I have interpreted the victory [1888 elections] to mean, the majority in this House and in the Senate to mean, that a revision of the tariff is not only demanded by the votes of the people, but that such revision should be on the line and in full recognition of the principle and purpose of protection." McKinley flexed, bent, and compromised, but held to the basics of protectionism against the Democrats, his own party, internationalists, free traders, Pan-Americanism, and some in his own district. No one has fought harder for an economic bill on trade.

McKinley was exhausted after his great and hard-fought battle. He now had only a few weeks to prepare for the fall elections where he faced his toughest competition in years. McKinley's defeat in 1890 was the result of a brilliant piece of politics, not the direct result of the Tariff of 1890, as many history books claim. First, in 1890, McKinley was again gerrymandered by a Democratic state legislature. McKinley's district this time included Stark, Wayne, and Holmes counties. The anticipated Democratic advantage was considered to be 3,000 votes. Wayne and Holmes counties were farming districts. Holmes was particularly problematic in that it was predominately made up of Amish farmers who voted as a block and usually Democratic. The block was estimated at 800 strong.[39] The state Democrats realized that farmers were hit hard by several factors. The years 1887 through 1890 had been terrible for farmers with severe blizzards and drought. The blizzards killed millions of cattle throughout the nation.[40] To complicate things, the price of wheat had been falling to around $.85 a bushel from its high of over a dollar. Corn fell from 63 cents a bushel to 28 cents a bushel. Combined with the price drop was a doubling of rates by the railroads to transport wheat and corn. Imports from Canada and Europe were putting pressure on wheat prices as well. The crop and animal failures caused the farmers an increase

39 Edward Thornton Heald, *William McKinley Story*, (Canton: Canton Historical Society, 1964), 61
40 Isaac Asimov, *The Golden Door*, (Boston: Houghton Mifflin Company, 1977), 82

in debt. In addition, there was a short but intense panic in 1890 which tightened money and credit. Not only was credit tight and interest high, but also inflation was raising prices on goods and supplies. The farmers were clearly in a depression. To make matters worse, the Congress was known as the "Billion Dollar Congress" because of its spending. The farmers, short on cash, overwhelmed by debt, and looking to place blame, would lead a "farmer revolt" nationwide in the 1890 elections.

Another problem nationally for the Republicans might be termed the capitalist revolt. The Congress had moved to help the farmers with the Sherman Free Silver Act in 1890, which used a silver base to dramatically increase the money supply and to hopefully reduce interest rates for the farmers. The Panic of 1890 was a rich man's panic, starting in the financial markets of Europe and hitting the American upper class hard. Many fortunes of the rich were lost, such as that of the Adams family. The crisis affected not only the 1890 congressional elections but also the presidential election of 1892. Ex-president Cleveland, now governor of New York, became the flag bearer of the gold standard, breaking with the mainstream of the Democratic Party. The break would gain him the support of America's wealthiest capitalists such as Andrew Carnegie and J. P. Morgan. Andrew Carnegie wrote Cleveland with his support: "You know that for several years my chief anxiety in public matter had been in regard to the 'silver question' and that I stated in the North American Review that if I were called upon to vote for a Free Trade Democrat who supported sound money, or a Tariff Republican who was not sound upon money, I should vote for the former."[41] The capitalist's revolt would eventually bring Cleveland back to the White House in 1892, but the farmers would rule the congressional election of 1890.

The actual impact of the Tariff of 1890 on the farmers that fall was only perceived or anticipated. It was applied about four weeks before the election too soon to have any real impact on prices. Furthermore, the bill contained tariffs on agricultural products that might actually have helped. The bill took duties off sugar, but this was done by joint committee with the Senate. McKinley felt deeply that sugar must stay on the bill, but James Blaine, then Secretary of State, addressed it with Republican senators and had it removed in the Senate. It was a positive for McKinley because the sugar tariff was considered the "poor man's table tax." McKinley himself had hesitated, but felt that in the long run a stronger sugar industry would reduce prices. McKinley increased the wool tariff which helped the depressed Ohio woolgrowers. The reciprocity amendments would ultimately open new South American markets, and the farm district represen-

---

41 Smith, 466

tatives had aided in the final passage due to these amendments. In other cases, McKinley tried to lower the tariffs on raw materials to help manufacturers. In the case of tinplate, he made a deliberate attempt to establish an infant industry in the United States. McKinley had wanted to take out the flag of his early mentor "Pig Iron" Kelly of Pennsylvania who, as Chair of Ways and Means, had fought twenty years to establish an American tinplate industry. Overall, the bill should have forged a unity of farmers and manufacturers.

The Democrats, however, seized the moment, calling for high tariffs on tinplate, which was the base for the farmer's tin ware. In tinplate, America was dependent on outside sources such as Britain, as Americans scrambled to make the investments. Tinplate was an embryonic industry that McKinley felt critical for the American economy, but it would need at least two years to stand alone. The tariff had focused on developing domestic tinplate to help reduce prices of tin ware down the road. In any case the merchants and peddlers did increase prices in anticipation of a price increase. In addition, Ohio peddlers, who resented the tariff, started to increase prices aimed at affecting the 1890 election. The actual tariff increases of the 1890 bill would take place after the election. The Democratic candidate even paid peddlers to raise prices. Holmes County peddlers even got encouragement (and probably help) from the Democrats to set prices as high as a $1 a pot and $.25 a cup, prices which would normally be $.25 a pot and $.05 for a cup. The prices were beyond what the farmers could pay, and though the peddlers didn't sell any, they achieved their goal. As farmers complained, they were told to blame it on the McKinley tariff. The issue was completely bogus with tinplate, and a Grange member noted: "I do not know of a single article that is higher than a year ago. Of course, it was less politic to say so from the stump."[42] Historical statistics support that there was no evidence of overall price increases.[43]

History would also vindicate McKinley, as a $40 million American industry was in place by 1896, generating tens of thousands of American jobs. The response of American steel companies represented a manufacturing miracle, but too late to help in the 1890 election. By the end of 1891, the tinplate industry had twenty plants operating and ten more under construction. By the deadline of 1896, there were 75 plants in operation. Furthermore, great industrial towns of Youngstown and Wheeling grew as a result of the tariff. Many credit the logistical successes of American doughboys in World War I to the existence of large tinplate industry due to the McKinley Tariff.

---

42 J. H. Brigham to A. J. Rose, September 4, 1891, Rose papers, Texas History Collection

43 Albert Rees, *Real Wages in Manufacturing 1890-1914*, (Princeton: Princeton University Press, 1961), 74-77

Sugar provisions were actually excluded (for six months) from implementation in 1890. The exclusion of sugar from the duty (should have helped) hurt the Republicans because it was not immediately implemented. The sugar tariff and its resultant higher prices was one item the consumers across America resented. Voters didn't realize that sugar prices would fall. Interestingly, the McKinley tariff on tinplate did establish American tinplate with over two hundred mills producing five million boxes of tinplate by 1901. Still, tinplate would be the focal point of the Democratic attack in McKinley's home district.

Mark Hanna was aware of the attack on McKinley and the Ohio congressmen that had supported the tariff. The distortions required an expensive educational campaign, and Hanna gathered the financial resources. Hanna was having trouble amassing the usual war chest, as many industrialists felt the Sherman Silver Purchase Act had sold them out. J. P. Morgan was outraged by the passage of the silver bill. The rich man's Panic of 1890 had also made cash short. Even with the McKinley amendments to favor the farmers, the farmers were being taken in by fear. It was the first campaign that industrialist Mark Hanna was highly involved in. He and McKinley had found common ground on the protection of American manufacturing.

Another problem was that Harrison was seen as unfriendly to labor and farmers, the very foundation of the old Greenback-Labor Party, and the alliance that McKinley dreamed of forming. In 1888, the Republicans had made inroads into the labor and Irish Catholic vote. Harrison was no McKinley ally; he took a hard line on Catholics and labor, which helped erode what the Republicans had gained in the 1888 elections. With his gold stand, he had no friends among the farmers either. Clearly, some of the Republican problems in 1890 were directly attributable to a Harrison backlash. Democrats, still smarting from the take down of their free trade representatives, targeted McKinley from a national perspective. McKinley's district always made him susceptible because of its Democratic registration.

McKinley was aware of the Democratic effort and ran one of his most active campaigns, making 30 speeches in 14 days. Beds were set up in railroad cars as he traversed the district. Still, he was hindered by a large registration disadvantage and a huge national Democratic trend. There is no question that had McKinley been in an industrial congressional district such as Pittsburgh, he would have had a lifetime seat, but his democratic leaning district dogged his whole career. Furthermore, in 1890, McKinley did not have a national organization yet. The 1890 election lived up to the name "farmer's revolt." It was a Democratic landslide as 78 of the 166 Republicans were defeated and the Democrats held their seats, leaving 88 Republicans against 235 Democrats in the House (with 9 Populists).

All Republicans in farm districts lost. The "Farmer's Alliance" of congressmen, or what we would call a caucus, consisted of 50 Democrats. McKinley lost by only 302 votes, a truly heroic effort. Ohio elected 14 Democrats versus 7 Republicans. Later analysis of the 1890 election suggests that federal spending, parochial schools, and temperance had as much an impact as tariffs.[44] Temperance and parochial school issues probably cost McKinley some votes.

McKinley's informal press release was as follows:

> Protection never was stronger than it is at this time and it will grow in strength and hearts of the people. The elections this year were determined upon a false issue. A conspiracy between importers and free trade to raise prices and charge it upon the McKinley Bill was successful, but conspiracies are short-lived and soon expire. This one has already been laid bare and the infamy of it will still further appear.

> Keep up your courage, strengthen your organizations and be ready for the great battle Ohio in 1891 and the still greater one in 1892. Home and country will triumph in the end.

McKinley had to endure the celebrations and taunts of Democrats on the floor of Congress, which he did with dignity. After the close of session, McKinley took his wife to Chicago for a vacation. Newspapers in Ohio almost immediately started to suggest that McKinley run for governor.

---

44 Morgan, 355

Chapter 8. Governor McKinley

Defeat this time was bittersweet for McKinley. He was well aware that he now had a national platform. Papers from Chicago, Pittsburgh, Cleveland, Buffalo, etc., were now routinely following him and his speeches. The large urban industrial districts and mill towns were in amazement that McKinley lost his congressional seat, but Canton was really an industrial oasis in a farm field. Duties of the 51st Congress kept him in Washington until March of 1891. An Ohio delegation spoke to him before he left Washington about running for governor in Ohio. He probably at least considered the idea of running for president at this point. The Senate seemed to be of little interest to him. In those days the power over money bills was in the House, not the Senate. He was still making appointments for speeches at national organizations such as the American Protective Tariff League, revealing that he had national ambitions. The defeat of McKinley was a serious blow for the nation's manufacturers, who now were leaderless in the protection effort. Personally, McKinley could have had the governorship with ease, as the Ohio Republican Party felt the need to keep him active. The governorship of Ohio offered national visibility and was considered a presidential stepping-stone. In the long run it would be the opportunity that indeed made McKinley presidential material. More importantly, the governorship was a management position. It would demonstrate that McKinley had managerial assets beyond that of a protectionist congressman. The state of Ohio needed a unity Republican candidate and McKinley fulfilled that need.

John Sherman and Mark Hanna had formed an alliance in the early 1880s that dominated Ohio politics. Sherman was the senior senator from Ohio, which tended to elect Democratic senators because of the farm base. Sherman was actually considered the founder of the Ohio Republican Party. He had attracted Mark Hanna because he was a gold bug and protectionist. Sherman had had a long career, having served as Secretary of the Treasury under President Hayes. In the Senate, as we have seen, Sherman was a floor leader. McKinley, however, had supported James Blaine over Sherman and the Ohio delegation for president in 1880. Blaine was a moderate protectionist compared to Sherman, who had other priorities. McKinley, over the years, had even perceived Sherman as weak on protection. In 1888, McKinley had given somewhat lukewarm support, but as a party loyalist he worked for Sherman's presidential efforts. Now Sherman was giving somewhat lukewarm support to McKinley for governor. Hanna showed the same lukewarm support but hoped privately that McKinley could rebuild the Ohio Republican Party. McKinley hesitated because of the poor conditions of his businesses, which were suffering from a lack of attention.

McKinley was always slow to make big decisions, and the decision to run for governor was no different. McKinley certainly had an array of options, including running for his old House seat. Even after his defeat in 1890, McKinley had declared no interest in a Senate run in 1890 or 1892.[45] He was not going to give up his tariff platform, and that was clear as he finished his congressional term in 1891. He could have waited and run again for Congress but would certainly tire of the battle each two years in a marginal district. He realized that his platform played better nationally and statewide. While he would always have ex-president Hayes's support, their political differences were such that he probably did not get Hayes's encouragement to run for governor. Still records suggest that Hayes anticipated McKinley's run for the governorship.[46] Immediately after his congressional defeat, national papers, such as the *New York Tribune*, *Philadelphia Record*, *Chicago Inter-Ocean*, and the *Cleveland Leader* believed his next title would be governor.[47] While Sherman-Hanna controlled Ohio from a national standpoint, McKinley owned the state organization. He had paid his dues in the state system, serving as chairman and on various state committees. McKinley had always stumped for Republican candidates throughout the state. More than anyone, McKinley had worked to repair torn relations in the state party between Governor Foraker and the Sherman-Hanna camp.

---

45 *Canton Repository*, January 2, 1890
46 Ari Hoogenboom, *Rutherford B. Hayes: Warrior & President*, (Lawrence: University of Kansas Press, 1995), 519
47 Phillips, 65

The Republican Party in Ohio was torn from the 1888 elections and the stunning defeats in 1890. Part of the problem was the rise of a young politician, Joseph Benson Foraker, who challenged Ohio's old Republican guard. Foraker's meteoritic rise was unsettling to the Grand Old Party that, since Hayes, had always favored paying your dues. Foraker used the force of his personality to win over the likes of John Sherman. Foraker was the antithesis of Sherman. He was colorful, dramatic, and likable. Foraker could also stand apart from years of scandal in the party. As a lawyer from Cincinnati, he had built a strong German following, which was critical to any Ohio Republican. These German ties gave him inroads into the farming vote as well. Foraker was an orthodox and conservative Republican, who offered no real new approaches to the standard issues. While Sherman was always wary of him, McKinley had supported him for governor in 1885.

Foraker's popularity became a threat to Sherman as Foraker looked at a possible senate run. Foraker had headed up the Ohio delegation to the Republican convention in 1888 and had supported Blaine against Sherman as the presidential candidate. While McKinley was torn between Blaine and Sherman, he was no friend of Foraker and ultimately supported Sherman in 1888. McKinley had brokered a meeting in 1887 to discuss Sherman's future, but had left Foraker out. Foraker would call Sherman-Hanna-McKinley alliance, the "combination," but focused his anger on Hanna and Sherman. The nomination went to Benjamin Harrison, but left the Ohio party split. Hanna particularly hated Foraker because he had downed Sherman's last hope for the presidency, and Hanna opposed Foraker's third run for the governorship. McKinley remained the party soldier and supported Foraker's third run for governor. Foraker released a set of forged papers suggesting some illegal business dealings of McKinley, Hanna, and Sherman. The incident caused a wider split in the party. McKinley, however, had the public trust, having never been implicated in any scandal over the years.

McKinley seemed like the right man to help heal the party split. McKinley, once he made the decision met directly with Foraker to ask for his support. McKinley risked some alienation by Hanna and Sherman, but he needed full Republican state support to win. At the state Republican convention in June, ex-Governor Joseph Foraker put McKinley's name in nomination. Foraker, acting as nominator, achieved the unity the state party had hoped for. Floor rules were immediately waived and McKinley was nominated by acclamation. Again the large continent of out of state newsmen augured the importance of McKinley as a national figure. State politics centered on the Tariff Bill of 1890. McKinley kicked off his campaign on August 22 in Niles after talking in Pittsburgh on tariffs. The Mahoning Valley and Youngstown now rivaled Pittsburgh and

Cleveland in steel and steel products, and McKinley found it to be the heart of protectionism.

The period around 1891 was one of economic growth in general. Cleveland and the Mahoning Valley steel mills were booming. The tariff on tinplate was spurring investment and job creation in Youngstown, Pittsburgh, and Wheeling. Coal mining was also booming in Ohio as the steel industry grew. In northwest Ohio, natural gas strikes had resulted in a mushrooming glass industry in northwest Ohio. The state race in such economic growth made it a sure thing for McKinley, but he took no chances, campaigning hard throughout the state. At one point, he made 12 speeches a day and recorded 134 speeches for the short campaign. The national press often outnumbered the state press. It was his greatest personal effort, and he did it without much help from Mark Hanna, who was tied up with Sherman's senate campaign. His opponent, Democrat James Campbell, was a traditional low-tariff, free silver Democrat, lacking any large urban support. Campbell did land some punches with free silver because tight money was still a problem in farming districts.

The farmers were at the peak of their power in the Gilded Age by 1891. Nationally the "farm alliances" had elected over 50 Congressman in the Democratic landslide of 1890. A new party was formed out of the success known as the "Peoples or Populist Party." The party had held its first convention in Cincinnati on May 19, 1891. While it did not have a state candidate, it backed Democratic Campbell. McKinley remained committed to the silver issue as a bimetallist. Amazingly, the issue that had been used against him was now a positive. Tariffs indeed had simulated an infant tin plate industry and jobs were being created in Ohio. Workers had "tinplate" and tin can dinners for him in the industrial districts, a political fund raising technique that would follow in his presidential campaigns. His supporters manufactured tin plate political souvenirs to distribute. Industrial workers formed long parades for him. In just a few years, Ohio had taken leadership in glass production, thanks to tariffs. He was asked to give a Labor Day speech in Cincinnati.

In the end, McKinley ran a tough, clean campaign based on the issues. The *Pittsburgh Gazette* and the *New York World* assigned full time reporters for national coverage, and in many aspects this was a national campaign. He depended on the state organization, having almost none of his own. He carried the state by 21,511 votes, and the Republicans took a majority of 50 in the state legislature. McKinley had taken Ohio against the trend. Industrial towns such as Cleveland, Pittsburgh, Chicago, Youngstown, and Buffalo saw it as a national victory. The national press started to promote McKinley as a future presidential candidate. With John Sherman over 70 and making his last ran for Congress, McKinley certainly was a national Republican figure. He had a solid labor vote in the Cleve-land-Pittsburgh corridor that no Republican before or after McKinley could ever count on. He was from them and understood them. And as governor, he would address their needs first.

While his platform was vague and touched more on national issues, his ac-ceptance speech got down to details. He recommended an appropriation for the Chicago World's Fair of 1893 (Columbian Exposition). The Ohio exhibit would be one of the biggest, and among the large industrial exhibits was Libbey Glass of Toledo, Ohio. He formed a commission to study the state's tax and the poten-tial upgrade of the canal system. He was in the end unable to gain any enthusi-asm for an improved canal system. He wanted a commission to look at the poor management of state institutions. He focused on the need for a state arbitration board to handle labor/management problems as well as taking an extensive look at working conditions including child labor and wages. McKinley called for the protection of unions to organize freely. Finally he called for better industrial safety laws.

He called in his friend George Westinghouse, and cajoled the state railroad commissioner to adopt a line of safety devices. This had been one of his lesser-known national quests as a Congressman. He called for legislation to improve the working conditions on railroads and in coalmines. He also drafted laws to improve general conditions for railroad conductors and brakemen. He enacted similar legislation for streetcar operators. Maybe more importantly, he designed an arbitration system for labor disputes, working with state labor leaders. He had some strong opposition from his own party on these labor laws, so he worked quietly behind the scenes. He used his personal influence to move the bill through the state legislation, gaining the respect of the national labor lead-ers. Another one of these bills required a six-month jail sentence and $1000 fines for employers who refused to allow employees to join a union. In this respect, he pioneered the model for management labor infrastructure in a democracy. His own party accused him of pandering to labor, but he had demonstrated that it was a core belief, rather than a merely political one. However, it was a strategic campaign of all-inclusive pluralism.

Congressman McKinley, as early as 1886, had spoken out on arbitration as a cornerstone for management-labor relations. In a speech in support of the O'Neill Bill for arbitration in interstate commerce he declared: 'I believe it is the true way of settling differences between labor and capital; I believe it will bring both to a better understanding, uniting them closer in interests, and promot-ing better relations, avoiding force, avoiding unjust exactions and oppression, avoiding loss of earnings to labor, avoiding disturbances to trade and transportation; and if this House can contribute in the smallest measure, by legislative expression or otherwise, to these ends, it will deserve and receive the gratitude of all men who love peace, good order, justice and fair play." Arbitration was how McKinley personally approached disagreements. He preferred direct, behind the scenes discussion, avoiding strong public stands. He believed that many of America's bloody confrontations were because of venting to the newspapers, a practice which backed people into corners. Arbitration represented a trademark of McKinley's style, and even political arguments were taken behind closed doors.

In 1894, the Hocking Valley Railroad was locked in a strike in southern Ohio. The strike was peppered with violence and had closed down the iron industry of the district. The American Railway Union and the company were deadlocked. McKinley had initiated early in his administration a state arbitration board but could not unlock the horns of this bitter dispute. McKinley brought the union, management, and the arbitration board to the governor's office. He brokered an agreement in eight hours. The management-union arbitration approach was considered uniquely American by McKinley, and was the answer to violent street riots. McKinley, realizing deadlocks would arise, felt the state should be the final arbitrator by using an impartial board. He had earlier worked arbitration into a number of state bills. Even as a national congressman, he had fought to add arbitration to labor bills. Arbitration was another area he found common ground with Mark Hanna. His passion for arbitration was yet another example of his strong administrative skills, which many biographers overlook.

As governor, McKinley exhibited adept executive abilities, which he had honed in the military. Furthermore, he demonstrated that the governorship was not just a stepping stone but also a position from which to leave his mark on Ohio. He worked hard behind the scenes on many controversial issues, often going against his own party. He reached his hand out to the Democrats in a conciliatory manner so he could advance his ideas. His behavior was far from that of the political puppet of the industrialists, which his critics tried to frame him as. In fact, he always kept to simple middle class values. His vision included good industrial jobs with wages that could give workers a future. He wanted to alleviate the twin fears of the middle class — debt and unemployment. He took on the industrialists often on safety and worker treatment. He wanted an industrial America, not a Big Business America.

His approach to relieve the heavy burden on middle class taxpayers was yet another demonstration of that vision. Real estate carried most of the state's tax income, while capital and investment carried none. His desire to form a commission to study state taxation found strong opposition from party heavyweights

Hanna and Foraker. McKinley had a deep belief that the wealthy should carry the tax burden, having seen the struggles of his own father to pay taxes in bad times. He took on the tax issue in Ohio just as he had the tariff issue on a national level. A corporate tax was part of his industrial vision and one that upset many of his capitalists backers. McKinley believed that corporations used the benefits of the state and should contribute to its finances. McKinley saw industry as the engine of the nation, which could improve life for workers and the government. He believed that the benefits of tariffs were not to support opulent parties, but wages, support of state government, and investment. This was far from the vision of the capitalists, which his critics said he was in bed with. McKinley saw part of the gains from tariff protection going to help finance state government. He opposed a federal tax on corporations and an income tax on the wealthy.

The tax issue would dog him throughout his terms as governor. He formed a bipartisan commission in the hope that it would defuse this issue. Still, Mark Hanna pushed against any new taxes on the wealthy. The commission affirmed his beliefs that corporations should be taxed, but he faced resistance from his own Republican majority in the state legislature. McKinley continued to work behind the scenes to formulate laws. He worked both parties in private meetings. His experience as a logistics officer paid off. He made no future enemies, stuck to getting the job done, and avoided public bullying. Less adept politicians would have gone the public route. In the end, McKinley got a tax on railroads and some other corporations such as telephone and telegraph companies.

He maintained an active schedule, dealing with state issues while taking requests to speak in America's industrial districts. He went to Indiana for the opening of a giant new tinplate mill, to Pittsburgh to talk to steelmakers, to Boston to speak on tariffs, to Indianapolis to speak on patriotism, and to Chicago to talk to workingmen. He was drawing crowds of thousands as his national popularity grew. He was a political workhorse for the national party, speaking on behalf of Republicans in almost every state while governor of Ohio. It appears clear that McKinley was thinking about the presidency in the long run, but this wasn't interfering with his duties as governor. In Ohio he built an infrastructure that would be a platform for future ambitions. McKinley exhibited more political savvy than most give him credit for, and he lacked a personal political manager during the period. The organization he built as governor was accomplished long before Mark Hanna came on the scene.

His personal life remained simple, only complicated by his wife's condition. Financially, McKinley's decision to become governor and forgo his career as a lawyer cost him thousands. His salary of $8000 a year left him struggling in the middle class. They lived in Columbus at the Neil and Chittenden Houses, since the governorship of Ohio did not include an executive residence. He rose early, did some work, breakfasted with Ida, and then took a walk to smoke his cigar. Ida seemed to improve by living in Ohio. Biographer Wayne Morgan noted the following: "His chief concern, as always, was Ida, and no matter what transpired, at 3 p.m. every day he opened his window to wave a white handkerchief toward the Neil House. Shortly an answering flutter would reply, indicating that she had seen his signal, an event that buoyed up her afternoon and proved that her 'dearest' thought of her even in the midst of state business." They traveled together whenever possible, but McKinley employed a full-time maid to help her. McKinley traveled extensively in 1892 to help refute Democratic attacks on the tariff bill.

Besides the numerous speeches on tariffs, the presidential election of 1892 required a lot of his time. McKinley was a delegate to the Republican National Convention in 1892. Benjamin Harrison, as president, was expected to get the nomination, but there was party strife. McKinley had some support and so did party deacons Blaine and Sherman. McKinley was probably interested, but he would not be part of challenging a sitting Republican president. Team playing was a touchstone of McKinley, and he, as always, waited his turn. He probably privately hoped for a deadlocked vote. Mark Hanna initially was still backing old Sherman, but Sherman declined to run. Hanna appears to have supported McKinley after Sherman backed down. The McKinley-Hanna team seemed to have emerged out of the convention. McKinley also attracted Chicago newspaper owner H. Kohlsaat's support. Enthusiastic young delegates generated floor demonstrations for McKinley. Blaine and McKinley each received 182 votes on the first ballot, but Harrison was re-nominated. McKinley left the convention with a strong team of future supporters and had made the first step to the 1896 presidential run.

McKinley, the loyal soldier, supplied strong support for Harrison. The support also came from a fear of Grover Cleveland who was running on tariff reduction. The Nebraska Republican Party paid for McKinley to take a Western campaign trip. Nebraska was the home state of populist William Jennings Bryan. The Republicans needed the Western states, but the Populists would take critical votes in the presidential election. The West could not go for Cleveland because of his absolute support of the gold standard. Most Republicans realized the tide was against them. In the Midwest, Democrats were pointing out prices as a result of the tariff bill. Harrison lacked McKinley's labor support, which almost assured his loss.

Late summer in 1892 saw problems between labor and capital. The battle broke out in Homestead near Pittsburgh over the closing of a steel mill of Andrew Carnegie. Henry Clay Frick was in charge of the company while Carnegie vacationed in Scotland. Frick used Pinkerton guards to move the workers out and a battle ensued. Guards and workers lost their lives, and the National Guard had to be called in. The whole affair hurt Harrison, who was perceived as anti-labor. Shortly, after the strike, an anarchist attacked Frick in his office. Frick and Carnegie were well-known Republicans, and this hurt the embryonic Republican gains with the steel laborers. This labor unrest further reduced Harrison's popularity in both parties. The local Democrats seized the moment, and Homestead, a traditional Republican stronghold, went Democratic in the 1892 elections. McKinleyism had built a labor alliance in Homestead, but the greed and abuse of capitalists such as Frick destroyed it in a few days. It was unfortunate, since Frick's actions didn't reflect the whole Carnegie organization. Harrison's unpopularity made it easy to target the blame for labor unrest.

In addition, the Republicans lost farm and Western support with the rise of the Populist Party. The Populist Party nominated James Weaver of Ohio, who had left the Republican Party. Weaver would get 300,000 votes in the election. Traditional Republican support faltered as the Eastern bankers supported Grover Cleveland, a gold supporter and friend of J. P. Morgan. The election followed the Republican setback of 1890. Grover Cleveland won by over 100,000 votes and carried the Electoral College 277 to 145. There were Democratic majorities in the House (218 to 127) and the Senate (44 to 38). The Democratic celebration would be shorted lived as the Panic of 1893 started to reach the factories of America. Cleveland set his sights on the repeal of the McKinley Tariff Bill, but the economy was already in trouble as he took office.

McKinley's speaking schedule for 1892 shows that he was running for president. He gave out-of-state speeches at Chicago, Ann Arbor, Providence, Pawtucket, Philadelphia, Minneapolis, Pittsburgh, Boston, and New York. He made train trips and tours in the states of West Virginia, Michigan, Nebraska, Missouri, Colorado, Indiana, Illinois, and Pennsylvania. These tours included his wife, maid, and family and friends. Everywhere he encountered large and enthusiastic crowds. The content of his speeches always concerned tariffs, jobs, and the economy. The following, from his October 4, 1892 in Boston is typical:

> The people believe in the industrial policy which promotes, not retards, American enterprises, and defines, not degrades, American labor, and they will take power away from any party that stands in the way of success of that policy. They believe in protection and reciprocity, and will give power to the party, which wisely and fearlessly maintains them, and power away from the party, which has weakened or destroyed them. They believe we should produce our own sugar, make our own tinplate, and we mean to do both. They believe we should do all our other work at home without being forced to pay labor starvation wages. They do not propose to give up

permanently anything they have gained in the industrial world in the last thirty years, and they would rather hold it by retaining a protective tariff than to hold it by reducing wages below the true American standard.

The Panic of 1893 had started, like most, as a financial crisis. The root cause remains debatable to this day. Part of the problem was a reduction of European investment in America. In 1890, the famous British investment firm, Baring Brothers, went bankrupt. Baring Brothers were a major stockholder in American firms. This financial failing caused investment to dry up in America. Another analysis is that Europeans pulled money out of America because the Sherman Silver Act caused them to lose confidence. Europeans were moving from bimetallism to a gold standard. Certainly that was a factor, but another view is that J. P. Morgan created it because he benefited by building his railroad trust and electric trust. Most of the failed railroads would come under Morgan's control. There was also a drain on treasury gold which Morgan attributed again to the Sherman Silver Bill. Another theory was that the generosity of the Republican pensions for veterans had drained the treasury. In fairness, however, the tariff revenues from the McKinley Tariff Bill more than covered the pensions. In any case, the first signs of a panic came ten days before Cleveland took office with the failure of the Philadelphia and Reading Railroad. Before the Panic of 1893 ended, a quarter of America's railroads would fail.

By summer, the stock market had crashed. Cleveland and Morgan blamed the Sherman Silver Bill and called for a repeal. Cleveland had the counsel of more capitalists than any Republican before him. Ike Hoover, head usher of the White House, called this constant flow of rich capitalists, the "millionaire's crowd." Cleveland pressured Democrats to hold them in line, but it was at a great cost to the party. He stood with Morgan on gold which resulted in a split in the Democratic Party. The Republicans and Populists united in Congress, but the overwhelming Democratic majority assured its repeal. McKinley gave some tacit support of the repeal, calling for an international agreement for bimetallism. Privately he believed that the recession seemed related to the silver question. Some of the problem was the resistance of the world to leave the gold standard, and since most exports went to gold countries, accounts were settled in gold. In addition, Cleveland blamed the Tariff of 1890 and moved quickly to reduce duties, but he wanted the gold standard back.

The public, like McKinley, hesitated on silver because of the recession. The highly prosperous years from 1882 to 1892 were years the country had been on the gold standard. McKinley probably favored the idea that the recession was silver driven rather than tariff driven. The repeal of the Sherman Silver Act passed the House 239 to 108 and the Senate 43 to 37, basically along party lines, but some republicans crossed over to gold. Its repeal slowed the gold drain on the treasury temporarily, but the Panic grew. In 1893 alone, 15,000 businesses failed, along with 158 banks. In the long run the public increased its demand to get gold for their silver certificates, which drained the treasury to the crisis point. The Panic of 1903 was a complex recession, more related to international tight money. The adoption of the gold standard in the United States probably caused money to further tighten nationally. Tariffs would have had a minor effect, except that when people are out of work, they tend to blame importation. Still, Europe started to lower prices and export into the United States as they had done before, to keep their factories running. McKinley, Cleveland, Democrats, Republicans, the Senate, and the House all lacked a complete answer to the Panic.

The national crisis soon turned into a personal crisis for McKinley. An old Youngstown friend, Robert Walker, faced bankruptcy, which would drain all of McKinley's assets. McKinley's ties with Walker went back to his days at the Poland Academy. Walker had loaned McKinley money to go to law school. Over the years, McKinley had co-signed for Walker's business notes. McKinley thought the notes amounted to $5,000, when in reality they amounted to over $100,000. This lack of attention to detail was typical of McKinley's approach to personal and business dealings. As President, he would have to assign his finance management to others because he could not keep up with them. Ironically, the Panic of 1893 put Walker's tinplate business in bankruptcy. When the Euclid National Bank called in the notes, McKinley found himself overwhelmed and far short of the assets to pay. Mrs. McKinley was forced to sign over the family home, and McKinley faced the probability of resigning as governor.

In March of 1893, as McKinley faced this personal and political crisis, industrialist Myron Herrick and Mark Hanna started to build a fund to help McKinley pay the debt. The group of twenty-five or more, including Judge Day of Canton, Henry Clay Frick, Philander Knox, George Pullman, George Westinghouse, Charles Taft, and Chicago newspaper owner H. Kohlsaat, quickly raised the funds to help. McKinley would not accept the money as a gift, and promised to pay the debt back. Kohlsaat, who owned several Chicago papers, was an old friend. Kohlsaat eventually owned the *Chicago Times Herald* and the *Evening Post*, and played a key role in getting good press coverage. In a letter to his friends, McKinley said, "I insist they hold it, as an obligation against me to be paid off as fast as I can do it. I cannot for a moment entertain the suggestion of having my debts paid in the way proposed or in any other way than I have herein indicated, so long as I have health to earn money."[48] McKinley, up to the day of his death,

---

48 McKinley to Messrs. H. Kohlsaat, M. Herrick, M. Hanna, W. Day, and T. McDougal, March 14, 1893, McKinley Papers

paid monthly out of his salary to Myron Herrick.[49] Herrick managed the fund and his friends refused payment. On his death the fund went to Mrs. McKinley to help her financially for the rest of her life.

The news of McKinley's problems was out, and Hanna came to his aid in handling the public relations. Hanna expected the charges to suggest that a man who couldn't handle his personal finances had no business being governor of Ohio, let alone President of the United States. McKinley was devastated by the problems, and he leaned heavily on Herrick and Hanna's friendship. Newspapers were generally sympathetic, and mail came from all over the country in support of McKinley, often with small amounts of money. McKinley returned the flood of money coming to him personally. He kept everything open and above board. McKinley had never been stained by a scandal, and he would not let this personal problem become a scandal. The affair actually buoyed McKinley's standing as one of the regular citizens, and though Hanna used the sympathy to build political capital, this sympathy was real and deep among his supporters.

One story in the *Canton Repository* related a meeting with some coal miners. While on a train trip to Pennsylvania, a group of miners met his train at Somerset. They wanted to raise money for him; he had initially refused the offer. The lead miner noted: "You helped us once and we have not forgotten it. If you ever want anybody to die for you, call on us."[50] This scene was common as McKinley traveled in 1893, making Mark Hanna's work easy.

It should be noted that Mark Hanna was a tough, shrewd politician. Hanna managed and groomed McKinley for the presidency as he had Sherman years earlier. Hanna was known for his direct and forceful manner. He also had the unusual desire to be a political "Kingmaker" rather than carefully defining any political policy. Of course, he believed in the basics of American capitalism and the American system, as did McKinley. Hanna was known to lean hard on people for money and recently he has been compared by many to Karl Rove. Hanna ran the campaign with little overseeing from McKinley. He did at times defer to McKinley's personal needs. However, Hanna was first a genuine friend that was noted by even the most critical of the McKinley biographers. Furthermore, Hanna's role was clearly that of a political campaign manager and financial manager, not a policy maker. The relationship with Hanna freed McKinley from dealing with details, which were not his strength. Often Hanna had to downplay McKinley's views to his wealthy contributors. The yellow press loved to portray McKinley as a wooden puppet created by Mark Hanna; the truth is far from that image, but it has been ingrained in history. Over the years, Hanna and McKinley had been

---

49 T. Bentley Mott, *Myron Herrick: Friend of France*, (New York: Doubleday, 1929)
50 *Canton Repository*, September 24, 1893

on opposite sides of many issues and had often supported different Republican candidates. McKinley differed on his approach to labor and eventually Hanna came to respect and even believe in McKinley's approach. McKinley differed on gold, but here McKinley would compromise a bit since it was not a core issue to him.

Hanna's support in the decision that McKinley should be president was probably made after the Cleveland victory. Hanna was a wealthy capitalist of the second tier from men like Carnegie, Vanderbilt, Frick, and Rockefeller; but like these men, Hanna believed in capitalism. He was part of a Gilded Age group of capitalistic philosophers who countered the socialists and anarchists of the period. These industrial lords wanted to spread the philosophy of capitalism. Carnegie wrote about this mythical capitalism, Frick preached it, and Hanna made it happen. Hanna himself was a major in their "army." He had started out in the 1850s at his father's Cleveland grocery store. Hard working and hard driving, much like Carnegie, he invested in other industries. By the 1880s, he was a regional power in coal, shipping, and steel making. He had become a dynamo of activity and that complemented McKinley's indecisiveness

Gilded Age chronicler H. W. Brands described the McKinley–Hanna team best: "Hanna realized that he possessed certain gifts McKinley didn't, including a greater quickness of mind and capacity for detailed planning. McKinley realized this too and felt little embarrassment in deferring to Hanna on matters where such gifts were essential. On the other hand, Hanna conceded a kind of moral superiority to McKinley."[51] Hanna had a strong belief that government and Big Business needed to cooperate for a strong economy. McKinley's concern for the laborer humanized this pure capitalistic view of Hanna. In McKinley, Hanna found a politician who believed in capitalism without being controlled by it.

While McKinley continued to campaign for a second term as governor, Kohlsaat took care of the trust fund to cover the debt and return the property to Mrs. McKinley. Mrs. Herrick became a true friend to Mrs. McKinley during this crisis. The McKinleys spent four weeks at the Herricks' home in Cleveland during the height of the crisis. They needed friends to support them and Herrick and Hanna proved their friendship. Myron Herrick also rallied the state party and Hanna continued to position him for a presidential campaign. As he campaigned, crowds grew and workers turned out to support him. The Panic had eased prices, renewed fears of factory closings, and cheap sugar started to have an impact as the trend turned toward the Republicans. McKinley carried Ohio by a plurality of 81,000 votes, the greatest Republican victory since the Civil War.

---

51 H. W. Brands, *The Reckless Decade*, (Chicago: University of Chicago Press, 1995), 266

CHAPTER 9. THE WORLD TURNED UPSIDE DOWN — THE CLEVELAND
ADMINISTRATION

The inauguration of Grover Cleveland in 1892 was marked by the number
of New York businessmen and bankers that arrived in a blizzard to celebrate.
It looked like a Republican celebration. Regardless of his tariff stand, Cleveland was a capitalist and a banker's friend. Woodrow Wilson would later claim
Cleveland was not a Democrat but a conservative Republican! Grover Cleveland
was the man that McKinley feared the worst; he stood for gold and low tariffs.
J. P. Morgan pressured Cleveland to address the gold standard quickly in 1893,
since the financial markets around the world were in crisis. Morgan was clearly
looking out for his own best interests, but he felt America had to stand with the
world markets and support gold. Cleveland was convinced, but his own party
was against him. Cleveland was also aware that the crisis had reached the factories with substantial closings under way. Cleveland decided he had to move
toward the gold standard. The Democratic successes had come from the farmers and Western state support, which were silver bugs. By June, the treasury
gold had dropped below the $100 million mark, which Morgan felt was the crisis
point. In 1893 alone, $89 million of gold was drained from the treasury. Cleveland
felt he had to follow Morgan, who was the premier financial analyst of the time.
    Cleveland had the ambivalent support of some capitalists such as Andrew
Carnegie. On hearing the news of the Cleveland victory, Carnegie wrote Frick:
"Cleveland! Landslide! Well we have nothing to fear and perhaps it's for the
best. People will think the protected manufacturers will be attended to and quit
agitating. Cleveland is a pretty good fellow." Carnegie especially liked Cleve-

land's strong stand on gold. Cleveland had also often praised Carnegie. They were friendly, and Carnegie often wrote him with ideas. In particular, Carnegie proposed a unique approach on tariffs to oppose Cleveland's income tax proposal. Carnegie proposed a tariff based on luxury items purchased mainly by the wealthy. When Carnegie Steel was fined for overcharging the government on armor and contract violations, Cleveland reduced the penalty. Cleveland's close ties to J. P. Morgan seemed to have endeared him to a number of key industrialists, who showed up to the inauguration. While there is no record of Carnegie campaign donations, Carnegie did donate a large sum to Princeton, where ex-president Cleveland was president of the Board. Ex-president Cleveland and Carnegie also became leaders in the Anti-Imperialism League opposing President McKinley in 1899. Cleveland's gold stand, however, was the root of all his capitalist support.

On June 30, he called Congress into special session to repeal the Sherman Silver Act. Cleveland did this in the midst of a personal crisis. At the same time, Cleveland left for New York to have a secret operation to replace a cancerous jaw diseased from years of chewing tobacco. Cleveland's advisors felt the operation might shake the confidence of the public, and it was kept secret (it remained a secret until 1917). The operation was done on a yacht and Cleveland was given a vulcanized rubber jaw. He returned quickly to Washington to start the fight to repeal the Sherman Silver Act. The Democrats still controlled the House and Senate, but many were Western, Southern, and farming "silver" Democrats. Cleveland and Morgan rallied some of the Eastern gold bug Republicans to offset the deflection of the silver Democratic. Cleveland caused further problems with his policy of punishing silver Democrats politically. Cleveland's gold standard pushed southern Democrats into the Populist Party. Cleveland had set the groundwork for the Democratic nomination of William Jennings Bryan.

To many, the world was turned upside down. Henry Adams put it beautifully:

> The Democrat party is also insane and disagrees with him [Cleveland], and he has no true admirers and supporters except the two Republican senators from Massachusetts... Cleveland has smashed my party into smithereens and is well smashed in return....Every debate is a four-sided fight; the Republican attacks the Democrat; the eastern Democratic flies into the throat of the Western Democrat; all three attack Cleveland. John Sherman bitterly denounced J. Pierpont Morgan.[52]

The repeal was a hotly contested floor battle in the House. The fight would bring some famous politicians to the limelight. Silver Republicans such as Henry Cabot Lodge and silver Democrat William Jennings Bryan made national news.

---

52 Smith, 492

In the House, Bryan tied to delay passage knowing public opinion was on his side. Cleveland addressed Congress in August for the final push. The repeal passed 239 votes to 108 votes on August 18, 1893. The Democrats were split for the future. It passed in the Senate 43 votes to 37. The gold issue had now become the most divisive issue since slavery, and the debate was far from over.

The repeal slowed the gold drain of the treasury, but the country slipped further into depression. Layoffs in the fall of 1893 were approaching a million, and 141 banks had failed. The smoke stacks of the Mahoning Valley and Pittsburgh were cold. Two old steel companies — Pennsylvania Steel and Oliver Iron and Steel went bankrupt. Railroads failed almost monthly forcing massive unemployment. One of the blames was that the railroads had overextended. Unemployment was probably around 25%. Wage cuts were causing a rash of strikes and the country declined further into a depression. Labor was now in the grip of the fear that McKinley had often worried about. Unemployment is always the root of unrest and upheaval in Democracies. The year 1894 would be the darkest of the Panic. Samuel Gompers estimated that there were three million out of work in 1894.

Historian Henry Adams chronicled the times: "winter is here and my perpetual miracle is that people somehow seem to go on living without work or money or food, or clothes, or fire. One or two million people are out of work; thousands of rich are cleaned out to the last shoe leather; not one human being is known to be making a living." Times were indeed tough. Even capitalists like Mark Hanna were feeling the pain.

The Panic of 1893 approached that of the Great Depression of the 1930s. The labor unrest, numerous socialists and anarchists made it a much more fearful time. Another description of the situation came in the book *The Growth of the American Republic:*

> Prices and wages hit rock bottom and there seemed to be no market for anything. Half a million laborers struck against conditions, which they thought intolerable, and most of the strikes were dismal failures. Ragged and hungry bands of unemployed swarmed over the countryside, the fires from their hobo camps flickering a message of warning and despair to the frightened townsfolk.

The unpopularity of the Cleveland administration built more national momentum for McKinley. McKinley opened his second term as governor with a focused speech on the economy. He was optimistic that the Republicans would win the Congress and turn things around. McKinley knew that Cleveland would push tariff reductions, and this remained McKinley's personal charge. His surviving the Walker financial crisis also buoyed him. He could do something few politicians could do-empathize with the struggling labor force. The depression and McKinley's popularity would put many demands on him to speak. In the end, he covered 10,000 miles, 20 states, and made 371 speeches in support of Republican candidates. The crowds were large and clearly the nation was already looking to McKinley. Mark Hanna was now a full-time campaign manager as both men eyed the presidency. The following of unemployed workers was even more amazing for this Ohio Republican. As governor of Ohio, the Democrats had no means to stop his national rise. It is doubtful that they could have been stopped anyway, considering the deep divisions in the party. Not far from McKinley's home in Canton, Ohio, a group of unemployed formed in Massillon that spring.

Jacob Sechler Coxey of Massillon formed the idea of organizing a massive march on Washington to protest the rising unemployment. Coxey owned a sand quarry that mined high quality silica sand for the steel and glass industry; it was closed by the Panic. Coxey had also run for Congress as a Populist candidate. The depression had idled his operation for months. Coxey had some unique ideas that would augur those applied in the 1930s. Coxey hoped to form a Christian nation based on charity. He called also for an eight-hour day and a minimum wage of $1.50 as well as a national bond issue to support the unemployed. Coxey suggested a massive influx of money and public works to provide jobs for the unemployed, but it was the idea of a national march that struck fear in the hearts of Congress. The idea of an army of tramps, socialists, and anarchists marching through the country struck a nerve. The politicians remembered the railroad worker revolt of 1877 and the more recent riots in Chicago and Homestead. Many believed the country was ripe for a socialist revolution like those seen in Europe.

The concerns were further stirred by the press which descended on Massillon, Ohio. The Chicago press was one of the first to arrive. While editorials denounced the march, the headlines promoted fear in a bid to move Congress. Money and support started to pour in from labor unions, populists, and probably a few Republicans. In the midst of the Coxey cry, Governor McKinley was dealing with an outbreak of worker violence. Coal miners from Stark County (including Massillon) were remnants of a settled national miners strike. The strikers were attacking trains carrying coal into Ohio from West Virginia. Rails were being torn up, trains shot at, and bridges burned. McKinley summoned John McBride, President of the United Mine Workers, to his office. McBride had noted he had "fourteen cannon pointed on one mine." His cajoling failed and McKinley ordered a massive call up of the National Guard. The show of overwhelming force ended the violence. One train alone carried twelve men and two Gatling guns.

Coxey's gathering forces remained peaceful as he used torchlight parades and speeches to muster his followers. Coxey started the march with several thousand men and thousands more converged with the main column along the way. The group reportedly reached 20,000 at its peak in Ohio. The march started on Easter Sunday with a plan to reach Washington on May Day. Coxey and his "officers" rode horses at the front of the column, along with a band. Hugh O'Donnell, one of the Homestead leaders, led the way. Reporters were astonished as they rushed reports to their papers. Headlines seem to rally more supporters from all parts of the country. Armies from Philadelphia, Pittsburgh, and Maryland mustered as well. Coxey's Ohio army followed roughly today's Route 30 to Pittsburgh. Towns offered food as the men passed through. By the time the army reached Pittsburgh on April 3, it had swelled to 300,000.[53]

Pittsburgh was the forge of the nation and the fortress of American labor. The winter of 1892–1893 had been the toughest ever for this industrial center. Hobo towns lined the great railroads leading into the city and the streets were filled with beggars. Immigrants in tent cities struggled to stay warm and to eat. The rich suburbs lived in constant fear of looting or attack. The city had emptied its coffers to supply relief. Andrew Carnegie kicked in an equal amount of about $125,000, and other capitalists chipped in another $100,000. The money was used for city work projects like those Coxey had been calling for. The army's appearance did lift the hope of the city. Bands and crowds gathered as if Coxey's division was a conquering army. But the ranks of the army dwindled quickly as it left Pittsburgh.

In Maryland, roads were mud from a rainy spring as the army bogged down. Food became scarce and towns less supportive. The local authorities restricted foraging as the army dwindled with each mile. It entered Washington with under a thousand hungry marchers. Grover Cleveland had braced for trouble, and Coxey was arrested for walking on the grass (trespassing on the Capitol lawn). Mounted police had an easy time intimidating the weary men. Some fighting broke out, but the police suppressed the men quickly. Populists in Congress read Coxey's petitions, and in the Senate a bill was unsuccessfully introduced. The New Deal in the 1930s would finally see many of Coxey's ideas implemented, and Coxey's march would be a model for the civil rights movement. Another army known as the "Industrial Army" formed in California and got some press as Jack London joined the march. In Montana, a group of 650 miners started another march, but by spring the marches were over. The unrest was, however, far from settled.

As Coxey's army failed, McKinley was managing labor problems throughout Ohio, mostly with the miners. McKinley dispatched troops to Cleveland and Ak-

---

53 Stefan Lorant, *Pittsburgh: The Story of an American City*, (Lenox: Donnelley & Sons, 1964), 551

ron to put down any violence. McKinley was firm but sympathetic to the workers. He often spoke out against the owners for their poor treatment of the miners. He also watched the troops closely to avoid anything that might trigger violence. He received telegraphs daily from the commanders. Overall he avoided any major violence. His office meetings with the leadership and speeches against the owners coupled with an overwhelming show of force won him the respect of all. McKinley's support for a presidential run actually grew among labor nationwide. President Cleveland, on the other hand, was rapidly losing labor's support.

The times brought the worst in race relations as well. Lynchings were on the rise nationally. Cleveland, in general, was no supporter of blacks. While Cleveland did not defend lynching, his attitude was problematic. Later in his career, Cleveland defined his attitude by saying, "I believe that neither the decree that made the slaves free, nor the enactment that suddenly invested them in the rights of citizenship any more cured them of their racial and slavery-bred imperfections and deficiencies than it changed the color of their skin."[54] In Ohio, William Dolby, a black man accused of raping a white woman, came under attack of a lynch mob. The guardsmen opened fire in the conformation. Several men were killed and wounded and the commanding officer was charged by the local authorities for murder. McKinley was clear: "Lynching cannot be tolerated in Ohio. The law of the State must be supreme overall, and the agents of the law, acting within the law, must be sustained." McKinley continued to speak out nationally against lynchings and support of civil rights for blacks. He personally believed the trend was an affront to the soldiers who had died during the Civil War. When Colonel Coit was acquitted at trial, McKinley sent congratulations and asked the state to pay the court costs. McKinley won praise for his tough but fair management of the unrest.

Violence would again erupt in Chicago. The once-hailed utopian Pullman Company and town would be the location of the breakout. The trouble started in June with a layoff of 3,000 of Pullman's 5,800 employees at the Chicago plant. George Pullman was labor friendly, but he was hardheaded and a poor communicator. In an effort to save jobs, he cut the wages of the remaining workers by 25%. Members of the American Railway Union asked that the rents in the Pullman worker town be reduced. Pullman ended up firing the union representatives, which brought union president Eugene V. Debs into the disagreement. Events escalated quickly to a strike as Pullman announced a regular dividend to its stockholders. The strike slowly started to spread along related railways, and as three-quarters of the rails moving in and out of Chicago closed. The combination

---

54 Robert Welch, *The Presidencies of Grover Cleveland*, (Lawrence: University of Kansas Press, 1988), 68

of rail lines was managed by the General Managers Association. The Association had strong ties in the Cleveland administration as well as with J. P. Morgan.

President Cleveland got involved, hiring 3,600 special deputies who had the full protection of the United States government. Cleveland thought it was less offensive than sending in Federal troops. The reputation of Pullman suggested that Cleveland would get labor support, but he did not. The newspapers supported Cleveland initially, but that was short-lived. Federal involvement inspired more rioting by the workers. The strike started to spread across the country. Cleveland was forced to get an injunction against the strikers. The strikers stood their ground.

Chicago began to attract socialists and anarchists to "help out." Ray Baker, second in command of Coxey's army, showed up in Chicago. The country seemed split between fear and outrage. Pullman refused arbitration; New York and other large cities supported him, characterizing the strike as an attack on society. As famous socialists and anarchists such as Emma Goldman joined the effort, many feared a rebellion in the large cities. The timing was poor for the strikers, as the president of France had just been assassinated by an anarchist. Mark Hanna, however, supported the workers, calling Pullman a "damn idiot."[55] Hanna would be one of those who exposed the fallacies of Pullman's utopia. Pullman charged rents 25% higher than surrounding neighborhoods. In addition, he purchased water from Chicago at four cents per thousand gallons and sold it to his town at ten cents. Emma Goldman would later inspire Leon Czolgosz, McKinley's future assassin. Goldman was an anarchist, socialist, Russian immigrant, and revolutionary. Meanwhile, McKinley sat by as industrial activity further declined due to shortages created by the strike. McKinley, as he had shown, would have forced arbitration, and his support was with the strikers. Mayors from over fifty cities asked Pullman to accept arbitration.

Samuel Gompers, one of the most enlightened labor leaders of the time, tried to meditate a settlement. He telegrammed President Cleveland only to have his offer rejected. Cleveland commented, "If it takes the entire army and navy of the United States to deliver a postal card in Chicago, that card will be delivered." Cleveland sent 14,000 Federal troops in, and the anger now turned towards him. Cleveland sent in the troops without notifying Governor Altgeld of Illinois. Governor Altgeld stated, in a letter made public, "I am advised that you have ordered federal troops to go into service in the State of Illinois. Surely, [the facts] have not been correctly presented to you in this case or you would not have taken the step, for it is entirely unnecessary and, as it seems to me unjustifiable." Cleve-

---

55 Smith, 522

land's use of federal troops was considered anti-workingman, when even capitalists had condemned Pullman for his hardheaded approach. The strike ended, but the courts took over to revenge the upheaval.

The result of the "Debs Strike" would change the landscape of American politics. Eugene Debs was sentenced to six months in prison and would later form the American Socialist Party. The Sherman Anti-Trust Act was used to support the conviction, and the Supreme Court upheld its use against labor. Socialists would oust Samuel Gompers as president of the American Federation of Labor. Cleveland lost the support of his party and would be forced to run as a third-party candidate. The Democratic majority lay in ruins and the elections of 1894 and 1896 would sweep in a Republican majority. McKinley's stock boomed as a supporter of labor and prosperity.

Cleveland had a distinctly different view on tariffs, stating, "A tariff for any other purpose than public revenue is public robbery." While there is no proof that the McKinley Tariff was a factor in the Panic of 1893, Cleveland had a deep belief it was a major factor. His advisor J. P. Morgan showed no interest in tariffs because his monopolies in transportation prospered from free trade, and his banking depended on international transactions. Cleveland's viewpoint was always that of the consumer, focusing on prices, which is the viewpoint of free traders. McKinley's viewpoint was that of the manufacturer, focusing on jobs. Within months of the repeal of the Sherman Silver Act, Cleveland moved on the McKinley Tariff of 1890. Cleveland viewed McKinley's scientific approach to duties as favoring special interests. Cleveland admired Andrew Carnegie and was encouraged by his change of heart in believing the steel industry could stand on its own. Carnegie was, however, unique in the industry in espousing this belief. Cleveland had started preparation with William Wilson, House Chair of Ways and Means, immediately after being elected president.

The bill that Cleveland and Wilson prepared was to be a step towards free trade. Cleveland espoused a new theory to help recruit labor. The basic argument in his theory was that duty free raw materials would reduce manufacturing costs and increase jobs. Based on this premise, coal, iron, wool, and sugar were to be on the duty free list. These, of course, had been the heart of McKinley's protective tariff. Cleveland also proposed tariff reductions on manufactured clothing. He also added a new twist in an income tax on wealthy manufacturers and capitalists. The bill, as proposed, would have caused a massive job loss in key industries such as iron ore mining, coal mining, wool production, textile mills, lumber, and sugar production. Cleveland caused a major backlash with the proposal of this bill.

Congress faired no better than Cleveland during 1894. Lacking any direction, they looked to tariff reform to keep busy. The American government had a $61 million deficit in 1894 as well. Cleveland and the Democrats had hoped to reduce the tariff rates, but the depression caused panic in the ranks. As what would be called the Wilson-Gorman Tariff Bill started in the Congress, the mood changed to more protection and more income. By moving quickly, Cleveland retained his support in the House, while others ran for cover — even in his own party. The base of the Democrats was the farmer who opposed the wool and sugar amendments. On February 1, 1894, Wilson moved the bill through with a vote of 182 to 106, but sixty-one congressmen were absent or avoided the record. The Senate stood ready to seriously amend the bill. Free silver Democrats and Populists felt Cleveland had sold them out on repeal of the Sherman Silver Act, and some farm Senators such as those from the sugar districts in the South opposed the bill. With job losses mounting across the country, cries from home districts were being heard in Congress. The break of so many Democrats caused a free-for-all to protect state interests.

The Wilson-Gorman Tariff was the result of sectionalism gone wild. The bill ended up raising the overall tariff, with 634 amendments from nervous senators and representatives catering to their geographic areas. It even took duties off wool, which McKinley's Ohio was the major producer. To appease the Populists, a 2% income tax was put on the wealthy and upper middle class to raise funds. The Supreme Court would rule the income tax unconstitutional in 1895. The overall tariff bill lacked the scientific approach of McKinley and resulted in major economic problems. Duties were put on sugar, which offended both Democrats and Republicans. Shortly after, a scandal involving sugar speculation and senators surfaced. Reciprocity agreements helping the farmers were dropped. Congress managed to destroy any more Democratic support with the base. The Senate went on to add 634 amendments including adding protection for coal, iron, and sugar, basically eliminating Cleveland's tariff-free raw material idea. Cleveland was furious, calling it "the abandonment of Democratic principles." The revised bill passed the Senate with a vote of 39 to 34 with twelve senators not voting. In conference, the Senate version remained unchanged.

The next step was the President's signature or veto. Cleveland was angry and would not sign the bill. Leaders in the senate warned Cleveland to sign the bill stating, "If you allow the bill to become a law without your signature, you abdicate the leadership of the Democratic Party . . . the present tariff bill is a Democratic measure."[56] Cleveland refused to sign and the bill went into law ten days

---

56 Robert McElroy, *Grover Cleveland: The Man and the Statesman,* (New York: Harpers & Brothers, 1923), 115

later. With the repeal of the Sherman Silver Bill, the passage of the Wilson Tariff Bill, and Cleveland's refusal to sign it effectively split the Democratic Party. The split opened the door to the rising career of William Jennings Bryan of Nebraska. Bryan built a coalition of Southern and Western Democrats.

Neither the repeal of the Sherman Silver Act nor the Wilson-Gorman Bill did anything to stop the depression. McKinley was in great demand to speak in the congressional elections of 1894. In a forty-day swing west, McKinley made 371 speeches, in 300 different towns, and 16 states. The bell tolled for the Democrats in 1894. The repeal of the Sherman Silver Act did not reverse the depression, in fact, it had gotten worse. In 1894, the Republicans regained control of the House 244 to 105 with 7 Populists, and the Senate 45 to 35 with 6 Populists. Cleveland knew it was time to turn things around or face another Republican landslide in 1896.

Cleveland for his part tried to ignore the economic problems throughout the period. In his 1894 State of the Union Address, he blamed the issues on silver and complained about the Congressional tariff reform. Cleveland stated: "The tariff act passed at the last session of the Congress needs important amendments if it is to be executed effectively and with certainty. In addition to such necessary amendments as will not change rates of duty, I am still very decidedly in favor of putting coal and iron upon the free list." The idea of taking tariffs off the country's major industries in the midst of a depression was political suicide. While the Wilson Tariff kept duties on raw materials, it reduced the duties by 15 percent, which pleased no one. The impact of the Panic on employment in these industries further opened an opportunity for the Republicans to strengthen their alliance with labor. McKinley quickly seized the issue and made it central to his campaign.

In early 1895, Cleveland had lunch with J. P. Morgan to try to stop the bleeding of the treasury. Lacking a Federal Reserve System, we have today required bankers such as Morgan to act as controller of the currency. Morgan was one of two or three bankers in the country that could back government bonds. He pulled together other bankers to float a bond offering. Morgan brought in 3.5 million ounces of gold (about 65 million dollars), most of it from Europe. Morgan also worked with Rothschild and with August Belmont to stop treasury gold speculation. J. P. Morgan probably saved the country from a crisis, but it came at a cost. Morgan pocketed a million and half dollars in profit. Morgan would later be investigated by Congress over the transaction, but the immediate effect was a backlash on Cleveland. Even his own party saw Cleveland as a tool of Wall Street. In reality, it may have been one of Cleveland's greatest moments, but few would understand. Cleveland and Morgan might have saved the country and world, but as always Morgan was well paid for his leadership. Historians have judged Morgan, for his part, much harsher. In general, Morgan gained throughout the depression in stock and money deals. The Morgan Empire expanded to the point many even believed he caused the Panic of 1893! The drain on the treasury slowed, but Morgan would be brought in again in late 1895.

In 1895, McKinley was now running for president, not a third term as governor. Mark Hanna was now his full-time campaign manager, and a full team of financial supporters was in place. Hanna started the informal campaign by a meeting with America's two most powerful bosses — Senator Matt Quay of New York and ex-Senator Tom Platt of Pennsylvania. Both men wanted a number of favors, typical of boss style negotiating. They looked at Hanna as a rank amateur. Platt, in particular, wanted Secretary of Treasury. Hanna dutifully reported the meeting to McKinley. McKinley was no amateur and was appalled at the idea that Platt wanted to manage the country's treasury! It wasn't so much the idea of a trading a political appointment as the idea of the "thief of Pennsylvania's Treasury" controlling the nation's money. Trading among politicians for Cabinet posts was and is common, but the idea of a political boss in such a position was too much. McKinley told his group of political managers: "If I cannot be President without promising to make Tom Platt Secretary of the Treasury, I will never be President." With that, McKinley set the limits and direction of the campaign.

Chapter 10. Pre-Presidential Campaign

> You shall not press down upon the brow of labor this crown of
> thorns, you shall not crucify mankind upon a cross of gold.
>
> — *William Jennings Bryan*

While the gold issue was prominent again, in reality the public, Congress, and even McKinley did not really understand it. Myron Herrick reminisced: "In 1896 William Jennings Bryan of Nebraska had been nominated by the Democrats for the Presidency because of his advocacy of 'free silver'; most people did not understand or could not understand why the gold standard was essential or what free silver meant; the advocates of the latter were arguing that it would spell prosperity for the poor and especially for the farmer, who had been having a difficult time for many years. Popular cries like the 'aristocracy of gold' and the 'democracy of silver' were invented . . . I believe at the beginning that McKinley did not really understand the gold question."[57] McKinley was surely not alone. Probably only J. P. Morgan and a handful of Eastern international bankers understood the full impact of gold or at least what it would do for them. McKinley knew better than most politicians that jobs and a good economy were the real issues to the laborers and middle class, not gold or silver.

McKinley would set the policy and direction of the campaign, but his campaign managers would handle the tactical assault. Mark Hanna was a godsend for McKinley. In 1895, Hanna alone financed McKinley's early campaign to the amount of $100,000. As a capitalist, Hanna had been very successful, but he al-

---

57T. Mott, Chapter IX

ways had good relationships with his workers. Hanna believed that unions were not needed if managers applied Christian principles. Hanna, however, was close to a broad array of robber barons of the era. Hanna and McKinley had not always been in agreement, but they shared the same vision of capitalism. McKinley would compromise politically, but he would not deal with political bosses. His approach to capitalists was less clear, but McKinley never sold out labor to the capitalists. He realized that he had the only alliance of labor and capital since Henry Clay, and that would be his personal platform. The plan was simple — use the money of the capitalists to fully deliver the labor and middle class vote. Compromise and bargain on political points but never on the principles of labor and Americanism.

In addition to Hanna, Cleveland industrialist Myron Herrick was part of the team, as well as Chicago newspaper owner Herman Kohlsaat. McKinley had strong editorial support in Ohio, Chicago, Pittsburgh, and Michigan. He could count on financial aid from most of America's capitalists, although some, like Andrew Carnegie, were concerned by his bimetallism. Many major labor leaders such as Samuel Gompers supported him, and often where he lacked the support of union leadership, he had the votes of the members such as the United Mine Workers and Knights of Labor. He didn't control the Irish Catholic vote, but he had enough of it to seriously hurt any Democratic candidate. From his earliest days, McKinley had worked with and supported the farmers' Grange. With the support of farmers, he also would take some votes from the Democrats. He owned most industrial areas and had a following even in the Western states. The Eastern bosses realized early on that McKinley's popular support was unmatched. Besides the Eastern bosses, he had other opponents such as J. P. Morgan and the Eastern bankers. Morgan thought McKinley had the "backbone of a jellyfish." Of course, Morgan had no time for bimetallism. The capitalist, bankers, and even the Democrats wanted the election issue to be gold versus silver, but McKinley wanted it to be tariffs and prosperity.

Before the National Convention, McKinley held to his bimetallism which focused on "sound money." "Sound money" meant whatever worked for the American economy's growth. McKinley's own advisors, like the party and nation, were split on the gold issue. McKinley's view was evolving, as was the nation's. Tacitly, McKinley gave his support to the gold standard in place. Eastern manufacturers tended to agree with McKinley that the gold standard alone would hurt the economy and lacked the inflationary punch needed to bring the country out of depression. Tariffs were something that most manufacturers, farmers, and consumers would rally around. McKinley's support and muscle support were in a triangle bounded by Chicago, Pittsburgh and St. Louis. This mid-continental anvil would be the forge of victory. In 1894 and 1895, McKinley traveled extensively outside that triangle to further establish his political octopus with arms radiating out of his mid-continental center. This early campaigning focused on the shortcomings of the Cleveland Administration-"Tariff-tinkering, bond-issuing, debt increasing, treasury depleting, business-paralyzing, wage-reducing, and queen restoring administration." In 1895, Hanna and McKinley planned a quiet southern campaign.

The South offered potential as silver Democrats were searching for an alternative to Cleveland. In the spring of 1895, Hanna set up a kickoff of the southern strategy at Thomasville, Georgia. Hanna had a home in Thomasville as did many northerners, and he hoped to bring southerners and northern supporters together. McKinley would then move to Florida vacation areas with a similar agenda. The short trip and McKinley's black vote resulted in a loss of 60,091 to Bryan's 94,600, but it was the closest a Republican would come till the 1970s. McKinley took 40 percent of the Atlanta vote. The strategy did not give McKinley the south, but it would not be until the 1990s that a Republican would do as well as McKinley in the state of Georgia. It also demonstrated how Hanna believed he could build voter alliances around McKinley's conservative and nationalistic beliefs.

One of the major problem areas was the east where the political bosses and bankers opposed him. In 1895, he refused a deal with the Eastern bosses to put them in the cabinet. He told Hanna that he would not have the corruption of these bosses near him. McKinley, not wanting to join the bosses, would have to fight. Hanna and McKinley used the slogans, "McKinley against the bosses," and "The people against the bosses in the 1895 pre-campaign. It would be a tough fight in the poor economy because the boss system provided a security network at the time. Bosses helped unemployed workers in return for their votes; it encouraged a type of economic co-dependency. McKinley opposed this system as much as he did socialism and paternal capitalism, which he saw as having similar roots. Many believed Hanna, as a capitalist, favored paternal capitalism, but like Westinghouse, Hanna argued that the best philanthropy was a high paying job. In the end, he believed that the American worker preferred a high paying job to the other options as well. The theme was popular with the press of the times. McKinley even won over Democratic papers such as the *St. Louis Post Dispatch*. This anti-boss approach won over young progressives and reformers such as Wisconsin's Republican governor Robert La Follette and Teddy Roosevelt. The timing was right as the boss system had been losing strength since the fall of Tammany Hall in New York a decade earlier.

Thomas Platt, boss of the New York Machine, was a tough opponent of McKinley. Platt had served as a New York Senator and had an extensive political network in the Republican Party. In many ways, Platt was the resurrection of the old Tammany Hall in terms of political power. Platt had strong ties to the New York bankers, who were against protective tariffs and for the gold standard. Platt confidently stated in the spring: "My opposition to Governor McKinley proceeds almost entirely from my belief that his nomination would bring the Republican Party into turmoil and trouble . . . . McKinley represents the most radical extreme view of protection. I foresee the greatest dangers to the Republican Party as the result of extreme tariff legislation . . . . He voted once for the free and unlimited coinage of silver. . . . This should remove McKinley from the list of Presidential possibilities.[58] Platt soon realized that the rank and file was solidly behind McKinley in the urban and industrial areas.

In fact, McKinley was popular throughout Eastern labor centers. His tariff effort had won him the rank and file as well as the labor leaders. Labor leaders started pledging support earlier in the campaign. Matt Quay, a Philadelphia boss, was his main opponent, but McKinley had grassroots support throughout Pennsylvania. Quay, at the time, was a Pennsylvania Senator. He was strongest in eastern Pennsylvania but carried little weight with the steelworkers of western Pennsylvania. Quay tried to put together an alliance of political bosses. Thomas Platt, New York boss, joined the "combine" against McKinley; but Hanna noted that as the bosses came out against McKinley, he gained even more support from the people. The bosses still had huge financial funds, but Hanna would pull in funds from hundreds of second-tier capitalists. The bosses started to search for a candidate who could stop McKinley's nomination, but they never fully rallied behind a single candidate. Furthermore, while they tried to unite, the bosses were city and county powers whereas McKinley had popular support. In addition, Hanna had a well-designed national strategic plan, which the bosses lacked.

The "combine" of bosses was a fearful thing. The combine included Thomas Platt who controlled everything in New York that Democratic Tammany Hall didn't. He was tough and old line with a history of using his power in New York to control national elections. New York had the biggest block of votes at the convention. He had a strong relationship with the New York bankers such as J. P. Morgan. Another New York boss, Levi Morton, was a protégé of Platt. Morton was governor of New York, a banker, and had been Harrison's vice president. Philadelphia boss Matthew Quay controlled Pennsylvania in a similar fashion. Speaker of the House Thomas Reed rounded out the great Eastern combine. In

---

58 Thomas Platt, *Autobiography of Thomas Collier*, (New York: Dodge Press, 1910)

the end, Reed and Quay remained favorite sons and did not pull their votes, but that was probably due to a realization that the attempt was hopeless. These Eastern bosses were the main part of the combine, but there were others such as Russell Alger of Michigan and Senator William Allison of Iowa. In the end, the combine counted for only 239 votes compared to McKinley's 661.

The "combine" did try to put together a united attack prior to the state conventions that would select delegates to the national convention (this was before primaries). The attack focused on the middle class/upper class Republican base, which tended to be anti-Catholic and anti-immigrant. The major organization of anti-Catholic bigotry was the American Protective Association (APA). The APA was a powerful organization, which many believed controlled the Republican Party. McKinley had never been a friend of the APA. His record of appointing Catholics as governor had raised the anger of the Ohio APA. McKinley believed the party had to include Catholics to establish an inclusive base for the future. McKinley also had the public support of many Catholic bishops who opposed what was viewed as socialist tendencies of the Democrats. The attacks spread rumors that McKinley had a grandfather buried in a Catholic cemetery, that Hanna was really a Catholic, that McKinley had numerous Catholics married into the family, and even that McKinley was a Catholic. Hanna was brilliant at turning these attacks into a plus for the Catholic vote. Still, for McKinley, it was a stand against many in his own party, and a profile in courage. The APA opposition offered a wedge that the Eastern Republican bosses could use. Hanna hired men to infiltrate the APA and fight from within, a move that outsmarted the bosses in the end.

One of the moves Hanna made at the convention was the selection of the opening prayer. It seemed simple enough, but with the bosses portraying McKinley as pro-Catholic it would be viewed as a signal. If Hanna picked a Protestant it would upset Catholics, and if he picked a Catholic, the bosses would use it against him. The bosses were sure they had Hanna in a corner, but Hanna exhibited the wisdom of Solomon. This was the type of thinking that became his hallmakr. He chose a Jewish rabbi, the first time a rabbi had ever opened a National Convention. Hanna had been just as brilliant in the pre-campaign run-up to the convention. In reality, Hanna had defeated the bosses long before the convention opened. This move was typical of how Hanna took McKinley's unpopular stands and either protected him from the opposition or turned the stand into a positive credential. It is clear that Hanna did not create McKinley, but he did create an election success for McKinley.

A more pressing problem of the 1895 pre-campaign was the lack of unity in the Ohio Republican Party. In 1895 McKinley and Hanna had an uneasy truce with Joseph Foraker. Hanna wasn't even on speaking terms with Foraker, believing Foraker had destroyed Sherman's last effort for the presidency at the 1888 national convention. McKinley was always willing to deal at the party level, and he had done so with Foraker before. Foraker controlled a key block in the state party, and McKinley would have to deal with it. Hanna even swallowed his pride and talked to Foraker, but with little success. McKinley had always had to deal directly with Foraker. The two were able to come to some personal compromise, although neither seemed to care for the other. Foraker was in control of the state convention in 1895 and was nominated for senator without any opposition by the McKinley faction. Asa Bushnell was the Foraker-backed candidate for governor. McKinley pulled behind Bushnell and campaigned for him. The result was a bigger plurality than McKinley's in the 1895 governor's race. It was a clear demonstration of the savvy of the McKinley-Hanna team.

Even before Harrison withdrew from the race in early 1896, McKinley's strongest opponent was Speaker Thomas Reed. Reed was the candidate of the Eastern Republicans and party bosses and had the support of powerful Republicans such as Henry Cabot Lodge. Reed's support of gold also gained the Eastern bankers, who looked at McKinley as "Wobblie Willie" on gold. Reed was from Maine, which he could count on for solid support, but New England industrial centers were his weakness. He also had strong financial support outside of his section, with the backing of Henry Clay Frick in Pittsburgh and Pennsylvania boss Matthew Quay. Hanna, focusing his publicity and literature campaign in these areas, decided to battle up from the rank and file. The Eastern bosses, however, saw Hanna as an amateur. Hanna focused on the Eastern industrial centers where McKinley's tariff had made him nearly unbeatable. For example, Hanna took cities like Pittsburgh away from Pennsylvania boss Matthew Quay, whose real strength was eastern Pennsylvania. Boston delegates went for McKinley over boss Reed of New England. Hanna's plan worked, and by April, Reed's support was weakening. Hanna's educational approach was different but worked against political machines. Hanna's pre-convention success shocked the bosses who felt unbeatable on their home turf. Political bosses started to hedge their bets with a possible dark horse — Levi Morton, the governor of New York. McKinley's ground support, however, seemed to be everywhere. The bosses realized too late that McKinley had really been campaigning for years.

The silver Republicans in the Midwest and West supported William Allison of Iowa, who had a strong record on silver. In reality, Allison was a bimetallist. Many believed that the Eastern bosses might support Allison in the end, but the bosses really were very divided. Harrison publicly remained neutral, but he was no friend of McKinley and privately favored Allison. Allison had some support from the Chicago bosses who were extremely anti-McKinley. But in boss-controlled Cook County, McKinley's grassroots supporters put fear in the bosses. The main driver in Chicago and Illinois was a young businessman and McKinley believer — Charles Dawes. McKinley had captured the young voters like no politician had before him. What these supporters lacked in experience they made up for in enthusiasm.

McKinley's pre-convention campaign was based on his strength — tariffs. He avoided his silver critics in the West and gold critics in the East with "sound money." Hanna flooded the nation with sound money pamphlets. The Democrats dogged his every move. The Democrats had shifted to "free silver" and turned against President Cleveland. The Republicans were more divided on the issue — the West for silver, the East for gold, and the Midwest for bimetallism. McKinley believed tariffs and sound money would work. He was counting on the industrial workers and conservative farmers of the Midwest. In the East, it would be the industrial workers. Hanna even believed they might carry the upper south. Even with a convention victory in hand, both McKinley and Hanna realized that Eastern moneymen would have to be pacified. McKinley also had gold supporters in his own organization such as Charles Dawes. Furthermore, the first tier capitalists such as Andrew Carnegie and Henry Clay Frick were demanding a gold standard. McKinley's first priority was winning the nomination, hoping he could then compromise on gold from a position of strength.

McKinley's position on gold had evolved over the years. He had believed in bimetallism as the best compromise for the middle class, farmers, and laborers. By the 1890s, the global operations of banking and the government did change things. Trade had become dependent on the currency basis between countries. McKinley became convinced that the country needed an international agreement on bimetallism, until then the government should stay with the gold standard. McKinley also saw that the country's best productivity occurred from 1882 to 1890 under the gold standard. The idea was to hold steady and try for an international agreement on bimetallism, something that was unlikely. This somewhat vague and middle-of-the-road approach allowed him to avoid the issue, which was not so much a political decision as a reflection of reality. The national convention would be weighed down with platform phraseology on gold. This approach also seemed to pacify the Eastern bankers such as J. P. Morgan.

The struggle between McKinley and J. P. Morgan remains controversial. It appears now that McKinley's advisor Myron Herrick met with Morgan in New York prior to the Republican National convention.[59] At the meeting Morgan said

---

59 Jean Strouse, *Morgan: American Financer*, (New York: HarperPerennial, 2000), 355

he found McKinley's waffling on gold "nauseating." Morgan had no time for compromise, but Herrick argued that the problem could split the party. Morgan, for one of the few times in his career, didn't hold all the cards; he had nowhere to go. The Democrats represented the worst case of free silver. In addition, they were making a scandal out of the gold settlement between Cleveland and Morgan. Mark Hanna, however, wanted full financial backing and had Herrick set up a meeting on Morgan's yacht, the *Corsair* (Hanna's first-ever meeting with Morgan). According to Morgan's biographer, Jean Strouse, Hanna reached a deal with Morgan prior to the convention. Later, it was suggested McKinley had submitted a draft of the platform to Morgan for his approval or at least suggestions. Election chronicler Stanley Jones confirms that Morgan was given a copy of the platform stand, but Morgan's response came too late for the convention.[60] It probably didn't matter; both Morgan and McKinley knew some type of support for gold was needed.

The national convention started on June 16, a Tuesday morning, in St. Louis. McKinley was in full control of all the committees and the majority of delegates. Hanna wanted a united front, however. McKinley remained in Canton, taking hourly telephone calls reporting on their progress. Hanna had a direct line set up to the McKinley house, allowing for constant communications. The main debate centered on the party plank and its stand on gold. It is disputed in history, but the term "gold" appeared in the plank, and it was a strong endorsement, as follows:

> The Republican Party is unreservedly for sound money... We are therefore opposed to the free coinage of silver, except by international agreement with the leading commercial nations of the earth....until such an agreement can be obtained, the existing gold standard must be maintained at parity with gold, and we favor all measures designed to maintain inviolably the obligations of the United States... the standard of the enlightened nations of the earth.

It was clearly a compromise that the Eastern bosses, bankers and manufacturers could live with.

The story of how the actual term "gold standard" versus the original "existing standard" got into the document became a matter of political interest, as today it is a matter of historical interest. There were seven McKinley men in the room in St. Louis's Southern Hotel that discussed the platform approval: H. Kohlsaat, Mark Hanna, Myron Herrick, Henry Payne, Melville Stone, ex-Governor Merriam of Minnesota, and Senator Redfield Proctor of Vermont.[61] The debate went

---

60 Stanley Jones, *The Presidential Election of 1896*, (Madison: University of Wisconsin Press, 1964), 167
61 H. H. Kohlsaat, *From McKinley to Harding*, (New York: Charles Scribner's Sons, 1923), 34

on for hours and probably included McKinley by telephone. At the end, according to Kohlsaat and Herrick, the term "gold" was inserted, after which Henry Cabot Lodge and Thomas Platt approved the draft. To improve their standing with their Eastern constituents and bankers, Lodge and Thomas leaked to the Associated Press that they were responsible for it. H. H. Kohlsaat answered with press releases claiming they had no part in it. It all might have been planned as a tacit concession to Eastern bankers. In retrospect, the public argument only eroded McKinley's weak support in the East.

Mark Hanna tried to appease the silver Republicans by suggesting McKinley was a bimetallist and would still remain open to some arrangement on silver. Senator Teller of Colorado read the minority report calling for a 16 to 1 ratio. The gold plank was upheld with an 818 vote to 105 votes. A number of silver Republicans left. Hanna would work behind the scenes to bring them back. Back in Canton, McKinley had a "war room" at his rented house on Market and 8th Street (where the McKinleys had lived 25 years earlier). The library had a telephone and a special telegraph set up. Ida was in the sitting room with Mother McKinley, while McKinley manned the library. A mass of reporters was on the porch, and McKinley would appear from time to time to talk with them. Canton residents were at the Repository listening to news bulletins as the convention approached a vote. The city had a number of company bands ready for the moment of McKinley's nomination.

Hanna had proved up to the task at the convention in preventing the "boss combine" from maneuvering and taking the nomination, which they had done many times in the past. First biographer and reporter summarized the success of Hanna:

> The movement for McKinley was skillfully presented as that of "the masses against the bosses." In some respects that was what it was. The bosses fought for others in the convention, but the will of the people carried. The pressure of the masses was for McKinley, and though the people stood on the outside the avalanche of popular opinion swept over all. The politicians opposed the "Ohio idea" and fought desperately. Platt, the most adroit of them all, threatened, cajoled, combined and bluffed. Reed's managers tried tact, diplomacy, compromise and all else available, the opponents of McKinley of all elements held all sorts of "star chamber" sessions time and time again, and on the night before the convention planned together until daylight endeavoring to fix some combination to defeat McKinley, but Mark Hanna, the manager of the McKinley campaign, kept in even tenor of his way, doing his work as past master of political strategy, smiled and feared not.

Much has been said of Hanna, but it was his focus on their goal that won the day. He used the rank and file to beat the bosses, and in the end that was how McKinley would win.

The nomination of McKinley was brought to the floor by previous agreement by Foraker, but it was Senator Thurston in seconding that would define McKinley's success: "On behalf of those stalwart workmen, and all the vast army of American toilers; that their employment may be certain, their wages just, their dollars the best in the civilized world; on behalf of that dismantled chimney, and the deserted factory at its base; that the furnaces may once more flame, the mighty wheels revolve, the whistles scream, the anvils ring, the spindles hum...I ask the nomination." This was to be the banner for McKinley — not gold or silver but iron and steel.

As the balloting started, McKinley's telephone hookup allowed him to hear the activity on the floor. Alabama started the vote with 1 for Morton and 19 for McKinley. McKinley steadily built a lead as the vote progressed. Iowa broke the trend with all 26 votes going to Allison, followed by another break with New York going for Morton. It would be Ohio that put McKinley over the mark. McKinley went to the next room to inform Ida and his mother. The bands broke out and crowds moved towards the McKinley residence. The final vote was McKinley 666; Thomas Reed, 84; Senator Quay, 61; Levi Morton, 58; and Senator Allison, 35. Senator Lodge moved to make it unanimous, which was approved. Finally, Garret Hobart of New Jersey was nominated for Vice-President. As trains arrived from Massillon and Alliance, the crowd swelled to 50,000. McKinley would also make his first "front porch speech" of the campaign.

McKinley's formal acceptance came after the Democrat convention and was written in Canton that August. It was a well-crafted strategic statement of the campaign. The longest part of the acceptance took the gold issue head-on with his support of gold being loud and clear. His strong support of gold appears as a bit of pandering to Morgan and the Eastern bankers who probably demanded stronger public support. McKinley also realized that the gold standard was not in his hands but those of Congress. It is clear by his later actions that he was at heart a bimetallist. He addressed the key points of the gold standard, silver and international bimetallism, avoidance of class warfare, and protectionism. The following are the key points made in his acceptance:

> *On Gold:* "Bimetallism cannot be secured by independent action on our part. It cannot be obtained by opening our mints to the unlimited coinage of the silver of the world at a ratio of 16 ounces of silver to one ounce of gold when the commercial ratio is more than thirty ounces of silver to one ounce of gold...It means the debasement of our currency to the amount of the difference between the commercial and coin value of the silver dollar...Until international agreement is had, it is the plain duty of the United States to maintain the gold standard... eighty-four percent of our foreign trade for 1895 was with gold standard countries. . . We never had greater prosperity in this country, in every field of employment and industry, than in the busy

years of 1880 to 1892, during all of which time this country was on a gold basis."

On Protectionism: "The Republican Party is wedded to the doctrine of protection and was never more earnest in its support and advocacy then as now. If argument were needed to strengthen its devotion to 'the American System,' or increase the hold of that system upon the party and people, it is found in the lesson and experiences of the past three years. . Another declaration of the Republican platform that has my most cordial support is that which favors reciprocity."

On Tariffs: "Our duties should always be high enough to measure the difference between the wages paid labor at home and in competing countries, and to adequately protect American investments and American enterprises. . .Our men at home are idle, and while they are idle men abroad are occupied with supplying us goods"

On Farmers: "Our unrivaled home market for the farmer has also greatly suffered, because those who constitute it — the great army of wage earners — are without the work and wages they formerly had. If they cannot earn wages, they cannot buy products. They cannot earn if they have no employment, and when they cannot earn the farmers' home market is lessoned."

McKinley's down home industrial economics were as powerful as Adam Smith's free trade village economics. The acceptance letter followed the strategic campaign plan of Hanna and McKinley, which would hit the money issue hard for 60 days then finish on the tariff issue. The major emphasis on gold and the currency was clearly aimed at the East. Overall it was a well-crafted document and Hanna distributed over two million copies.

Chapter 11. The Campaign of 1896

The Democrat candidate William Jennings Bryan is probably better known to today's readers for his involvement in the 1925 Scopes Trial on evolution. In the 1890s, he was considered America's greatest orator, and in the campaign of 1896 he focused all his talents on silver issue. McKinley had hoped to avoid the silver issue, but the nomination of Bryan by the Democrats left him no choice. Bryan combined the silver Democrats, old populists, and farmers to offset the conservative Eastern Democrats that had brought Grover Cleveland to power. Bryan would give his famous "cross of gold" speech in acceptance of the nomination. The Democrats nominated Eastern banker Arthur Sewall for vice-president. Bryan struck fear in the hearts of capitalists and caused a river of donations for McKinley. Even so Bryan proved to be a great orator with massive crowds. Furthermore, the youthful Bryan planned a railroad campaign of over 13,000 miles to take his silver message to the people.

The Democratic platform centered on free silver and opposition on the gold standard. It called the gold standard a "British policy" leading to "financial servitude to London" to secure its Irish vote. Bryan's main concern was to make the link between the silver standard and good times for all. After that foundation, the platform tried to offer a little something for everyone. It supported the Wilson-Gorman revenue tariff and the income tax. It stated that protective McKinley tariffs were a "breeder of trusts and monopolies." It opposed immigration as a way to protect American labor, which had been the strong stand of the

Republican Party. The platform opposed a third term for any president, probably to justify dumping Cleveland. It also called for various reforms in civil service, which was a popular theme of the time.

Bryan surprised many by getting early traction on the silver issue. The difference between gold and silver was more a matter of how the politicians played it. Bryan had made it the issue, and Hanna realized it could not be ignored. Hanna would excel in the educational campaign waged against the Democrats. He focused on the industrial centers where the Republicans could not afford to lose any support. Manufacturers and labor leaders were asked to distribute informational packets on the issue. Flyers and notices were even put near the machines. Foremen were given training and educational seminars on the subject. Notices and sometimes warnings were put in pay envelopes to tell of the dangers to industrial centers of free silver. Talks by experts were given during lunches and where possible at union halls. Hanna dispatched expert speakers to the big plants, such as Baldwin Locomotive in Philadelphia, Carnegie Steel in Braddock and Homestead, Pullman in Chicago, Standard Oil in Cleveland, and Westinghouse Electric in East Pittsburgh. This direct approach to industrial workers had never been so well planned and coordinated. Bryan supporters countered with copies of *Coin's Financial School,* but lacked the funds to even come close to Hanna's pamphleteering. Carnegie's *ABC's of Money* was reprinted by the millions to support gold. McKinley picked up another surprising ally in these industrial districts. A lot of Catholic priests feared Bryan's support of socialism and even preached for McKinley, while down the street Protestant minister were preaching McKinley to their bosses.

McKinley and his team were struck by the rising tide of Bryan support in the early going. Hanna felt that McKinley should counter with a whistle stop campaign, but McKinley differed, feeling he could not pull it off. The bigger factor was that McKinley believed the candidate should remain at home as had been the practice for decades. Furthermore, McKinley thought it would appear weak to counter Bryan with a break from Republican tradition. Hanna and Dawes in Chicago demanded that McKinley take to the road. It was McKinley that overruled his staff and decided on a front porch campaign. The reasons were varied; clearly McKinley felt he could lose in a head-on confrontation, which Bryan excelled at. Other factors included the health of his wife, who would want to travel with him, his concern for the dignity of the office, possibly his own stigma, and McKinley realized his porch was the geographic center of the electoral votes needed. Chicago was actually selected as national campaign headquarters, while McKinley himself would remain in Canton. An ancillary headquarters was set up in New York, probably to remain close to Eastern financial interests. Interestingly, the Democrats set up their national headquarters in Chicago.

At first look, Hanna was counting on the East to deliver the votes and money. The gold and industrial states of New York, Pennsylvania, New Jersey, Maine, Massachusetts, and Connecticut seemed safe for McKinley, where he had a base in the industrial cities. Bryan appeared unbeatable in the silver states of Colorado, Nevada, Montana, Utah, and Wyoming, especially since the silver Republicans had bolted the convention. Bryan was also strong in the south, but Hanna believed he might take Florida and the upper South such as Kentucky and Tennessee. The Great Lakes bloc of Ohio, Indiana, Illinois, Minnesota, Michigan, and Wisconsin presented 97 of the 224 electoral votes, and were considered key to winning in the Gilded Age. After the election, Bryan calculated that a shift in a mere 20,000 votes in California, Oregon, Kentucky, Indiana, North Dakota, and West Virginia would have given him the election.[62] Such reconstructions, while interesting, are not necessarily reflective of the election.

Hanna set the strategy of the first 60 days on the currency issue. McKinley wanted to make tariffs the issue, but the Democrats avoided this, sticking to the currency. McKinley didn't stick to the currency issue as Hanna suggested, moving to tariffs often. The campaign became an asynchronous talking past each other, instead of a debate on the issues. Bryan's railroad campaign would be countered with flooding areas with pamphlets and speakers, which had worked so well in McKinley's nominating campaign. Charles Dawes managed the Chicago office, and he was the first to realize that Bryan could win. Dawes also told McKinley funds would be less than in 1892. The business community started to think of a Bryan revolution and started to withhold funds. Hanna stopped arguing and started to build the campaign on McKinley's restrictions: a tariff focus and the front porch location. He looked to ways to counter Bryan with education and literature. The expenses of the Hanna literature strategy were enormous. Over 250 million documents were sent out by the end of the election with five million receiving weekly material. The Chicago office statistics were staggering with over a million and half mail packages going out.[63] Much of the material was printed in German as well. Hanna brought out smaller papers when necessary, but Bryan's speeches drew thousands. Still, Bryan was landing hard punches. McKinley avoided any direct debate in response to Bryan's points.

Some capitalists, such as Henry Clay Frick, kept the donations coming, but in general in early August, there was great concern. At first, overconfidence had slowed donations, followed by an almost panic of impending doom. The East

62 Paul Glad, *W. McKinley, Bryan and People*, (Chicago: Ivan R. Dee, 1991), 137
63 Morgan, 229

was again McKinley's nemesis. There were old wounds in the Eastern bosses and bankers, and a lack of enthusiasm for McKinley personally. Reed was also still bitter about his defeat at the convention. Hanna realized he needed more support from the Eastern moneymen. He established himself at the New York headquarters and purchased a special telephone line between New York and Chicago (a rarity at the time). He decided the wounds between the bosses had to be patched first. Hanna looked East for the money, realizing McKinley had the votes in the East. It was Chicago and Canton that were badly in need of money. Chicago expenditures would approach $4 million, while the Midwest donations were more moderate. For example, Marshall Field gave $4,000 and John "Bet-a-Million" Gates gave $12,000. The real money was, however, in the East. Hanna now needed the bosses and bankers he had defeated in the nomination campaign. The plan was to heal the Eastern divide by highlighting the danger of a Bryan victory and a return to silver.

First, Hanna and McKinley healed the differences with Reed and turned him into a stump campaigner. Hanna and Reed started to turn the psychology in the East to a positive confidence. Hanna met secretly with boss Platt of New York, and agreed with McKinley's approval that Platt would run the machine in New York. McKinley met with Matthew Quay of Pennsylvania in Canton in an effort to improve relations. Hanna and McKinley forged an uneasy alliance, but one good enough to start money flowing. Improved relations with the Eastern bosses, Hanna's cheerleading, and a mounting fear of Bryan finally opened the purses of Carnegie, Frick, Morgan, and Rockefeller in amounts of $250,000. Hanna also looked to the bankers of Philadelphia, Pittsburgh, and New Jersey to help. Estimates are that Hanna raised over $4 million from the East, which would be needed since expenditures of the Chicago office alone were over $3.5 million (mostly for literature and pamphlets). Rockefeller kicked in over $250,000 as Hanna requested. More typical was a Philadelphia banker who donated $25,000 stating: "We have never before contributed a cent to politics but the present crisis we believe to be as important as the war."

The bosses clearly underestimated both Hanna and Dawes, who put together a brilliant Midwest strategy. There was a special department at Chicago Headquarters for the Germans.[64] German Lutherans were key to the rural Midwest, and German Catholics were key to the urban Midwest. Dawes put money into German language newspapers in Chicago and Wisconsin, which paid off in votes. Dawes's banking background made him an excellent administrator. The bosses were thrown off balance since no organization had ever tried to "end run" them.

---

64 Charles Dawes, *Journal of the McKinley Years*, (Chicago: Lakeside Press, 1950)

Dawes courted and counted delegates like a pro during the campaign for the nomination, and he similarly counted votes during the campaign. Both men put together a print campaign that was unmatched. Bryan, however, benefited from the sales of *Coin's Financial School*, which supported silver and sold over a million copies. This book with its straightforward talk won many votes for Bryan in the West and Midwest.

Bryan's private train continued rolling, and Hanna and the staff once again begged McKinley to get onto the road. McKinley steadfastly refused, with this account recalled by Bentley Mott: "I announced that I would under no circumstances go on a speech making tour. If I should go now it would be an acknowledgment of weakness. Moreover, I might just as well put up a trapeze on my front lawn and compete with some professional athlete as to go out speaking against Bryan." The front porch campaign was the traditional approach considered statesman-like and dignified. It had one advantage of concentrating newspapermen for a steady flow of reports. Hanna would re-invent the old front-porch campaign of Harrison and other presidents to play McKinley and the organizations' strength. Hanna in the end turned Canton into a tourist attraction. He got the help of the railroads to bring the people to McKinley as they had brought them to the World's Fair in 1893. Daily parades and picnics were prepared for train arrivals. Vendors lined the streets selling food and souvenirs.

Hanna planned to make Canton into a Mecca or Holy Land for pilgrims. Hanna's work with the railroads was said to make a trip to Canton "cheaper than staying at home." Special discounts were given for groups of forty or more. Canton became a county fair with hot dog stands, souvenir hawkers, lemonade stands, and cigar stands lining the streets from the train station to the McKinley home. At the home, reporters and visitors mixed on the front porch, and in her good moments Ida McKinley served lemonade and McKinley shook hands. Reporters stayed in Canton, and every speech was clearly prepared and printed for their easy use. Reporters following Bryan were forced to take shorthand notes of his fast-moving speeches. This gave McKinley a powerful edge in the big national newspapers, and he more effectively reached the masses, which remains one of the little known strengths of the front porch campaign. In person, McKinley's speeches seemed a little stiff and statistical, but the point was that they were written for the newspaper. McKinley was really a much better pamphleteer than orator. Because Hanna supplied full-page text to reporters, the full text often appeared in newspapers. Bryan's speeches became repetitive towards the end of the "whistle stop campaign," and coverage tapered off. McKinley, by writing them out, honed his speeches better for each audience and supplied punch along with statistics. Hanna continued to be creative and strengthened the front-porch approach throughout the campaign. Saturday speeches were the longest and best prepared, realizing they would appear in the next day in the Sunday papers having huge circulations compared to the weekdays. Hanna coordinated the delegations based on a Saturday priority.

Hanna made Canton a popular stop for family vacations. Steelworkers from Pittsburgh often brought their kids for an outing. Westinghouse employees actually designed it as a Sunday family picnic. There were bands and soldiers as well as open-air picnics with tinplate tableware. At night electricity lighted the way from the train station to the McKinley home. Tinplate dinner pails were sold with the slogan, "the advance Agent of Prosperity." Over ten thousand souvenir dinner pails were sold throughout the United States. Bars and saloons sold "the McKinley," which had been made popular at the Republican convention. "The McKinley" was a mix of bourbon, lemonade, and sugar. Carnations were available for labels at the McKinley home. Souvenirs focused on the tariffs by the use of tinplate products, badges of raw wool, and glass canes.

More instructive than the McKinley souvenirs were the gifts to the McKinley. One plate mill presented a sixty-foot roll of tinplate, while another gave him the largest piece of galvanized iron ever made. Food came in an endless stream of cakes, cheese, cookies, pies, and candy, all of which was used to feed the staff. Flowers poured in daily. Kegs of Scotch whiskey were a popular gift from capitalists like Carnegie and Frick. H. J. Heinz sent pickles and ketchup. Pet eagles and stuffed eagles named after McKinley and Hanna were common. A steel tube cane made by the new seamless welding process, a polished tree stump from Tennessee, and a gavel made from a log from Lincoln's home were received as gifts. Glassmakers brought beautiful art pieces. These gifts often represented thank-yous from factories saved by the tariffs, and they clearly reflected McKinley's strength with industry and labor.

Steelworkers poured into Canton, not by the thousands but tens of thousands. Carnegie's rail mill at Braddock alone sent thousands. Carnegie and the Pennsylvania Railroad offered special trains for workers and families. Braddock's Edgar Thomson was one of the largest factories, producing most of the steel rails for the booming railroad expansion. The mill had started in 1875, and owed its very existence to the Republican tariffs. Over 90% of rails were imported at the time Edgar Thomson started up. Thanks to tariffs, it survived and thrived, overtaking the domestic rail market by 1882. In 1889, British steelmakers hailed Edgar Thomson Works as the most productive mill in the world. By the end of the 1890s, Edgar Thomson Works would have made more steel rails than the rest of the world combined. When the crews visited McKinley they presented him with a gold-plated piece of steel rail, which he cherished.

Support was not only coming from the mill at Braddock; a huge delegation from the troubled Homestead Works came by thirty-three special train cars in September. McKinley avoided any reference to the 1893 labor lockout, which had generated Democratic criticism, as McKinley had no ties to that strike. McKinley was still popular with steelworkers; even the Homesteader visit was paid for by Carnegie Steel. Carnegie's right hand man, Charles Schwab, headed the delegation. Charles Schwab, like Bill Jones at Braddock, was an extremely popular boss with the men. A large parade was organized to march the Homesteaders from the train station to McKinley's home. The Homestead speech exemplified the model of the front porch campaign. McKinley used what would later be called the "rhetoric of silence": he avoided the local issue and keyed in on a national and future path. It was a well-prepared speech, with hard statistics that could be printed in national newspapers. The strength of McKinley with the steelworkers was amazing; the remnants of these Republican steelworkers would remain into the 1980s. It was the same appeal Bryan had with the Western farmers. The real difference in rhetoric was that Bryan was the superior orator, but McKinley's speeches gained leverage through publication throughout the nation. Such use of newspapers was the cornerstone of the front porch campaign; while Bryan spoke to hundreds, McKinley "spoke" to tens of thousands. The front porch campaign allowed for McKinley's staff to do much of the work for the reporters, passing out copies of the speeches. Reporters were daily visitors and camped near by. Mrs. McKinley served them lemonade. For the reporters, it was a great assignment compared to chasing Bryan around the country, and would lead to the implementation of a 'White House press corps" when McKinley was president. Bryan's railroad campaign may have been legendary, but McKinley's front porch campaign was just as powerful.

Delegations and groups came in endless streams, varying in size from hundreds to thousands. McKinley's neighbors organized the "Home Guard," as horse mounted guides at the train station. Civil War veterans joined the "Guard" in large numbers to help out. The Guard not only escorted delegations but also controlled traffic and rode ahead to alert McKinley's staff. The McKinley staff was well prepared with names, personal details, and hometown statistics. Bands were directed to play the appropriate regional song such as "Dixie" for southerners. Campaign songs were written to emphasize protection and prosperity. McKinley readied variants of his speech themes to address regional concerns. McKinley was then briefed to be able to speak informally with the members of the delegations, though he himself prepared his more formal speeches. Other speakers were enlisted and writers prepared their speeches with a final review from McKinley. On one day alone McKinley gave nine speeches. For large delegations, Hanna would set up tents to food and entertainment.

The delegations represented workers, trade associations, unions, companies, and sometimes even cities. McKinley also attracted a number of non-political church groups including African-American church groups, revealing his popularity with blacks. McKinley's all-inclusive approach never conceded any voter group to the Democrats. Pittsburgh delegations flooded Canton in September. Steelworkers from Pittsburgh mills were a common sight throughout the campaign every week. Trains were set up so that often commercial travelers found themselves in Canton. Daily totals often ran as high as 20,000 to 40,000, comprising a true sampling of the population. McKinley sensed early on that it was necessary to deviate from the plan and bring out the "heavy artillery." He was quoted as saying: "The people — I mean the masses — are most deeply concerned about the tariff. 'Give us a chance to earn some money,' is what they are saying just now, and they are not grumbling about the kind of money." McKinley would go into the tariff issue with industrial and urban visitors. By the end of the campaign, McKinley had successfully combined the two. To workers from Carnegie's Braddock mill, he called for "good work, good wages, and good money." If McKinley was struck by the crowds that Bryan's speeches turned out, Bryan must have feared the sight of laborers pouring into Canton, Ohio. McKinley proved flexible at speaking, as well, which was required as the Democrats drove home the silver message.

The battle for the Great Lakes states such as Michigan, Minnesota, and Wisconsin was also problematic. These states had a large urban population of Catholics (about 35% of total vote) and a large rural Lutheran German population (about 30%). Some cities such as Milwaukee, Wisconsin had large populations of Catholic Germans. It required a balanced approach of factors important to farmers, Catholics, urban workers, and Protestants. McKinley had learned to balance this approach with the Germans from his congressional runs in Ohio, and he got a boost when Catholic Archbishop John Ireland of St. Paul gave him his backing. McKinley focused on gold with the rural Germans. These German farmers were a bit different, having experienced the failure of silver in their homelands. Also, 1896 had brought a major rise in wheat prices due to a crop failure in India. Farmers now had high crop prices, low goods prices because of the recession, and gold was the standard. Maybe silver was not the answer. Interest rates seriously concerned farmers. Estimates suggest as many as 80% of farmers were mortgaged at rates of at least 9%. They really didn't care about gold, silver, or paper as long as it could buy sausages and beer. The tariffs didn't play well with them either, since they equated them to high prices. Bryan miscalculated by playing to the Republican Protestants in the German population. In the final analysis, fewer Republican Protestants shifted to the Democrats than Catholics switched over to the Republicans. McKinley's Stark County gerrymandering experiences and battle scars had paid off. Bryan's Protestant strategy worked in southern Illinois, Indiana, and Ohio, but not enough to overcome the Republican edge. The Protestant strategy of Bryan also worked well in Southern Michigan, but again not enough to carry the state.

While Bryan spoke with the fire of a preacher, mainstream religions leaned toward McKinley. Catholic leaders feared anarchism with the preaching of Bryan. The fact that men like Eugene Debs and Edward Bellamy campaigned for Bryan seemed to confirm their suspicions. McKinley's middle class values crossed all religious lines, and his fairness appointing government workers regardless of religion paid dividends. McKinley had a proven record of ecumenism, which was part of the overall "McKinley Realignment." McKinley consistently viewed the combination of the civil rights, equality, and upward mobility as the cornerstone of prosperity. McKinley had strong support from Midwest Catholic bishops, such Bishop Elder of Cincinnati, Bishop Horstmann of Cleveland, and Bishop Ireland of St. Paul. While a Mason and devout Protestant, McKinley carried as much as 45% of the Catholic vote. Presbyterians were strongly for McKinley as well as Methodists. Religious German farmers became strong McKinley supporters based on McKinley's religious values in an age of corruption. McKinley proved stronger at bringing farmers to his side than Bryan did in bringing workers to his side. A large part of that was the result of McKinley's religious values.

Hanna proved a true visionary in campaigning. Historian Lawrence Goodwin noted: "In sheer depth, the advertising campaign organized by Mark Hanna in behalf of William McKinley was without parallel in American history. It set the creative standard for the twentieth century."[65] He was one of the first to use political polls, and their use helped him identify an early boom for Bryan. He was the first to use the telephone extensively, paying for lines where needed. Hanna used news summaries to stay informed on editorial comment across the nation. Never before had literature been used so successfully. Earlier elections had focused on political speakers, but Hanna found pamphlets to be almost as effective. Hanna printed the pamphlets in many languages. Later in the campaign, public opinion polls clearly defined tariffs as the issue in the Midwest, silver in the West, and gold in the East. Hanna used the mill owners and managers to get the pamphlets in the hands of workers. He brought in speakers who spoke the native tongue of the workers and advertised in special nationality newspapers.

---

65 Lawrence Goodwin, *The Populist Moment*, (Oxford: Oxford University Press, 1978), 282

The tariff issue played well with the industrial workers, and pamphlets added focus and local color. Polls also helped Hanna catch the shift towards McKinley in late August. The shift allowed McKinley to hammer home the tariff issue, which the Democrats did not respond to. McKinley and Hanna used regional speakers in a masterly way. These speakers were often Senators and Representatives, a role McKinley had played for Hayes, Garfield, Harrison, and Blaine. McKinley used Terence Powderly, former Grand Master of the Knights of Labor, to maintain his edge with labor. Bryan lacked the money to put speakers in the field and depended too much on himself to carry the message.

As the trend went towards McKinley, more funds poured in. Hanna's "Canton World's Fair" got even bigger. Hanna shifted to patriotism by planning a nationwide "Flag Day." Millions of flags were distributed to major cities. Hanna played on McKinley's war record and recruited veterans to march in all cities. The parades were meant to contrast the revolutionary and socialist nature of Bryan. Democrats were angered and responded by tearing down flags, which played into Hanna's propaganda machine. It was in New York that Hanna's new relationship with Boss Thomas Platt paid off. Platt, like McKinley, seemed to make friends out of necessity. Platt delivered the parade crowds for Hanna, who supplied the money. More than 150,000 participated in the New York parade and 750,000 looked on. Large parades were also put on in Chicago, San Francisco, Boston, and Pittsburgh. San Francisco had become a McKinley stronghold by the time of his death in 1901. Flag Day continued to be celebrated for many years. In the meantime, Bryan was bogged down by commercial train schedules, only getting his own rail car at the end of the campaign.

Dirty tricks were common throughout the campaign. McKinley was pictured as a "cook" who never saw the enemy during the Civil War. Many accused him of being a drunkard and a wife beater. Bryan got his share, too. He was pictured as a revolutionary and an anarchist; he was called mad, a foreign agent. The most vicious attacks were directed at Ida McKinley, who was accused of insanity as well as being a Catholic. Others accused her of being part black. Most observers and historians have noted that there was relatively little fraud and corruption. However, there is evidence of some owner coercion at some factories, as well as restrictions on black voters in the border states. Hanna's strength was not dirty tricks but showmanship. The shows kept getting bigger as the campaign progressed. Finally, Hanna and McKinley put together a strong finish as many noted a tired Bryan falling off. Bryan was the better orator, but Hanna countered this strength with the best use of the technology of the time.

McKinley went to vote early on the morning of November 3 in his home First Ward. Both McKinley and Hanna were confident at this point. McKinley was said to have chain-smoked cigars into the early morning as he awaited returns. By 4 a.m. on November 4, 1896, the results showed the greatest presidential victory since Grant. McKinley received 7,101,401 popular votes and 271 electoral votes to Bryan's 6,470,656 popular votes and 176 electoral votes. The voter turnout was 80%, which put to rest the idea that a front-porch campaign could not generate interest. It was a tough fight to the end. McKinley carried the Eastern and Middle Atlantic states. In these areas the McKinley Labor alliance carried the day. The South and West went to Bryan, but McKinley took the battle ground states of the Great Lakes and upper South. These states showed McKinley's strength with Midwest farmers by carrying Ohio, Indiana, Iowa, Michigan, Minnesota, and Wisconsin. Cleveland had carried the Midwest, so McKinley's success was hailed as a new realignment. McKinley even chipped away at the "Solid South" with Bryan becoming the first Democrat to lose the former slave states of Kentucky, Delaware, Maryland, and West Virginia since the end of reconstruction.

It was a great victory, but there were some disappointments. McKinley's Ohio was carried by only 48,494 votes (smaller than his margins in Wisconsin and Illinois). The Ohio vote was probably affected by Bryan's focus on that state in October. Bryan found large crowds in Akron and Cleveland. McKinley lost South Dakota by 200 votes and Wyoming by 300. His effort in the South fell a bit short, losing Virginia, North Carolina, and Tennessee by 19,000, states which he probably would have won if all three had had full black voting rights allowed. While he carried the industrial immigrant vote, he failed to crack the hold of Tammany Hall on the Irish vote in the East. He did break the Democratic farm alliance. The Republicans took the House as well and established a majority in the Senate. McKinley had proved that his protectionism represented the will of the people. He now faced the difficult task of turning the economy around.

The McKinley realignment was really an extension of the 1894 elections, but McKinley built the labor alliance and broke the farm alliance. The new realignment brought together the middle class and rising lower class from all regions. Every state that McKinley carried, with the exception of Kentucky, would remain Republican until 1912. McKinley had a simple message of prosperity and equal rights. Historians talk about the "battle of the standards," but McKinley knew it was the economy, not the methodology. It was a vote for capitalism versus socialism (which Bryan represented). Labor wanted better conditions and more money, but jobs had to come first. McKinley's victory heralded the end of the People's or Populist Party, which never again challenged at the national level. McKinley had demonstrated his labor support early on with the miners, and they never forgot it. He did the same with Catholics and blacks. America and its principles were always put first. He became synonymous with the American flag. He had avoided scandals and was a member of the middle class that loved him. He had built a foundation that would provide decades of Republican dominance.

Bryan's organization put a good spin on the election, but on November 5, McKinley was president elect. For McKinley, the issue now would be tariff legislation, but the first order of business was the filling of his Cabinet. Cabinets in those days were a combination of rewards for support and positioning for driving legislation. McKinley could be assured that the bosses would show up, at least to give their opinions, and McKinley had only a one-vote margin in the Senate. Eastern boss Thomas Platt held that vote, and would have to be pacified by a presidential appointment. McKinley also had to repay the second tier capitalist bosses he had created, such as Hanna in Ohio, Dawes in Chicago, and John Porter in New England. McKinley would have calls from his Ohio base as well, and certainly some capitalists would have opinions as well as labor leaders. McKinley first problem was what to do with the man who many people felt had been responsible for his victory. Hanna was said to have stayed out of the decisions initially, but he clearly expected a key position. Hanna's business background might have qualified him for Secretary of the Treasury as the newspapers speculated. Usually presidents looked to bankers and first tier capitalists for the position of Secretary of the Treasury. In any case, it appears that Hanna did not want a cabinet position, although McKinley certainly wanted him there.

Hanna appears to have wanted more than anything to be a senator. The road to getting him that position was complex, even for a president of the United States. The string of events required McKinley to appoint Ohio's senior senator John Sherman to Secretary of State, thus opening a senate seat. McKinley could then pressure Governor Bushnell to appoint Hanna senator. McKinley managed to pull off the difficult arrangement. The deal was done only to gratify Hanna, since the 88-year-old Sherman offered little to the cabinet. McKinley backed Sherman with his old friend Judge Day of Canton as assistant secretary. The Treasury Secretary was a surprise. The Eastern gold Republicans would watch his appointment closely, but McKinley put tariffs ahead of gold. In addition, McKinley's Chicago campaign manager, young Charles Dawes, wanted the job. McKinley felt Dawes was too young, but he did give him Comptroller of the Currency. Illinois Senator Allison wanted his friend appointed but McKinley didn't think he was qualified. A dark horse candidate, banker, and friend of Kohlsaat, Lyman Gage was selected. Gage said he believed in McKinley's protective tariff, but would impose any tariffs that would help monopolies. Gage is a clear example that McKinley opposed monopolies that would take advantage of tariffs. Gage was a gold bug and Democrat, which was a concession to the East. McKinley also liked Gage's support for labor and Gage's work in Chicago for labor and capital cooperation.

Even stranger was McKinley's selection of General Russell Alger of Michigan to head the War Department. The appointment of Alger made no sense except to repay Michigan's support, which had not been a major factor. To satisfy Eastern supporters, Teddy Roosevelt was appointed assistant Secretary of the Navy. Many feel that Roosevelt was positioned as a rebuff to Platt, who disliked Roosevelt. He repaid California by selecting Judge Joseph McKenna as Secretary of the Interior. McKinley appointed James Wilson, Secretary of State, on the request of Senator Allison. With the cabinet in place, McKinley focused on the tariff as his first priority. A number of minor appointments were made to put Platt in his place, such as Teddy Roosevelt as assistant Secretary of the Navy. McKinley, in doing so, initiated the end of many Republican machines. The reformer Teddy Roosevelt had long been an opponent of Boss Platt in New York.

Roosevelt, however, did satisfy all the Eastern Republican bluebloods such as John Hay and Henry Cabot Lodge. Lodge offered McKinley a wedge into the East as well. Lodge and McKinley had had adjoining desks in the house and had developed a friendship, even though Lodge had supported Reed in the Republican primary. The alliance with Lodge would serve McKinley well in the Senate. The Roosevelt assignment included some behind the scenes horse-trading. Lodge and Hanna had Roosevelt remove the blackball on Thomas Platt's membership in the upscale and very blueblood Metropolitan Club. Membership in the Metropolitan Club, a hub of Washington and international power broking, was just the gift for a political boss like Platt. The Metropolitan Club would become a type of think-tank for imperialists and expansionists. Many believed membership was more valuable than a cabinet position or Senate seat. Like the Sherman-Hanna deal, the Roosevelt assignment served a multiple political purpose. In general, McKinley's cabinet was older, with most in their sixties and one in his seventies (several died within a few years), but they were highly experienced. Most of them were political compromises with the exception of Henry Payne, who was refused because he was a lobbyist. McKinley's eye was on the Congress more than his Cabinet, and his selections reflected this.

CHAPTER 12. PRESIDENT MCKINLEY

His Inaugural Address started by focusing on the quest for international bi-metallism as opposed to a strong affirmation of the gold standard. Manufacturing was to be the solution for the depressed economy: "The depression of the past four years has fallen with especial severity upon the great body of toilers of the country, and upon none more than the holders of small farms. Agriculture has languished and labor suffered. The revival of manufacturing will be relief to both." His bimetallism gave tacit support to the Eastern bankers, but they worried about McKinley's unwillingness to commit fully to the gold standard. The switch to a lower key approach to gold had to be disturbing to J. P. Morgan, who feared this would happen after the election. What McKinley was saying to the bankers was that, if the gold standard of their trading partners was critical to international trading, they could as well move those trading partners to bimetallism instead of meeting their gold standard. At the end of the speech, he sent out the call for a special session of Congress to consider tariff reform. Thus McKinley returned to his core strength and belief. McKinley informally let it be known that there would be no government appointments until the tariff reform bill was passed. Chairman Nelson Dingley gaveled the House to order on March 15, 1897 to consider this crucial issue.

The focus on the tariff was not isolated strategy, as the President hoped to use the duties to lower French tariffs on American products as well as to pressure France to support the international commission on bimetallism. McKinley was now convinced of the necessity of reciprocity in tariff reform. France, in particular, had high rates on American canned goods and lumber. McKinley saw reciprocity and bimetallism as the key to lifting the nation out of the depression, and France was the weakest link in Europe's golden chain. McKinley had already studied the tariff and had proposed some key objectives for Congress. He wanted to expand the American manufacturing surplus by reciprocity and favorable rates. Secondly, he wanted the president to have a free hand to enact reciprocity agreements. McKinley's view on reciprocity had evolved since he had battled Blaine and Harrison in 1890 on South American reciprocity. This was really one of his strengths, the ability to be flexible and open to change. On the rates themselves, McKinley was willing to increase rates on wool, hides, and metal ore to help the West. Wool had been taken off the list during the Cleveland administration, almost as a slap in the face to Ohio and McKinley. Lastly, McKinley had his diplomats working in France and Europe on support for bimetallism in return for favorable rates.

McKinley was confident in the House where the margin was 204 Republicans to 153 Democrats, but some compromises were necessary with the Western silver Republicans. The Senate posed a bigger problem for the Republicans with only 42 Republicans to 38 Democrats, enough to win but not enough to prevent endless regional amendments that had defeated the Wilson-Gorman tariff of 1894. The House version had high rates on French goods and they lobbied hard in the Senate for reciprocity or an outright pledge on bimetallism. McKinley got personally involved by having afternoon smokers for congressmen. The hard work was done by Vice President Hobart who lunched, cajoled between sessions, and held dinners. McKinley had great respect for the body he had evolved in. He would never bully or threaten, but he worked hard behind the scenes. The strategy centered on the West and Midwestern states where farm products, wool, ore, and hides were duty free or had low duties since 1894. Republicans could satisfy both the some Democrats and silver Republicans with protection on these goods.

The bill moved quickly through the House and was carried by a vote of 205 to 122. As the bill moved to the Senate, an endless array of amendments was expected, but the press kept the pressure on as the country wallowed in recession. The silver Republicans continued to be problematic, wanting to introduce currency legislation with the tariff bill. McKinley, Hobart, and Secretary Gage spent days trying to keep the Silverites in line. There was public pressure too. The economy had taken another downturn. McKinley had very good press relations, one of the side benefits of the front porch campaign. There were endless negotiations between the White House, House, Senate, and even diplomats. In the end, the bill passed with strong protective planks and reciprocity clauses. The clauses gave the president wide latitude to negotiate trade treaties and impose rates when necessary. The bill, known as the Dingley Tariff Bill, passed the Senate on July 7 by a vote of 38 to 28. It then went to conference in the more protectionist House. The bill came to McKinley's desk and was signed on July 24 and was signed by McKinley.

While McKinley pressed to move the bill quickly, he wanted a scientific approach to the tariff schedules reminiscent of Alexander Hamilton rather than across-the-board hikes. Nelson Aldrich of the Senate Finance Committee was also a believer in scientific tariff management and an ally of McKinley. The scientific approach demanded research on specific products within industries. For example, steel plate needed more protection than steel rails where American technology had given the industry an inherent advantage. Aldrich surveys of key steelmakers such as Carnegie and Frick resulted surprisingly in no need for increases in the steel schedule. This scientific and weighed approach helped avoid trade wars, retaliation, and kept consumer prices down. The key to the success of the McKinley Tariff as opposed to the Democratic tariff of 1893 was to be found in this scientific approach. The government needed a tariff at least at the level of revenue. The income of the government in 1896 consisted of customs duties of $160, 022,000, alcohol taxes of $114,454,000, tobacco taxes of $30,712,000, and stamp taxes of $260,000. The income tax promoted by Cleveland had been struck down in the Supreme Court. Andrew Carnegie had suggested publicly that tariffs be raised on luxury items as opposed to having a tax on income. These luxury duties on were increased in the Dingley Tariff during the McKinley administration. Duties on pieces of art, art glass, and silk rose under the Dingley Tariff. These revenue-producing tariffs helped McKinley turn around four years of treasury deficits under Cleveland.

The bill gave the president wide latitude in increasing or lowering duties based on concessions from other countries. The French almost immediately retaliated with tariffs on cottonseed oil and pork products. McKinley entered into months of negotiations, which the new bill allowed for, and was in the end successful at gaining a reciprocity agreement. The reciprocity agreement was also able to use possible concessions to help gain French support for a commission on international bimetallism. The initiative on bimetallism failed because of the reluctance of countries such as India and Britain. Critics have said that McKinley never put his heart in the effort for bimetallism, and there may have been some truth in this. McKinley probably personally had come to believe the bankers concerning the gold standard or had tired of the issue. For McKinley the tariff bill was the real economic issue of the time.

An early biographer, Alexander McClure, summarized the immediate impact of the Dingley Tariff:

The new tariff proved the Rubicon of the advancing good times. That passed, the indications of a coming industrial boom were everywhere to be seen. They grew and expanded, they rose and swelled, until such a wave of prosperity swept over the land as this Western world had rarely seen. Never in the history of the world had there been a more marked contrast of bad and good times than between the second Cleveland and the first McKinley administrations. And let what may be said, the fact stands largely self-evident that this wondrous change in conditions was due to the opposed fiscal measures of the two administrations, the Wilson tariff for revenue and the Dingley tariff for protection.

The Dingley Tariff had a very swift effect as imports dropped and exports increased. After years of a trade debit, the trade balance developed into surplus of $257 million. The growth in exports presented proof for the McKinley scientific approach to tariffs. From 1896 to 1901 exports surged from $833 million to $1.49 billion. The surplus grew every year under the tariff, reaching $664 million in 1901. As the economy grew, imports even increased slowly each year. The raw statistics were hard for free traders to pass off as an anomaly. Our heavy industries of steel, iron, glass, and machinery hit new production records and dominated the world in technology and production. The scientific approach to setting duties by industry and economic value worked extremely well. The reciprocity clause allowed negotiation in order to avoid trade wars. Furthermore, trade wars did not develop because of the size and value of the American market. Countries were happy to pay the tax to gain entry. The Treasury grew as the duties produced revenue again. Amazingly, prices went down as industry invested in process improvement and plant expansion. McKinley and the manufacturers were turning their interests toward finding expanding markets for their surplus production.

McKinley got a break in 1897 with the finding of gold in South Africa and Alaska. The new production of gold increased the money supply just as the Silverites had hoped to do with Western silver. The issue behind the silver–gold controversy probably was always the money supply. Silver was attractive at the time because of the production of American silver mines. By the second half of 1897, the economy experienced a definite upward turn. The expanding gold supply expanded the world's currency, and America began increasing its exports as a result. The turnaround was the result of gold production, tariffs, and the new confidence of American businessmen. The fall crop was solid with high prices in 1897. Farmers saw profits jump. The nation's mills and businesses started to plan for prosperity. Too little credit is given to the upbeat and optimistic nature of McKinley. He dug in on problems, always believing they could be resolved. The likable and friendly McKinley could get people to accomplish things. The Republicans could finally unite under a gold standard and high tariffs.

The $50,000 salary changed McKinley very little, other than he gave his wife expensive gifts, something that had not been possible previously. The constant visitors, tourists, and guests were something the McKinley had gotten used to during the campaign. They were also used to moving into rented and new surroundings. Mrs. McKinley seemed to maintain herself in her new role. She certainly enjoyed the closeness of her husband as well as the constant availability of a physician. It certainly relaxed McKinley, who had spent years being the primary caregiver. Ida did fulfill most of her duties as First Lady, although McKinley sometimes would handle the longer and more formal engagements himself. At dinners McKinley broke with protocol and had Ida sit beside him so he could watch over her. He was probably the last president to freely walk the streets of Washington in the evening. In December, McKinley's mother died at 89. This was a blow since, like Ida, she had been an emotional support in the tough times.

As the tariff bill progressed through Congress, McKinley started to look to the future. The nation was just coming out of a depression, and McKinley was thinking into the future. He believed America would soon reach a point of overproduction and surplus with the tariffs in place. Even in his inaugural speech, he had noted the need to rebuild the merchant marine. The American Navy had started a rebuilding program as far back as the Harrison Administration. Exports had been rising and many industries, such as the steel industry, were ready to aggressively export goods. Part of the McKinley strategy was to move towards the gold standard, which was based on a foundation for expanded exports. Exports of machinery, transport equipment, and metals had been surging since the 1880s. McKinley's friend George Westinghouse was manufacturing railroad brakes in Pittsburgh for the world, and this was the future McKinley envisioned. In a few years, as McKinley correctly forecast, the amount of exports would be double that of imports. His effort for a merchant marine bill stalled in the House as Midwest representatives objected to the use of Federal funds.

McKinley saw an analogy in the growth of the merchant marine to that of his hero Henry Clay and the canal system. Like Clay, McKinley thought the role of government was to facilitate manufacturing and trade by developing transportation infrastructure. He kept up his quest to expand the merchant marine throughout his career. McKinley's final speech in Buffalo would be a call to expand the merchant marine. In the Senate, the improvement of the merchant marine was the pet project of Mark Hanna; it was a concept that the Midwest refused to pay for, since it favored the East and West Coasts. The Midwest farmers also feared that it would facilitate a flood of farm imports. Part of this concept was the building of an isthmus canal for Atlantic–Pacific trade. As early as 1897, McKinley formed a committee to study Nicaragua as a possible route for the canal. Progress had started in Congress but the debate on a possible Panama lo-cation slowed things. McKinley more and more assumed the role of the forgotten Henry Clay. McKinley's vision of America's new role as a sea power seemed to play into what his critics would see as imperialism. Unfortunately, foreign affairs would put these transportation issues on the back burner.

McKinley had campaigned solely on domestic issues but foreign problems quickly became part of the administration's focus. Cuba had presented a mount-ing problem for a decade as rebels called for freedom from Spain. Hawaiian an-nexation had surfaced first in the tariff debate in Congress because of its stra-tegic position in American trade and sugar production. The Hawaiian Islands were the stopping point between Japan and California. In the 1870s, Hawaii had been made a coaling station for stream ships. President Tyler had even included Hawaii in his view of the Monroe Doctrine. Reciprocity trade agreements with Hawaii dated back to the Grant Administration. American traders and business-men saw Hawaii as a key to trade in the Pacific. Germany and Japan also started to use Hawaii and fears rose of rivalries between nations. Republicans under President Harrison had pushed for annexation, but the effort died during the Cleveland Administration. In 1896, it was put back in the Republican platform. McKinley fell short of pushing the Hawaiian annexation through as he used most of his power for the tariff legislation. McKinley also fired up an old enemy in Speaker Reed, who opposed any American expansion.

The idea of expansion and imperialism had deep roots in the Republican Party and included businessmen, nationalists, bluebloods and imperialists. In particular, five Republicans fathered this movement: John Hay, Henry Cabot Lodge, Teddy Roosevelt, Alfred Mahan, and Elihu Root. All of these men were influential with McKinley, but McKinley was not really an imperialist. John Hay had been an advisor to Republican presidents going back to Lincoln. He would be Ambassador to Great Britain and Secretary of State under McKinley. Henry Cabot Lodge was a Republican blueblood and powerful Senator from Massachu-setts. Teddy Roosevelt was first McKinley's Assistant Secretary of the Navy and future Vice President. Elihu Root, a blueblood with strong ties to the bankers and capitalists, would become Secretary of War under McKinley. Alfred Mahan was a Navy strategist who was behind the growth of American Naval power. Mahan's book, *The Influence of Sea Power upon History*, was a source book for the na-tion and for Republican presidents.

Cuba, however, was being pushed on McKinley from all fronts. The press, led by William Randolph Hearst in the West, was constantly running stories of Americans being beaten and tortured in Spanish Cuba. Americans supported the rebel cause to overthrow what appeared to be oppressive Spanish rule. McKinley was trying to hold down expansionists in his party, just as Henry Cabot Lodge and Teddy Roosevelt coupled with the drumbeat of the press towards war. The supporters of war with Cuba became known as "jingoes" from an English term in 1878 when the British government was trying to decide whether to defend Turkey against Russia. McKinley is often called an imperialist and expansionist, but with Cuba he actually did more to stamp down the push. Critics viewed it as indecisiveness, but in any case, he resisted the call for war. The drive had really started under the Harrison Administration with the rebuilding of the American Navy and expansion of the merchant marine. This Naval expansion slowed but continued through the Cleveland Administration. The economic pressure was building for expanded trade in the Pacific as a means to relieve production surplus as well. The Republican Party and the Democratic Party had called for support for Cuban independence in the elections. McKinley came into office with all ingredients in the pot being stirred. Annexation offered no problem for McKinley, but he fiercely opposed war or use of the military.

There was strong opposition toward war including Republican Speaker of the House Thomas Reed, Secretary Sherman, Andrew Carnegie, Mark Twain, and Samuel Gompers. The anti-imperialists cut across the population and included prominent businessmen. Annexing Hawaii was considered a separate issue; while expansionist in nature, it did not require armed conflict. Even McKinley's future Secretary of War, Elihu Root, had publicly opposed the war but favored expansion in general. Hanna also was against American expansion, but the base of the Party tended to be for war. The anti-war movement never developed into a political faction as the yellow press pushed for action in Cuba. The Metropolitan Club with Roosevelt, Hay, Lodge, and Root found an ally in William Hearst on Cuba. Personally, Hearst hated the blueblood Republicans such as Roosevelt. McKinley did not want war over Cuba and was discussing plans for a possible purchase. McKinley wanted an industrial empire, not a military one. Hanna suggested that business in general opposed war, but this was probably wishful thinking considering the opportunities for world trade.

Early 1898 brought more problems as rebel violence increased in Cuba, and the rebels tried to pull the United States into the struggle. In early February, Hearst's yellow press published a letter from a Spanish minister calling McKinley "weak, and an abider for admiration of the crowd." Then on February 15, 1898, the *Maine*, an American warship was blown up in Havana Harbor. McKinley again kept his powder dry, as the press screamed for the United States to take action, with headlines like, "Remember the *Maine*." A Naval Commission was assigned to make inquiry into the nature of the explosion. The source remains unknown to this day, but the press and public assumed it was caused by

Spanish loyalists. McKinley did everything to avoid war, even going so far as to try to buy Cuba. McKinley and Spain negotiated until April 11, when McKinley sent a war message to Congress. In the meantime, McKinley sent an ultimatum to Spain for an end to control over Cuba. War was declared on April 24 (it was backdated to April 21).

The declaration caught Spain a bit off guard. Spain was 5,000 miles from Cuba, but its fleet was even further away tied up in another insurrection in the Spanish Philippines. While sizable, the Spanish Navy was considered to lack firepower and possessed many obsolete ships. America, on the other hand, had a new and retooled Navy. In addition, the main American Fleet was ideally located in Japan, thanks to the foresight of Assistant Secretary of the Navy Teddy Roosevelt, who had sent them there to be close to the Spanish main fleet in the Philippines, just in case. The American Army faced a much different problem; it only had 28,000 soldiers, while the Spanish had 155,000 soldiers in Cuba alone. A call went out immediately for volunteers, and 200,000 poured into the army. The pay would be the same as McKinley's during the Civil War: $13 a day.

McKinley ordered the Navy to attack the Spanish fleet in the Philippines as the Spanish launched another fleet towards Cuba. Admiral Dewey and the American fleet engaged the Spanish at Manila Bay on May 1, 1998. Within five hours every Spanish ship was sunk and 381 Spaniards killed. The victory was a triumph of America's might with American steel armored ships cutting down the Spanish wooden ones. The steel armor was a product of the Homestead Steel Works. On May 19, the other Spanish fleet reached Santiago, Cuba. Here the Americans blockaded them as they prepared to mount a land attack on Cuba. The American troops landed on June 30 and proceeded on two fronts. The Americans quickly won two battles and Teddy Roosevelt's volunteers, the "rough riders," made a name for themselves. The Spanish fleet, sensing defeat, made a run for it on July 3. The American fleet quickly engaged and destroyed every Spanish ship, killing 474 Spanish. The Spanish Army surrendered on July 17 in Cuba, followed by Guam Island and Wake Island in the Pacific. Insurgents took Manila in late July and the war was over.

McKinley assumed his role as Commander-in-Chief, and set up a war room in the White House where he followed the action around the clock. The war room had a switchboard of twenty telegraph lines, and McKinley could exchange information in twenty minutes with the commanders in the field via these lines and American cables to Cuba. There were fifteen telephone lines for Administration communications. By the end of the war, McKinley had telephone connections to the battlefield. It was the type of war armchair commanders dream of: quick and flashy victories with low causalities. The war lasted less than four months, with only 385 battle related deaths, although 2500 additional soldiers died of disease after the August ceasefire! The Peace Treaty in December forced Spain to give up Cuba, Puerto Rico, Guam, Wake Island, and the Philippines. The United States offered $20 million to cover property damages and the damage to Spain's national pride.

In the fears of the early war, McKinley pushed and got Congress to annex Hawaii. While McKinley generally had the favor of the public, there were partisan issues since it was a congressional election year. McKinley and particularly Secretary of War Alger were criticized for lack of medical and troop supplies. The outbreak of typhoid fever devastated the heroes of the Cuban battles. The Democrats were calling for congressional inquiry as stories of the sick soldiers mounted. The debate of what to do with the war booty was also under way. McKinley decided to keep the Philippines, but critics used his words against him. But this would not happen until two years after his death when a reporter recalled McKinley's description of the decision: "I walked the floor of the White House night after night until midnight; and I am not ashamed to tell you, gentlemen, that I went down on my knees and prayed Almighty God for light and guidance more than one night. I don't know how it came — but it came." The decision was to keep the Philippines and "civilize and Christianize them." Liberal historians have pointed to this statement as proof of McKinley's rationalization to justify imperialism.

The political impact of the war on McKinley was probably more positive than negative. The firing of Secretary of War Russell Alger took some of the heat out of the medical crisis of the troops. McKinley replaced him with Elihu Root, publicly moderate on expansion, and a man of solid administrative skills. Root's appointment helped calm anti-imperialists for the short term. Root, however, would side with the expansionists in the long run, which is where his true feelings lay. McKinley was able to convince labor that he was not planning to import cheap labor from the Philippines and that counted most of all in heading off Samuel Gompers' opposition.

The war had little effect on the booming economy, but Republicans feared a backlash from the poor management of the troops. The midterm elections went against the usual swing against the incumbents as the Republicans increased seats in the Senate and held a majority of 53 to 36. In the House they lost a few seats but held a majority of 185 to 163. McKinley tried to take some short vacations for a rest, but the Philippines dogged him. The Filipinos resisted the occupation for over three years and America became caught in their first insurgency war. Expansionists wanted the Philippines as a gateway to the East. While not considered a war or part of the Spanish–American War, 4230 American soldiers died in the three years of fighting.

The Philippines would haunt McKinley throughout the balance of his presidency, but with Cuba settled, he moved on to addressing the banking and currency system of the country. The 1898 elections had pushed out many Silverites in both parties. The strong economy and the increase in the gold reserve from $170 million to $250 million at the end of 1898 seemed to have ended the battle for silver. Gold production was increasing nationally and internationally, which allowed for monetary and industrial expansion. McKinley had been converted to the ideal of a gold standard, but he still hoped that international bimetallism might be an option in the future. McKinley also wanted a better national banking system, realizing that dependence of the nation on a few Eastern bankers was not a good idea. The pressure mounted for the gold standard to become formalized, and that had to come first in Congress. McKinley had hoped to move a bill through Congress by the end of 1899, but problems and debate mounted. McKinley was also working on reciprocity treaties as part of his overall economic plan. The Gold Standard Act was tied up for over a year in Congress, but McKinley signed it with a gold pen in early 1900.

In the summer of 1899, he planned a "holiday" of three months in Canton. He had finally gathered enough money to buy his old house on Market Avenue. He was very proud of his middle class home (which Teddy Roosevelt thought was beneath the dignity of the president). McKinley appeared happier than ever as he planned improvements and gardens. McKinley noted: "I am happy as a child to have it back. It's a fine old place." Canton always had a restorative effect on Ida, and that alone helped McKinley relax. He loved to get up and walk, then have breakfast while reading the local newspaper. The evening could be spent on the front porch. It was a reminder of McKinley's middle class roots and his enjoyment of simple pleasures. The McKinleys made a few day trips for picnics and relaxation. They enjoyed the nearby small lakes and rural towns such as Zoar, Ohio. The McKinleys talked of their eventual retirement in Canton.

In September 1899, more foreign problems mounted as the Philippine Insurrection continued along with the debate on what to do with the islands. This time it was China. The merchants of the world had their eye on China's huge market. European nations were locked in a fight over control of trade with the giant. They were negotiating "spheres of influence," but the United States was demanding an "open door" to all. China was trying to keep them all out, preferring to remain in isolation. But Japan invaded China in 1894, launching the Sino-Japanese War, and in the end China not only lost territory, she was forced to make a number of concessions, including opening up to foreign trade. The foreign control of China stirred up Chinese revolutionaries. A secret society of Chinese fighters rose up, known to the Chinese as the "I Ho Ch'uan" or "Righteous and Harmonious Fists" because of their fighting style. (The Westerners preferred the term "Boxers.") On June 29, 1900 the Boxers killed the German Minister and surrounded other diplomatic buildings including the Roman Catholic Cathedral.

An international expedition was launched which included Germany, Great Britain, Russia, France, Japan, and the United States. At the time, the status of the United States embassy was not clear. The rescue force relieved the surrounded embassies in August of 1900. For McKinley, the American role was over, leaving the Europeans to debate the status of China. Peking was under occupation by the international force, and the United States reduced its presence to that of an embassy guard. McKinley demanded only that the open door policy remain, as McKinley held off strong pressure from business to be more active in China.

Big Business, with the exception of Carnegie and some special interests, showed little interest in the Spanish–American War. China was a different story. China represented a huge market for American goods. Exports to China had gone from $1,741,000 in 1895 to $7,489,000 in 1897. The potential was huge for cotton goods, steel, wheat, and kerosene. A large consortium of American companies, including Carnegie Steel, had won a contract for a railroad in China from Hankow to Canton. As the Germans captured key Chinese ports in late 1897, many business concerns called for "immediate action." Business journals, such as the *Philadelphia Manufacturer* and the *Cincinnati Commercial Tribune*, called for an alliance of Britain, Japan, and the United States to offset the Russia/German alliance. McKinley adroitly avoided any military struggle in China against the demands of the expansionists, realizing that Cuba and the Spanish colonies were more then enough to manage. Again, McKinley did not play the role of being the tool of Big Business or an imperialist.

Through the war and the issues with the Philippines, McKinley worked hard on the reciprocity trade agreements permitted him under the Dingley Tariff. He had evolved toward strong support of reciprocity, which James Blaine had introduced him to in 1890. Reciprocity had roots going back to Alexander Hamilton and the Federalists. McKinley appointed John Kasson of Iowa to handle reciprocity agreements for the State Department. Kasson negotiated hard, but found resistance in the Senate, which had to ratify treaties. Conservative Republicans on the Senate Finance Committee such as Senator Nelson Aldrich of Rhode Island had opposed higher tariffs in 1897 and resisted reciprocity. McKinley was being called a liberal because of his enthusiasm for reciprocity, but he well understood the need for future exports. Reciprocity was an outstanding tool to control and manage trade. Old line Republicans including Henry Cabot Lodge, Nelson

Aldrich, and William Allison tried to organize resistance to reciprocity. When McKinley called for a reciprocity agreement with Puerto Rico, the conservative Republicans found allies with Democrats who were linked to the sugar trust.

CHAPTER 13. THE LAST TERM AND A NEW VISION

McKinley's dream of an industrial empire had come true by 1900. It was followed by a rise in patriotism and nationalism. Americans were proud of their economic might. One magazine hailed it: "Almost incredible that we should be sending cutlery to Sheffield, pig iron to Birmingham, silks to France, watch cases to Switzerland . . . or building sixty locomotives for British railroads."[66] National pride and consumer confidence could be seen everywhere. The quick victory over Spain and the triumph of American naval strength further caused a wave of nationalism. Industrial production was at record levels and prices had fallen. Exports were at record levels as well. American art reflected the industrial empire. Free traders and Silverites were both at a loss to understand how tariffs could have led to such an economic boom? Had McKinley found the Rosetta stone to the economy? Even today economists scramble for reasons to avoid crediting scientific tariffs. The McKinley boom had delivered the full dinner pail and more. McKinley's biggest problem was how to sustain the boom. There was just one issue that was threatening economic stability — that of trusts.

In his 1900 annual address in January McKinley addressed head on the growing problem of trusts:

> Combinations of capital organized into trusts to control the conditions of trade among our citizens, to stifle competition, limit production, and determine the prices of products used and consumed by the people are justly provoking public discussion, and should early claim the attention of Congress. . . . There must be a remedy for the evils involved in such organizations. If the present law can be extended more certainly to con-

66 Judy Crichton, 1900, (New York: Henry Holt and Co., 1965), 30

trol or check these monopolies or trusts, it should be done without delay. Whatever power the Congress possesses over this most important subject should be properly ascertained and asserted.

Many critics called this a smokescreen for the elections where the Democrats would surely make it an issue.

The rise of the trusts was not a fully unexpected event. McKinley had studied the problem for years, as tariff critics had used it since the 1880s. The Sugar Trust had caught McKinley's eye in the formation of the 1890 Tariff. However, the real rise of problematic trusts occurred in the last months of the 1890s and the early 1900s. The public attention throughout most of the 1890s was sporadic. From 1898 to 1901, trust formation doubled. McKinley, Dawes, and Hanna anticipated the problems. McKinley's Comptroller of the Currency and campaign manager, Charles Dawes, noted in the following March 28, 1899 meeting: "I talked over the matter of the unprecedented growth of trusts with the President and the position in reference to them and their evil tendencies which our party should assume. He told me he expected to call the attention of Congress to the matter in his next message and would lead the movement for their proper restriction."[67] Dawes and McKinley had a number of conversations in early 1899. McKinley did follow up with his 1899 address to Congress. McKinley, however, did not see trusts as systematically bad. Trusts, in his mind, could just as easily be good. He was slow to move in any case, seeing some value for the overall economy. As the combinations increased, McKinley tried to put public pressure on their be-havior, but it would become a point of attack by the Democrats in the upcoming elections. The formation of United States Steel took the headlines in 1900 and a new interest by the press. In addition, the popular press had taken up the idea of anti-trust legislation in late 1898. The Republican platform of 1900 took on the trusts, stating that the Republicans favored, "legislation as will effectually restrain and prevent all such abuses."

McKinley did not wait for the summer platform to address the issue of trust abuse. He pushed Congress to hold hearings and establish an Industrial Com-mission. He wanted Congress to take on this issue. Unlike Roosevelt, who fol-lowed him, McKinley did not see a role for the executive in attacking the trusts or the use of aggressive legal action. McKinley did discuss his role with his At-torney General to review legal recourse. Attorney General John Griggs felt the Sherman Anti-Trust Law of 1890 had little application since the 1895 Supreme Court ruling (*United States vs. E. C. Knight*), ruled legal action required both the monopoly of manufacture and a monopoly of interstate commerce. Griggs felt the ruling even prevented action against Standard Oil. The ruling actually gave

---

67 Dawes, 185-186

the green light to business to form large corporations. Chief Justice Fuller wrote the court's opinion in the case:

> Contracts, combinations, or conspiracies to control domestic enterprise in . . . production in all its forms, or to raise or lower prices or wages, might unquestionably tend to restrain external as well as domestic trade, but the restraint would be an indirect result.

Furthermore, an 1899 Court decision (*United States vs. Addyston Pipe and Steel*) actually encouraged mergers. The Addyston Pipe decision showed the court would be harsh against pools and cartels, but lenient on mergers. Future president William Howard Taft gave the definitive ruling on Addyston. McKinley adopted a minimal legal policy, opting for a legislative strategy, and accepting Griggs's advice. The Democrats kept up the drumbeat in the midst of America's greatest economic boom, but McKinley hesitated to aggressively take on the trusts. Again in retrospect, it's hard to decide if McKinley's indecision was because the course was unclear or McKinley lacked the aggressive approach needed. Providence again seemed to favor McKinley's indecision.

The trusts of the late 1890s seemed to work at the time for the growth of the general economy. McKinley and Hanna's concern with trusts came in part from the control of banks. These were not combinations of manufacturers who would focus on jobs, investment, and technology, but the creation of bankers. Combinations like United States Steel created huge and immediate profits for J. P. Morgan and Wall Street. The bankers had a reputation in the railroad trusts and more recently the electrical trusts for pushing out the old operational lions. These old lions had a great distaste for bankers. The focus moved from operational efficiencies and productivity to financial returns. This approach threatened job creation, the very point of McKinley's approach. The image of the businessman as inventor, innovator, and risk-taker became viewed as one of exploiter of the workers. This, coupled with the rise of socialism, the yellow press, and the overspending of capitalists would lead to the Progressive movement in the early 1900s. McKinley was just at the beginning of the real problem, and he realized this would have to be addressed in the future. In fact, the philosophy of restraining abuses was the first point to be incorporated in the Republican platform.

The Republican Convention found a strong and popular president in the White House, but the question was the vice presidency. Vice President Hobart had died in November, so there were new opportunities for upcoming Republicans. Teddy Roosevelt was popular with the rank and file, and he had the support of some key Easterners such as Senator Henry Cabot Lodge. Also, the Eastern machine bosses such as Senator Platt wanted him out of New York. McKinley didn't really want Roosevelt, but he remained neutral, at odds with Hanna, who wanted nothing to do with Roosevelt. Corporate interests feared Roosevelt's anti-trust stand and threatened to withhold campaign support. Hanna tried to mount several anti-Roosevelt efforts against the wishes of McKinley. Hanna was National Chairman, but the pre-campaign was not what it had been in 1896 and the bosses again had control. Henry Cabot Lodge was the Chairman of the Convention and was Roosevelt's biggest backer. McKinley was now an insider and was running a traditional campaign of political trading.

Hanna became obsessed with keeping the "damn cowboy" away from the White House. McKinley rebuked him a couple of times, but he persisted. Charles Dawes became concerned about the split in the McKinley camp. Hanna worked directly with Roosevelt to get him to pull out, but the draft movement was huge. Finally, McKinley had to be perfectly clear with Hanna by telephone. After the conservation with the president, Hanna angrily stated: "McKinley won't let me use the power of the administration to defeat Roosevelt. He is blind, or afraid, or something." The politics were complex, but the bosses like Tom Platt and Mathew Quay actually did not care personally for Roosevelt. They just didn't want him in New York politics. Roosevelt had made his career as a reformer, but he was also a Republican blueblood with strong political ties in the party. The bosses would actually filter more money into the campaign than in 1896 as part of the deal. McKinley had always been willing to accept the will of the convention, so he brought Roosevelt in with grace. McKinley was much more interested in directing the platform and ultimately national policy. Again Hanna and McKinley had differences, Hanna wanting a more positive framing of trust issues. McKinley was clear that he was going to take on the abuses of certain trusts, and he wanted the platform to reflect that approach.

The arguing and differences between McKinley and Hanna are interesting. They clearly show that McKinley was in charge. Fundamentally, the differences were not great. Hanna might have even seen Roosevelt as a long-term threat to his own future run for the presidency. McKinley didn't care for Roosevelt, but he also didn't care for playing political boss either. Roosevelt was also given a free rein by McKinley to attack the abuses of trusts in his speeches. As to the trusts, Hanna had come to see the positive side much as J. P. Morgan had. Hanna didn't care for their methods, but he had said years earlier that he saw no way to prevent their growth. Still, Hanna's reasoning that trusts were a natural outgrowth of prosperity was really hopeful thinking. He agreed with McKinley that abuses existed. Hanna was a friend and loyalist who did come back to give McKinley the platform he wanted.

The 1900 platform was, with a few exceptions, crafted by McKinley, Hanna, and Dawes. The major points were:

- Legislation against the abuses of the trusts
- "Renewed faith in the policy of protection and the associated policy of reciprocity
- Raising the age limit for child labor
- Labor injury insurance as well as worker rights
- Legislation to improve the merchant marine
- The construction, ownership, control and protection of a Isthmian Canal by the government of the United States
- The gold standard (although many variously took credit and denied credit for the inclusion of this clause)

The key points left out were Hanna's desire for subsidies for the merchant marine, because of Midwestern opposition, and McKinley's desire for full rights for Puerto Rico. After the Roosevelt nomination, the convention went smoothly.

The best-crafted section of the platform (while idealistic) was that on trusts, which stated:

> We recognize the necessity and propriety of the honest co-operation of capital to meet new business conditions and especially to extend our rapidly increasing foreign trade, but we condemn all conspiracies and combinations intended to restrict business, to create monopolies, to limit production or to control prices, and favor such legislation as will effectually restrain and prevent all such abuses, protect and promote competition and secure the rights of producers, laborers, and all who are engaged in industry and commerce.

Interestingly, the platform recognizes the need for large combinations in order to compete in international markets, and in particular, the great cartels of Europe. The language reflected McKinley's personal view and was consistent with his beliefs, but again it lacked the specific legal or legislative approaches hoped for by party reformers. The overall platform was united under a pro-export stand, business expansion, job creation, and improved worker rights. Still, the McKinley plan was to stay the course, which had given America its best economy in its history.

The Democratic Convention, on the other hand, was confused and split. Bryan would easily win the nomination, but the platform was the problem. Bryan supporters still wanted to make silver the issue, but the rank and file saw it as a dead issue. The McKinley prosperity and the gold standard seemed to have really ended the usefulness of the issue. Trusts seemed more promising, but the full slate of the public opinion was still a few years away. Imperialism seemed to provide a stronger basis to attack the Republicans and the platform focused on it. The Democrats hoped to attack the colonialism of McKinley, but again it lacked the priority in public opinion. Bryan also insisted on maintaining the silver issue. His running mate Adlai Stevenson was also a strong Silverite. Democrats lacked one single issue, and instead took on a basket of issues. Attacks would highlight the ties between Big Business and the Republicans, monopolies, and railroad abuses of the Interstate Commence Act. McKinley easily countered with "four more years of a full dinner pail." Hanna confidently stated: "Let the other fellows have the fiddles and barbecues! Our argument exists per se at the bench, in the workshop, at the desk, in the counting room, at the chair by the fireside." It was one of those rare moments in American history where the incumbent would stand on that he delivered what he promised.

Not all was unity in the Republican Party; below the surface was the split between imperialists and anti-imperialists. The fight over the vice presidency of Teddy Roosevelt represented this subsurface split. While the platform was the handiwork of McKinley, most of the convention rhetoric focused on expansion. Chairman Lodge's speech was nationalistic, imperialistic, and expansionist. He characterized the Spanish–American War as, "a war of a hundred days, with many victories, and no defeats, with no prisoners taken from us and no advance stayed, with a triumphant outcome startling in its completeness and in its worldwide meaning." Manila in the Philippines was called "a prize of war" that "gives us inestimable advantages in development of trade." He further hailed trade expansion and world markets demanding an "open door" policy in China. Lodge seemed to link tariffs with a world strategy, much closer to Roosevelt's view than McKinley. Still, all left the convention united on the surface and ready for battle.

McKinley, learning from Hanna's front porch strategy, had developed and nurtured strong relationships with the press. McKinley set up the first pressroom in the East Room of the White House. His personal secretary, John Porter, gave press briefings at noon and 4 p.m. Christmas and holiday receptions were held for the press, and accommodations were made for the press on all Presidential trips. Reporters' needs were catered to like never before. In particular, this contrasted with the almost oppressive years of Cleveland and Harrison. McKinley was adept at remembering the names of reporters. Press releases were distributed to make their work easy. Telephones and telegraph were made available to reporters. Porter made it a two way street, using reporter feedback to put together the daily news summary. McKinley won favorable editorial support across the nation, and even Democratic papers hailed the openness of the White House. The approach toward press relations was clearly an extension of the successful front porch campaign.

The openness to reporters spilled over to the public in general. McKinley's popularity grew, and was similar to that of Henry Clay with its wave of baby naming. Visitors to the White House were encouraged as opposed to discouraged under President Cleveland. He held noon hand shaking receptions for visitors. McKinley was always at ease with the public, and his first years in the White House appeared as an extension of the front porch campaign. As they had at Canton, visitors poured in with gifts for the president. Congressmen found the same ease in visiting McKinley. McKinley was known to use his personal charm on problem senators with great success. Most felt it was just hard to not like him. Congressmen were encouraged to bring the whole family to the White House for a visit. McKinley preferred small dinners with wives included to large formal dinners. This quality of openness and the economic times uplifted the whole nation.

The 1900 election came at the peak of American prosperity. The economic power of America had reached new heights by 1900; it led the world in steel, coal, and oil production. Its exports flooded the world and the treasury's surplus surged. It was the world's second largest trader, only slightly behind Great Britain. Exports had more than tripled between 1860 and 1900. The economic miracle of the 1890s had drawn 3,700,000 immigrants in that decade alone. The population stood at 75,994,574, behind China, India, and Russia (the order remains the same today). The urban population surged from 22,106,265 in 1890 to 30,160,000 in 1900. New York now had 3,400,000 people. Population almost doubled from 1870 to 1900. The most populous states, in order, were New York, Pennsylvania, Illinois, and Ohio (all of these had solidly supported McKinley). The workforce had risen from 23,740,000 in 1890 to 29,070,000 in 1900. Major cities were being powered by the introduction of electricity, and industrial plants were turning to electrical power. America was also the world's leading energy consumer in 1900. The United States led, too, in mass media, with newspapers and magazines.

The largest employer was the railroads, which had over 245,000 miles of track. Manufacturing had become the dominant sector of the economy. The average workweek was fifty-nine hours and the average annual income was $462. Union members had risen to over 500,000 and had been successful in improving working conditions. Union members worked six fewer hours a week and earned about $1 more a day. Prices had even fallen slightly during the expansion of the late 1890s, but wholesale prices had actually dropped as much as 50% since 1870. The money supply had reached a new high. A new industry was on the horizon, which put 14,000 automobiles on the road. The biggest car production occurred in 1900 of which 1,681 were steamers, 1,575 were electrics, and 936 were hydrocarbon driven. McKinley was the first president to ride in an automobile; it was a Stanley Steamer (he had refused to ride in an electric car for the inauguration parade). McKinley did ride in an electric ambulance after being shot in Buffalo. Electric trolleys had created the American suburb. He was the first president to have a fully electrically wired White House. In 1900 there were over 1.5 million telephones in use. While not the first to use the telephone, McKinley and Hanna had pioneered its long distance use in elections and administration. During the Cuban War, McKinley had a telephone line put down to connect him to the battlefield. He might have even been the first president to enjoy bottled water (he loved to have Apollinaris mineral water with dinner).

One of the major concerns of the 1900 election was how to hold the votes the Republicans had gained with the Midwestern Germans. The concern was over an effort by the Democrats to portray the McKinley Administration as anti-German. The root of this had been a growing tension between Germany and the United States. German-Americans were strong anti-imperialists, but they still cherished some feelings for the fatherland. Within a few days of his great Manila Bay victory, Dewey had confronted what he thought was threatening behavior by the German fleet. Dewey addressed them boldly: "Tell your Admiral, if he wants war, I am ready." The Germans, of course, angrily backed off. The challenge was overplayed in the press and "media." Thomas Edison made a short movie rec-reating the battle of Manila, which further highlighted Dewey's remarks. The Midwest Germans were still very sensitive to attacks on their fatherland. Dewey continued with anti-German speeches and the Kaiser demanded an apology. McKinley adroitly reprimanded Dewey in public, defusing the issue. In the end, the strong economy would hold these votes.

Apathy remained a problem for McKinley, while Bryan searched for an is-sue over which to launch an attack. Bryan probed the silver issue in a West-ern campaign swing and found no interest even in the silver states of old. The economy was just too good for both the urban and rural areas. Bryan found some interest in the trusts, especially in the large cities, but the socialist candidate Eugene Debs was more likely to get most of these votes. Labor unrest and strikes were building, but the time was not ripe for this issue to come to a head. The continuing military involvement in the Philippines and the mounting death toll could have been a possible issue if Bryan could have garnered the support of the press. Amazingly, the death toll of over 4,000 American soldiers is lost to his-tory because of the lack of press interest. The press of giants such as Pulitzer and Hearst were imperialists who downplayed the Philippine Insurrection. Im-perialism in general struck a note with the public, but it never overcame the McKinley prosperity. The nation as a whole was a bit more to the imperialist side. Andrew Carnegie and Grover Cleveland had formed an Anti-Imperialism

League to counter McKinley, but again it never really amounted a serious threat to McKinley's campaign, except for the loss of Carnegie's money. Money was the least of McKinley's problems, however, and even without Carnegie, the Republican Fundraising machine was unstoppable. McKinley even stunned Rockefeller by returning $50,000 of unused funds.

McKinley basically stayed at home without the front porch campaign. Roosevelt and Hanna did most of the campaigning. The economy sold itself. McKinley had assigned future president William Taft to manage the territory of the Philippines. The Taft Commission report in September was very positive and took the wind out of the sails of Bryan's attack on the "war." Hanna did seem to tire of his role, and disagreements between him and McKinley were common. Roosevelt was a huge asset as crowds came to see him and his "touring rough riders." Roosevelt's enthusiasm seemed driven by his belief that he would be the presidential candidate in 1904, and he developed the same type of following McKinley had done during the Cleveland Administration. People began to joke about Bryan chasing any cause to become president. Hanna mounted a special train campaign that turned out bigger crowds than Bryan. Most Republicans were confidant that nothing could beat the McKinley prosperity and national pride. The quick victory in the war encouraged nationalism and expansionism. The Spanish–American War was indeed a "splendid little war," the dream of any Commander in Chief. The insurrection in the Philippines was becoming problematic, but the war victories brought short-term benefits at home that were deemed to out-weigh the future problems.

Bryan had gained some momentum earlier on, with the attack on trusts. The press had made trusts a bigger issue than might normally have been the case, given the overall prosperity. A battle was beginning to be waged between Henry Clay Frick and Andrew Carnegie, who had had a strained relationship since the Homestead Strike of 1892. The ugly court battle was gaining headlines. Hanna went to Carnegie to ask for a compromise, and George Westinghouse approached Frick. Other capitalists and Republicans got involved and hammered out an agreement. Hanna relaxed after getting this scandal off the front pages in key McKinley industrial areas.

Hanna took no chances, however, mounting a broad and expanded publicity campaign. He refined his tactics, with two million "news releases" and documents going to five thousand newspapers each week! In total he published 125 million documents and sent out 21 million postcards. His organization had "departments" to focus on voting blocs such as German-Americans, Catholics, blacks, organized labor, unorganized labor, farmers, and Protestants. He published documents in German and Polish for the nationality papers in cities like

Chicago. This effort dwarfed the document campaign of 1896. Posters summarized the Republican platform and were distributed throughout the nation. Speakers were the traditional campaign mode, and Hanna organized over six hundred for 1900. Teddy Roosevelt became Bryan's match in speaking. These speakers covered cities and voting groups. Bryan lacked money and issues to counter Hanna, whose courting of the press became a major campaign strength. Teddy Roosevelt also found great favor with the press.

The election of 1900 confirmed McKinley's domestic and foreign polices. He became the first president since 1872 to win re-election. His vote count was 200,000 higher than the margin in 1896. The popular vote was 7,206,777 for McKinley and 6,374,397 for Bryan. This time McKinley carried six of the Western states, as the Solid South held for Bryan and added Kentucky. As might be expected in such good times, the turnout fell to 72%. The electoral vote was 292 to 155 (21 votes higher over 1896). His coattails were extremely long as the Republicans increased their House majority from 151 to 197 members, and the Senate majority from 35 to 55 members. McKinley gained in all economic classes of votes as well as in the large ethnic groups. While the McKinley realignment seemed complete, there was one signal of a problem. Socialist Eugene Debs collected popular votes for his growing Socialist Party, but it was still far from a real vote-getting movement in 1900. Bryan's socialist appeal cost him heavily with the Catholic vote. McKinley responded with: "I am no longer President of a party; I am now the President of the whole people." The election was not a landside, but it was a mandate.

The Cuban issue came to the forefront again in 1901 as McKinley and Congress tried to come to terms with what to do about the island. McKinley spent the first months of 1901 pushing Congress to accept Cuba's independence as an American protectorate. This hopefully would prevent any foreign influence in Cuban politics. In addition, the United States would be given three naval bases including Guantanamo. The Philippines were set up as a dependency subject to Congressional authority and under a governor general — William Taft. In May, the Supreme Court ruled that Puerto Rico and the Philippines were new possessions but their people were not United States citizens, which was essentially how McKinley looked at it.

On April 29, McKinley started out on a grand American tour of the South and West. The trip was to stress tariff reciprocity and build momentum to take on the trusts. It was to be a six-week tour by special train. The crowds were huge and enthusiastic all along the route. The flowers and crowds brought some to call it a triumphal procession. Ida McKinley contracted an infection during the trip, and her health deteriorated on the West Coast. Mrs. McKinley's illness required the party to return to Washington, canceling the final stop at the World's Fair in Buffalo.

McKinley spoke throughout the trip on trade reciprocity, but hit it hard at New Orleans and the West Coast launching of the *Ohio*. In New Orleans he laid out the theme: "We can now supply our own markets. We have reached that point in our industrial development, and in order to secure sale for our surplus products we must open new avenues for surplus." At the launching, he tied world peace to commerce: "There is nothing in this world that brings people so close together as commerce. There is nothing in this world that so much promotes the universal brotherhood of man as commerce. . . . The nations are close together now. The powers of the earth are tied together. We have overcome distance." Interestingly McKinley hoped to achieve the same goal as that of free traders, but with reciprocity and treaties. America's power and economic might was building resentments throughout the world. McKinley believed the future was in reciprocity and fair trade through treaties. A lot of the Midwestern Republicans were not convinced that reciprocity was a good strategy. McKinley looked at it as more of a necessity against retaliatory tariffs. His June 6 speech at the Pan-American Exposition in Buffalo was to tie his tariff and trade vision together, but Mrs. McKinley's illness caused it to be postponed until September. McKinley would not chance leaving her side. He re-scheduled for September 5, realizing a technological World's Fair would be the ideal place to set a new course on trade and reciprocity.

By July, Mrs. McKinley had improved and they went to Canton for the rest of the summer. His secretary, George Cortelyou, went with them to work on the September speech and the new direction. Other than developing his integrated vision for America's economy, the summer at Canton was laid back and informal. They had a few small dinners, played euchre on the front porch with neighbors and took short evening walks. The McKinleys had never been part of the fast social life in Washington, always preferring to be at home in Canton. His last summer was one of his most enjoyable, but there was policy work hanging over his head. Many in his own party were questioning reciprocity. McKinley wanted to tie tariffs, reciprocity, and world peace together. This approach was typical of McKinley, who liked simple and common themes versus multiple objectives. The importance of reciprocity increased throughout the summer as he discussed it with his cabinet and advisors. Arrangements at the Fair were discussed a number of times with both Hanna and Cortelyou, who worried about security at such a large event.

In late August, McKinley's assassin Leon Czolgosz was 60 miles away from the McKinley house, attending a lecture by socialist leader Emma Goldman. A few days later, while Czolgosz was in Chicago to attend more socialist meetings, he read of McKinley's upcoming visit to the Buffalo World's Fair, the Pan-American Exposition. He admitted that, at the time, he was thinking of killing the president but lacked a full plan. On August 30, he boarded a train to Buffalo, sensing that the Fair would be the best opportunity to make his attempt. He stayed at the hotel and saloon on Broadway Street owned by John Nowak, a socialist sympathizer. September 5 was to be President's Day at the Fair and the first of two days of events for McKinley. Czolgosz made a number of scouting trips to examine the fair grounds. McKinley arrived on Wednesday night, September 4, 1901, at the Buffalo Station. Czolgosz couldn't get close enough to see the him.

Presidents Day, September 5, 1901, lived up to the expectations and fears of McKinley's staff. The paid crowd numbered 116,000 with over 50,000 hearing McKinley's speech at the main plaza. McKinley delivered what most consider one of his best speeches. He clearly defined America's need for scientifically-calculated tariffs and for reciprocity. A photograph of McKinley giving this speech was used for the sculpture of McKinley at the monument at Canton. Czolgosz was in the crowd with a 32-caliber pistol but could not get close enough for a clear shot, and he left even more depressed.

On the evening of his speech, McKinley and his wife went to rest at the house of John Milburn, the president of the Pan-American Exposition, where they were to be guests while at the Fair. After a light dinner, the President and Mrs. McKinley returned to the Fair to see the electrical illumination and fireworks. The next day, a trip to Niagara Falls was planned to help relax Mrs. McKinley, who became nervous on trips. The short trip was made by his special train so that she could rest. They saw most of the tourist attractions, and while Mrs. McKinley rested on the train the President toured the new powerhouse at the falls, which was the pride of George Westinghouse's company. The power plant at Niagara was the largest in the world and was the reason for the selection of Buffalo as the site of the World's Fair. What McKinley observed that day was the start of the second Industrial Revolution. The Niagara Falls power plant was generating more electricity than all other American power plants. It supplied enough power to create a new industry of aluminum manufacture.

After the tour of Niagara, the train took McKinley to the Exposition for a public reception in late afternoon. Mrs. McKinley had been weakened by the heat and returned to the Milburn house to rest. At the Exposition's Temple of Music, people had been forming a line to see the president since morning. Leon Czolgosz was one of the first in line that morning, and he waited through the extreme heat of the day until late afternoon. The reception had just started when shots rang out. Czolgosz got off two shots before a black waiter, James Parker, threw himself at the assassin. Parker had been waiting in line right behind Czolgosz. Parker's action almost saved the president; he prevented the third shot. Almost immediately, an electric ambulance was summoned. McKinley, still conscious, asked that the assassin not be harmed.

At the Exposition hospital, six doctors were ready to attend to the President. An hour-long operation proceeded to remove the bullets. The President was taken to the Milburn house to recover, and a New York specialist was called. The report at 10:40 p.m. that night read: "The President is rallying satisfactorily and is resting comfortably. Temperature, 100.4; pulse 124; respiration 24." Things seemed positive as McKinley passed peacefully through the night. At the same time, Czolgosz was undergoing questioning. He admitted shooting McKinley and declared he was an anarchist and a disciple of Emma Goldman. Further investigations never established a direct link to Goldman, other than his being inspired by her speeches. At the time of the interrogation of Czolgosz, anarchists across the country including Goldman were being brought in for questioning.

The Saturday following the shooting, McKinley was stabilized, and then on Sunday his temperature rose to 102 and his pulse to 122. The newly invented X-ray apparatus was brought from Thomas Edison's lab, but unfortunately it was never used. Updates were posted hourly, and by Monday, he had improved rapidly. By evening, Mrs. McKinley was confident and left his side to go for a brief ride. On Wednesday, the President took solid food and requested a cigar, which doctors denied him. On Thursday, six days after the shooting, the president relapsed. Friday morning, September 15, it was clear the president was not going to recover, after which the family, and the Cabinet members came in one by one. The president moved in and out of consciousness throughout the day and evening. Just before he lost consciousness for the last time, he told his wife, "It is God's way, not our will, but Thine be done." Moments later in a low voice he said: "Nearer, my God, to thee." He died at 2:15 a.m., Saturday, September 14, 1901.

CHAPTER 14. A TALE OF TWO CITIES: SOCIALISM AND CAPITALISM

> Socialism has never and nowhere been a first working-class move-
> ment. It is a construction of theorists.
>
> — *Friedrich Hayek*

In the late 1800s, Carnegie Steel had built two great mill cities — Braddock
and Homestead. While they were separated by the Monongahela River, they
were quite different. Homestead had dominated the headlines in the 1890s, but
before Homestead, Carnegie had built his first steel mill in Braddock in 1875. The
mills had many similarities but offered a stark contrast in political outlook. Both
cities were dirty and had slums of immigrants. Residents on both side of the river
said the sun rose in a smoky sky at 11 a.m. and set at 2 p.m. While both cities had
thousands of Slavs, Hungarians, Austrians, Poles, and Italians, Braddock had an
Irish Catholic core of "natives." To a large degree, these natives defined the party
domination before 1893. Braddock tended to be Democratic while Homestead
voted Republican. Braddock had always been part of the Carnegie family since
its start up in 1875. It had some Knights of Labor but generally lacked a union.
Homestead had been purchased by Carnegie in 1889 and had the old roots of
the Amalgamated Iron and Steel Workers. Immigrants of Braddock started in
slums but within a generation moved out to better surroundings. Homestead's
workers were more trapped in the slums, often taking two generations to move
up the social ladder. Most of Braddock's managers at the Edgar Thomson Works
had risen through the ranks. Employee advocate Bill Jones was the famous plant
manager at Edgar Thomson. Transferred Carnegie managers, reflecting the dis-
ciplined style of Henry Clay Frick, managed Homestead. Under Jones, Braddock

had tried the eight-hour day suggested nationally by the Knights of Labor. Jones found that, given the choice, the men actually preferred the financial opportunities of the twelve-hour day. Homestead experimented with the sliding wage scale more, adjusting for market downturns.

Braddock remained calm throughout the turbulent 1890s while Homestead was involved in one of America's bloodiest strikes. The difference was slight but important. Braddock had labor issues, but grievances were listened to. In the 1880s, thanks to Bill Jones, union leaders had their grievances heard by Carnegie himself, often with little success other than the airing the problem. Bill Jones and Carnegie often clashed over the running of the mill. Braddock had a tough anti-Amalgamated Union policy — requiring employees to pledge that they would not join. Braddock was more tolerant of the Knights of Labor that promoted a social hierarchical structure for upward mobility.

As an enlightened manager, Jones understood both Carnegie's need to keep wages low and the men's need for money. Jones countered with the idea, "It should be the aim of the firm to keep the works running steadily." One of the big problems was the up and down nature of the steel industry, where workers lacked a consistent pay envelope week after week. As another measure, Jones asked that "the company should make the cost of living [for the worker] as low as possible." To that end, cooperative company stores were opened and help with mortgages was offered. Homestead management offered no options but cold rhetoric on business conditions. The managers under Jones at Braddock often helped workers financially and attended worker weddings. These managers knew the families and might give an injured family member a light work assignment or a lifetime job. The difference was clear. Not only did the great Homestead strike signal its failure, but Homestead attracted socialists, while it would have been difficult to find one in Braddock. Jones, like McKinley, understood that socialism was a shelter for the disenfranchised.

Braddock had another advantage over Homestead. It had developed from an unoccupied battlefield to a one-company mill town. Braddock started and grew up as a Carnegie Steel town, while Homestead had glass plants and steel plants before Carnegie Steel moved in. Braddock's social networks were therefore more integrated between the steel mill and town. There were "natives" such as English, Scots-Irish, Welsh, and Irish, in Braddock; it was more open to the immigrants than Homestead. Braddock, in that respect, had its "native" roots. Braddock had better-evolved social networks of churches and nationality clubs. These networks spread to the steel mill so that an immigrant had a way to enter society. Certain sections of the mill were controlled by certain nationalities and job agreements were often made informally at social clubs. Braddock had also developed a type of civic pride in being known throughout the industrial world. Braddock managers and workers had many problems, but they had grown up together. In Homestead, Carnegie managers often took the attitude that they had to change the mill and town.

The Catholic Church, which was the church of the workers, played a bigger role in the town of Braddock, and Carnegie and his managers donated churches and aid. Catholic education was actually promoted because of its anti-socialism stand. McKinley had also supported Catholic education nationally, seeing Catholics as allies, not the enemy as blueblood Republicans saw them.

Anarchism rebelled against authority of any kind; thus organized religion of any type was the enemy of anarchism. Furthermore, the Catholic Church looked at the political movement of socialism as a stepping stone to anarchism, and the Church worked to keep its immigrant worker members in line, away from both socialism and anarchism. McKinley realized that Catholics, something of an oppressed minority themselves, had to be included in the American dream if socialism was to be suppressed, and McKinley worked hard to achieve that end. In inoculating Catholic immigrants against the appeal of socialism, McKinley left the movement struggling to find members.

Like the "model" town of Homestead, Hanna and McKinley saw Pullman City as a sham, while they hailed the enlightenment of George Westinghouse. Pullman offered low wages but "gave" social and housing benefits. Westinghouse by contrast offered good wages and helped the worker with living needs. Both maintained the towns as examples of cooperative and corporate models. Pullman offered housing but profited from the mortgage. Westinghouse offered to help with mortgages, with repayment required but at no profit to the company. Water and electricity cost more in Pullman City than in nearby Chicago, with profits going to Pullman. Westinghouse believed in helping those who helped themselves, while Pullman operated more of a corporate plantation; in fact, a modern form of feudalism. Westinghouse promoted the transition to the middle class thorough hard work and fair wages. Socialists tended to flock to both towns, but in Pullman City they rioted, while in Wilmerding they joined the democratic elections.

Wilmerding also had a strong social network developed by Westinghouse through private caregivers such as the YMCA. Westinghouse attributed his use of the YMCA to his congressional relationship with William McKinley. Westinghouse supplied buildings and meeting places for the YMCA, using his capital to fund social services. Through a variety of programs the YMCA helped immigrants assimilate into society and in general focused on building society. Westinghouse Company and the YMCA also offered skills courses such as typing, grammar, and mechanical arts. Westinghouse employees were offered, in addition, a full selection of college level courses. There were opportunities to move up the social ladder by these educational opportunities. When foreign industrialists visited the White House, McKinley often set up a railroad trip for them to Westinghouse's Wilmerding and East Pittsburgh factories. Interestingly, many socialists moved to this industrial utopia and saw that, under these ideal (if difficult to replicate) conditions, their concern for the population's social welfare could be addressed within the capitalistic system.

The upper class saw socialism and anarchism as European threats to take away their enormous advantages; they looked to a political and governmental solution and often over reacted forcefully. McKinley perceived socialism and anarchism as an economic barometer. Socialism gained in appeal as jobs became scarce, wages went down, and class mobility was restricted. McKinley saw that releasing the pressure was more effective than causing an explosion. The more certain groups of Americans were excluded from access to a share of the country's prosperity, the better socialism looked. Wealthy Republicans weren't the only politicians that missed the point; Bryan looked for a regulatory solution. Bryan even tried to cast it as a type of gold versus silver class warfare. Though Bryan courted the socialists, they were looking for more, as shown by Eugene Debs's 900,000 votes in the 1907 election. Democrats didn't see that their support of white supremacy was just another energizer of the socialist movement. America's prosperity had to be all-inclusive, and Protestant Republicans needed to adjust their anti-Catholic views.

The most dangerous branch of socialism was the radical and revolutionary anarchism. Call for anarchism arose in countries such as Russia, Spain, and Italy where trade unionism was outlawed. The anarchist manifesto of 1878 declared: "Let us arise, let us arise against the oppressors of humanity; all kings, emperors, presidents of republics, priests of all religions are the true enemies of the people; let us destroy along with them all juridical, political, civic, and religious institutions."[68] The terrorist Johann Most brought these radical views to America in 1882. In 1883, Most called for a meeting of anarchists and radical socialists in Pittsburgh (known as the Black International). The result was the famous "Pittsburgh Manifesto," which made these points:

- Destruction of the existing rule
- A cooperative organization of production
- Free exchange of equivalent products

---

68 Louis Hacker, *The World of Andrew Carnegie: 1865-1901*, (New York: J. B. Lippincott Company, 1968), 142

- Organization of education on a secular, scientific, and equal basis for both sexes
- Equal rights for all
- Regulation of public affairs

While written in Pittsburgh, it found almost no support among the Catholic immigrants that worked in Carnegie's mills. In particular, the Catholic Church aggressively opposed all branches of socialism while supporting trade unionism, which sought some of the same protections for workers — only within an approved structure. The anarchist faction had to find its home in Chicago, where the "Pittsburgh manifesto" was better known than in Pittsburgh.

McKinley was well aware of the failure of socialism to take hold in the steel making districts of Pittsburgh, Youngstown, Niles, Cleveland, Detroit, and Wheeling in the 1880s. The key factors that suppressed the socialist movement were the growth of trade unionism, the opposition of the Catholic Church, a higher ratio of Eastern European to Western European immigrants, an economically strong steel industry, upward mobility of the working class, and conservative values of the workers. The movement failed to appeal to some groups of workers who were anti-black, anti-immigrant, and anti-feminist. Furthermore, many immigrants had left these types of political theories behind in Europe and now were interested in the potential opportunities of America. McKinley's all-inclusive pluralism offered a viable option to radical socialism. Anarchists, however, while a small group, contained the seed of violence and provided more of an intellectual "religion" that did appeal to some people.

Some terminology is needed to have an understanding of socialism and anarchism. First, in the 1890s, the average American did not really understand or care about the philosophical nuances in the various forms of socialism. Socialists were followers of Karl Marx, who wanted social revolution — that is, a revolution that would favor society as a whole, not just those at the top. The revolution, however, did not need to be a violent overthrow of government. In fact, socialists were more interested in replacing the structure and form of government than in eliminating it. Socialists focused on political activism aimed at political parties and unions. Socialists believed that the capitalists used and abused the lower classes, and believed that the struggle between social classes was fundamental to the industrial movement. Anarchism is a radical extension of socialism that believes no government will be equitable and advocates "action" to break up the exploitative system. Karl Marx had rejected the movement because he saw a socialist government as the ultimate solution. McKinley's assassin Leon F. Czolgosz was an anarchist. Russian socialists had first developed the "propaganda of action," which highlighted violence and political assassination as a means to force a change in social relations between the haves and have-nots.

Anarchists were terrorists; utterly frustrated and in despair, they found that violence was the only way to make sure their message was heard. The bloody Haymarket Strike was a result of anarchists in Chicago (1887). Henry Clay Frick's would-be assassin in 1892 was an anarchist. President Carnot of France had been killed by an anarchist in 1894 as had been Czar Alexander of Russia in 1881. An anarchist assassinated Elizabeth, Empress of Austria, in 1898. On July 29, 1900, an anarchist assassinated King Humbert of Italy. Attempted assassinations seemed be occurring on a monthly basis worldwide. While socialists published political tracts, anarchists published pamphlets on bomb making. The social unrest created by the excesses of the ownership classes could breed both socialists and anarchists. When violence of any sort was promulgated, the term "anarchist" was used.

The Haymarket riot of 1886 in Chicago was often linked with both the socialists and anarchists. The story of the Haymarket is fundamental in understanding the rise of anarchism in the United States. For several years there had been an upswing in the ranks of America's largest union, the Knights of Labor. The 1880s also saw a concentration of immigrant socialists in the Chicago area. The Knights had called for a national strike over the eight-hour day in 1886. The strike would peak in Chicago on May 1, 1886. Some 350, 000 were on strike across the nation and about 60,000 in the Chicago area alone. Strikes (and battles) had occurred before the lead up to May Day. The Knights took a holiday on May 1 but all appeared peaceful as crowds took to the streets of Chicago. Incidentally Eugene Debs, head of the railroad union, called for a strike but he didn't fully convert to socialism until he was jailed for his role in the Chicago riot.

The strikes lingered on after May 1 in the Chicago area with strikes and walkouts at the McCormick Reaper Works and Pullman Railroad Works. A small group of anarchists, labor leaders, and socialists, such August Spies, Eugene Debs, and Albert Parsons, prolonged the unrest for days. A large gathering May 4 at Haymarket Square exploded into violence and bombs were tossed into the crowd and the police returned fire. There were deaths on both sides. The investigation reportedly found anarchist bombs throughout the city. A number of people were arrested as anarchists and eventually four were executed. These executed men became "Labor Martyrs to American Capitalism," and were remembered in May Day celebrations around the world for decades. There was a great deal of sympathy for the "martyrs" and a number of organizations built a monument in 1893. International sympathy for the "martyrs" caused an increased interest in anarchists and socialism. Men like Eugene Debs took the movement to unionism and social democracy, but young anarchists lacked organization. It wasn't until the 1907 elections that socialists found enough votes to be considered a national movement. The McKinley boom had suppressed its growth. Anarchists, while small in numbers, made headlines and spread fear with their violence.

The heart of both the American socialist movement and anarchist movement was in Chicago. For the anarchists, Chicago may well have been world headquarters. The official paper *The Fire Brand* was published in Chicago and circulated around the world. Evidence suggests that the assassination of King Humbert of Italy was planned in Chicago. Czolgosz was in Chicago eight days before the assassination of McKinley, and this has led to conspiracy theories, but none were ever proven. Anarchists were feared by all segments of society and even the socialists tried to distance themselves. McKinley's death heightened fear of the anarchist movement. Roosevelt called anarchists: "not the outgrowth of unjust social conditions but the daughter of degenerate lunacy, a vicious pest," one that threatened, "to uproot the very foundations of society." Without necessarily addressing the concerns that drove people to such lunacy, Roosevelt recommended they be "speedily stamped out by death, imprisonment, and deportation of all anarchists."

Czolgosz was typical of the American anarchist. His background was Polish and he admired Russian-style anarchism. He was born in Michigan around 1870 but had lived in Chicago, Pennsylvania, and finally Newburgh, Ohio (a suburb of Cleveland). Newburgh was a Slav community where his parents had found a comfortable living. Socialism had found roots in the German, Slav, Polish, and Russian communities. German based communities tended to adopt the philosophical points of socialism, while Russian communities found some appeal in anarchism. The community of European immigrants of industrial Newburgh was a typical setting for the evolution of socialism as well. The industrial burgh supplied labor to Cleveland Rolling, a wire mill on Fleet Street. The area had been the home of several wire mills going back to the 1870s. The Polish immigrants had been used in the early 1880s to break a strike of skilled Welsh rollers. Technology had dumbed down the available jobs. Once a few Polish families had made a beachhead in the area, Slavs followed. Czolgosz was representative of the first generation born of these immigrants that traveled around the country in search of better work. He had started as a blacksmith helper, then worked in a glasshouse in Western Pennsylvania, and then returned to work at Cleveland Rolling Mills. This pattern of wandering from industrial city to industrial city was typical of young anarchists. His father, Paul Czolgosz, had also tried many different jobs, but had successfully made it into the middle class.

Paul Czolgosz probably earned less than $700 a year in the factories of Detroit, but the family saved and purchased a small farm. Failing in farming, the family moved to Cleveland to work in the rolling mills. The family saved enough to own a small bar as a side business. This was a typical path for families to move out of the slums next to the mills. Henry Chisholm, a friend of Mark Hanna and a donator to McKinley's debt fund when McKinley was governor, owned Cleveland Rolling Mills. The company was a pioneer in new rolling techniques for Bessemer steel. The cheap steel wire opened a new market in nail making from the wire. Production at the wire mills boomed, requiring more immigrant labor in the 1880s. The company broke the union effort in 1885, but the movement grew with the increase in production. The Panic of 1893 hit hard. A strike at about the same time got Leon blacklisted for his union activity. It was about this time also that Czolgosz lost faith in America's good intentions toward the workingman. His depression led him to the philosophy of socialism as a possible alternative. Czolgosz recalled these times to the Buffalo police in 1901: "During the last five years ... I suppose I became more or less bitter. Yes, I know I was bitter. I never had much luck at anything, and this preyed on me." The words of Czolgosz describing his unemployment, depression, and eventual acceptance of anarchism were typical of anarchists over the world.

Leon Czolgosz changed his name after he was blacklisted to Fred Nieman. He frequented the anarchists' informal network of saloons and bars in industrial cities, particularly Chicago. An international meeting of anarchists had been held in Chicago in 1893 in the shadow of the World's Fair.

Czolgosz stated: "What started the craze to kill was a lecture I heard some little time ago by Emma Goldman. . . . She set me on fire...Her doctrine that all rulers should be exterminated was what set me to thinking so that my head nearly split with pain."

Emma Goldman had become well known through her support of the Haymarket anarchists, but maybe more so from her connection with the attempted Henry Clay Frick assassination in 1892. The would-be assassin Alexander Berkman was Emma Goldman's lover. While Berkman went to prison for fourteen years, Goldman made a martyr out of him with the Haymarket anarchists. It remains doubtful that Goldman would have suggested McKinley as a target. Like Roosevelt, Goldman even wondered, "why had he chosen the President rather than some more direct representative of the system of economic oppression and misery."[69] Furthermore, Goldman even questioned Czolgosz's real commitment to the cause, although she agreed it was an anarchist act. Czolgosz was very

---

69 Eric Rauchway, *Murdering McKinley*, (New York: Hill and Wang, 2003), 105

much like today's terrorists. He was inspired by the movement but acted individually. After the assassination, famous anarchists were rounded up across the country, but no real link to Czolgosz was ever found.

Anarchists were problematic because of their doctrine of violence and assassination. They believed that Big Government was no better than Big Business in offering the worker better working and living conditions. Anarchists tended to be restless terrorists without real direction. Socialists desired to overtake unions and the government in order to establish a worker's paradise while anarchists wanted the elimination of government. The one thing that McKinley and the anarchists agreed on was that government is not the answer. McKinley preached industrial democracy, but he was not sure about how to address the abuses of industry. McKinley's industrial democracy had found acceptance with many labor leaders, and even socialists saw hope in McKinley's view. McKinley believed that Christian principles would eventually lead the way, an approach that Czolgosz had rejected. McKinley did not want to risk increasing unemployment by overzealous attacks on American industry.

Czolgosz's family did not share the hatred of capitalism that Leon had. His father was middle class, but probably the low end. Besides good steel workers wage, he saved and had owned a saloon and a farm. The Czolgoszs put the whole family to work and managed to save money. Many steelworkers had taken the same path out of the slums by saving. Leon Czolgosz was Catholic, but he gave up his faith for the doctrine of socialism. This was typical of socialists, who saw the Church as a tool of the rich. Czolgosz noted in the trial his low esteem of the Church and priests. The American Catholic Church had played an important role in restricting the growth of socialism. Sunday sermons were often against the rising socialist movement. McKinley had also seen the role of the Church as important in industrial democracy and that was the reason for his ecumenical efforts. Cardinal Gibbons's eulogy of McKinley left no doubt about the Catholic view of anarchism. "The most effective way to stop such crimes is to inspire the rising generation with greater reverence for constituted authorities and a greater horror for any insult or injury to their person. All seditious language should be suppressed. Incendiary speech is too often an incentive to criminal acts the on part of many to whom the transition from words to deeds is easy. Let it be understood, once and for all, that the authorities are determined to crush the serpent of anarchism whenever it lifts its venomous head."

The anarchist Pittsburgh manifesto of 1882 stated their philosophy: "But if the landowners, the manufacturers, the heads of state, the priests, and the law are our enemies, we are also theirs, and we boldly oppose them. We intend to reconquer the land and the factory from the landowner and the manufacturer; we mean to annihilate the state under whatever name it may be concealed; and we mean to get our freedom back again in spite of priest or law." To the anarchist, all were the enemy. They tended to be bitter and angry. They were similar to terrorists of today. This is not to justify the abuses of society now or then, but their goal was to tear down, not improve. Leon Czolgosz was clearly more driven by the philosophy than economics, which was typical of the anarchist.

The capitalists made matters worse by embracing "social Darwinism" as a philosophy. Carnegie, in particular, adopted this idea of Darwinism, which dominated his Museum of Natural History in Pittsburgh. The idea that survival of the fittest was a natural law of economics created an appearance of coldness. Carnegie became a follower of Herbert Spencer, who developed the idea of social Darwinism. There was another bias against unions that was held by even the best of the capitalists, such as Westinghouse, Charles Schwab, and others. McKinley, unlike Carnegie, who mouthed some support for unions, saw unions as necessary. McKinley, the labor lawyer, was well aware of the propensity of the owners to put profits ahead of workers. McKinley, the middle class politician, wanted a harmony between capital and labor, and he believed democratic laws and unions could best achieve this. He stood almost alone in these beliefs for most of his career. The socialists were rejected in their efforts to take over trade unions as well. The unions were more interested in wages than political ideas. George Bernard Shaw noted, "trade unions were not socialism, but the capitalism of the working class."

McKinley lacked answers for many of the abuses of capitalism, but he believed that the Golden Rule would have to be followed in an industrial democracy. What Marx called the "opium of the masses" McKinley sought to use as a unifying force that could help labor and capital speak the same language. He believed that the goals of socialism and capitalism could meet where there were fair wages and long-term employment.

These very problems took Czolgosz out of the mainstream. Samuel Gompers came from the same basic view. Gompers stated wage emancipation simply: "The way out of the wage system is through higher wages." McKinley, like Gompers, saw American unionism and law as providing necessary checks on the propensity for capitalists to take advantage of the work force. They both agreed that it would take checks and balances in industry, as in the government itself, to keep the American society flourishing.

Besides the Catholic Church, another ally of McKinley's against socialism was American trade unionism. Samuel Gompers, like the Catholic bishops, took to the pulpit to preach against the ills of socialism. Unions offered both a political outlet and a means to address grievances as a united group. The socialists realized early in the 1880s that they could not compete with trade unionism and changed their strategy to one of infiltration. The strategy had only moderate success. The socialists failed to achieve much success with the Knights of Labor, which was hierarchical and capitalistic in its own structure. The Knights represented the craftsman more than the common laborer. Socialists needed to take control of the American Federation of Labor and ousted Samuel Gompers for his failure to endorse Bryan in the 1896 election. The economic boom of the McKinley years actually caused a decline in both unionism and socialism. McKinley, however, saw trade unionism as a unique and very successful characteristic of American capitalism. Even as a labor lawyer in Canton, McKinley realized that unionism was a necessary check on capitalism, similar to the checks and balances found in the American Constitution. He knew firsthand the propensity of the capitalists to put profits ahead of concern for the worker. McKinley was the first pro-union president and this was fundamental to his overall vision of Clay's American System. Trade unionism was McKinley's contribution to that system.

McKinley realized that unions were needed to stand up for the rights of workers. He also hoped that a few good managers would aid in the progress. Carnegie's plant manager Bill Jones was one of those enlightened managers who worked with the unions. Jones convinced his boss to try the eight-hour day at the Edgar Thomson Steel Plant. By the way, the switch to the eight-hour day was not always hailed by workers, whose pay went down with a reduction in working hours. Jones was known for his ability to listen and work with the laborers. His untimely death in the late 1880s in a furnace accident brought out over 10,000 workers to line the streets of his funeral procession in Braddock, Pennsylvania.

Czolgosz was placed on trial September 23, 1901, less than two weeks after McKinley's death. Investigators were satisfied that he had acted alone, and there was no link to a conspiracy. The jury found him guilty the next day, and he was sentenced to be executed.

McKinley fully believed that industrial harmony was possible if neither interest group had a monopoly of power. The relationship between owners and workers had to be based on mutual respect. That is an ideal that still requires constant work and constant balancing in today's societies.

In his utopian belief that the right balance could not only be achieved but maintained, McKinley struck many as naive. However, he knew far more of the hard realities of life than his contemporaries such as Teddy Roosevelt and Grover Cleveland. McKinley could understand how socialism might attract an unemployed worker or how a disenfranchised youth such as Czolgosz might turn to anarchism.

CHAPTER 15. DINNER-PAIL REPUBLICANISM — MCKINLEY'S INDUSTRIAL LEGACY

Dinner-pail or lunch-pail Republicanism has become linked with the industrial policy of William McKinley.[70] It peaked with the famous McKinley Tariff Bill of 1890 and carried into the 20th century, but Republican senators had been increasing tariffs since 1882. The struggle to protect American industry can be traced to Henry Clay in the 1830s. But Abraham Lincoln, a fan of Clay, brought tariffs to the newly formed Republican Party during the Civil War. Lincoln, though, saw tariffs as providing federal revenue more than protection. McKinley, like Clay, was committed to the use of tariffs for protectionism. McKinley had even as a boy, coming from a manufacturing family, debated Lincoln protectionism with local Democrats in Ohio. Since there was no income tax at the time, tariffs could be used as a fiscal tool to regulate the economy.

After the Civil War, the Congress without Clay once again debated tariffs. The focus was on pig iron, which allowed "Pig Iron" William Kelly to take the protectionist torch from Clay. Kelly represented the 4th congressional district of Philadelphia, Pennsylvania from 1860 until his death in 1890. In 1866, the debate to remove duties on pig iron heated up. The Special Commissioner of the Revenue, David Wells, made a controversial report to Congress. It created a firestorm, with Republicans calling for Wells to be fired and his report destroyed. Wells made the classic argument of free traders of high profits of pig iron producers with a loss of jobs in industries that used pig iron. He wildly speculated that without the tariffs, the shipbuilding industry would have built

70 Dinner was the term used for lunch in this period of history.

191

another 600 ships and employed 30,000 more workers. His over-inflated number of 30,000 would have been two and a half times the actual employment in the pig industry at the time. Worse yet, Wells was a Republican appointee who initially was a protectionist. Kelly defended the need for tariffs for American producers and took the leadership of the high tariff movement. The Congress passed a small reduction on pig iron but increased the tariff on steel rails. Kelly got the high tariff back in 1875. The Kelly–Wells debate would continue for another fifty years and even continues today among economic historians.[71] Applying mathematical models to post-Civil War data, economists suggest that had tariffs on pig iron been eliminated in 1867, the domestic production would have been cut a "modest" 15 to 30%, the problem being that a "modest" 30% decrease in production means a deep recession for an individual factory. Furthermore, efficient and low cost production of pig iron, glass, and steel is dependent on high volume output. A 30% reduction in volume would have mneant a steep increase in production costs, which would have made American products less competitive.

McKinley had been part of this legislative effort to increase tariffs from 1877. As a young congressman, William "Pig Iron" Kelly of Pennsylvania adopted McKinley. Kelly taught him the principles of high tariffs and high wages. Kelly, then Chair of Ways and Means, started to groom McKinley for the chairmanship. As a member of the Ways and Means Committee, McKinley was instrumental in the formation of a Tariff Commission and became a framer of the 1882 Tariff Bill. McKinley's floor speech was eloquent, as usual: "Free trade may be suitable to Great Britain and its peculiar social and political structure, but it has no place in this Republic, where classes are unknown and where caste has long since been banished; where education and improvement are the individual striving of every citizen, no matter what may be the accident of his birth or the poverty of his early surroundings. Here the mechanic of today is the manufacturer of a few years hence. Under such conditions, free trade can have no abiding place here. We are doing very well; no other nation has done better or makes a better showing in the world's balance."

The debate between Democrat free traders and Republican protectionists seemed endless from 1870 to 1930. In an 1888 floor debate, McKinley argued the danger of foreign domination of product manufacture. He pointed out the loss by fire of the Missouri Glass Company, the sole American glass producer of cathedral glass. McKinley noted: "Within ten days from the time that splendid property was reduced to ashes, the foreign price of cathedral glass advanced 28 percent to the American consumer. Showing whether you destroy the American

---

71 Robert Fogel and Stanley Engerman, " A Model for the Explanation of Industrial Expansion during the Nineteenth Century," *Journal of Political Economy*, June 1969, 306-328

production by free trade or by fire, it is the same thing; the prices go up to the American consumer, and all you can do is to pay the price the foreigner chooses to ask." In an earlier debate McKinley made a similar point:

> The expectation of cheaper clothes is not sufficient to justify the action of the majority. This is too narrow for a national issue. Nobody, so far as I have learned, has expressed dissatisfaction with the present price of clothing. It is a political objection; it is a party slogan. Certainly nobody is unhappy over the cost of clothing except those who are amply able to pay even higher price than is now exacted. And besides, if this bill should pass, and the effect would be (as it inevitably must be) to destroy our domestic manufactures, the era of low prices would vanish, and the foreign manufacturer would compel the American consumer to pay higher prices than he had been accustomed to pay under the "robber tariff."[72]

McKinley was describing a fundamental law of markets over the years. The British had used this tactic after the War of 1812 with iron products — at first dumping iron products and driving out domestic competition, then raising prices as a monopoly. Britain used it again in the glass industry in the 1850s and with steel and irons rails in the 1860s. The benefits of "free" market trade can quickly be lost once all domestic competition is eliminated. And once the domestic industry is gone, the American government has no power or jurisdiction to restrict price increases.

McKinley's example is not an artifact of the 19th century but a common economic process that would find even Adam Smith in agreement. As recently as the 1980s, when most American steel rail producers went out of business, the result was similar. The once-cheap Japanese rail steel suddenly rose dramatically in price in the absence of domestic competition. Free trade will usually result in lower prices — until the competition is eliminated; then the price soars.

As Chairman of the Ways and Means committee, he again brought protectionism to the forefront. In 1890, McKinley framed a tariff act which would bring tariffs to their highest level. After the Democrats reduced tariffs in the early 1890s, as President McKinley restored and even increased them. McKinley believed in protectionism and rigorous management of the tariff schedules. No one in government understood the tariff schedules and their effect on industry better than McKinley. He successfully avoided trade wars by his studious approach to apply duties. He protected infant or foundational industries and effectively used the leverage of one of the world's great markets. His approach actually resulted in industrial employment and lower prices.

The McKinley Tariff Act of 1890 is still pointed out as a triumph of the policy of protectionism, but it was not always so. In fact, it cost McKinley the only major election he ever lost — the congressional election of 1892. In that election,

---

72 *Congressional Record*, 1887

the Ohio Democrats used the very name "Dinner-Pail Republicanism" against him. Dinner pails of the time were products of the tinplate industry, along with tin ware for canning and house wares. The tariffs of 1890 protected the infant tinplate industry in America, but an ancillary result was a short-term price increase in tin products such as dinner pails. Democrats seized the moment in the election of 1892 by sending out tinplate peddlers to sell overpriced tin ware in McKinley's Ohio district. When rural consumers asked why the price for such things as tin cups cost so much, the answer was "the McKinley Tariff," when in fact the timing of the passage and implementation of the tariff would have made it impossible for higher price tinplate to be in products at the time. Democratic storeowners also increased prices on imported and import-based products to artificial highs. Again when the customer inquired about the high prices, the answer was the same — "the McKinley Tariff." The Democrats claimed that big business was favored by the tariffs, but one of the biggest American companies suffered the most. The real opposition to the "tin plate tariff" was Standard Oil, whose five-gallon kerosene cans made it the world's biggest tinplate user. The tariffs forced makers of tinplate cans to become more efficient. McKinley ran a close race in the industrial base of Canton, Ohio, but gerrymandering left him short in the election of 1892 after his legislative success with protectionism. McKinley held strong to his beliefs and the long run success of tariffs, and history bears him out.

McKinley had learned what Henry Clay had known before him. Protectionism, while good for the nation's overall manufacturing, was many times industry-specific and region-specific. Voting to protect American industry often had a backlash in the other regions. Protectionism, like its antithesis free trade, works as a political policy, not as a set of economic principles. Political compromise and trade-offs would always be required. Even Adam Smith made exceptions for British shipbuilding in order to pacify critics.

McKinley would learn to compromise, in the future, suggesting reciprocity with certain nations and products. Furthermore, McKinley believed with Henry Clay that Congress's function included reviewing and monitoring manufacturing tariffs. Both Clay and McKinley developed a congressional committee to oversee the tariffs. Still, in the end Congress preferred debate to the work of monitoring.

Even today economists still point to the tinplate industry of the 1890s as a failure of protectionism.[73] Tinplate, however, is a biased example. In 1890 tinplate was made from mostly imported rolled high quality iron; two thirds of their costs were in rolled iron, mostly from England. Thus a tariff on imported rolled iron products drove tinplate prices high as well. Most of the tin came from Wales; the world's largest tin deposit was at Cornwall. In effect, Wales had an international monopoly on tin and tinplate. In the short run, the McKinley tariffs did increase the price of tinplate, but in the long run the high price spurred exploration for tin and increased technology investment in tinplate and canning. The tinplate industry itself became a major employer in the United States, and prices dropped as the industry matured. Welsh tinplaters immigrated to the United States to set up shop, further building the domestic American tinplate industry. The Welsh brought their "secret powders," but Americans learned fast, and in the end the McKinley Tariff broke a world monopoly and cartel on world tinplate.

Prior to 1890, there were a handful of tinplate manufacturers in the United States, but by 1892 there were 200, producing 13,000,000 pounds of tinplate! As domestic production increased, importers could no longer charge as much as they liked. The mills "found" the technology that free traders said America lacked. Fifteen months after the passage of the Tariff of 1890, McKinley toured a new state-of-the-art tinplate mill built in Ellwood, Indiana. The price of tinplate dropped dramatically by 1895 as the McKinley tariffs created a very competitive iron industry and technology improved through putting profits back into the business. As the price increased, American investors poured into the tinplate and canning industry. McKinley, as a Union Army quartermaster, knew well the shortage of canned food to supply the army. The tariffs not only brought investors into tinplate but into the biggest use of tinplate — canning. During the Civil War a tinsmith could make sixty cans a day; by 1880 a two-man machine could produce fifteen hundred in one day. In general, the period from 1880 to 1910 saw one of the greatest growth rates for American industry ever. By 1900 McKinley had turned the public perception around; one of the slogans for McKinley's presidential reelection would be a "full dinner pail."

Coming from an iron manufacturing family in Niles, Ohio and representing an industrial congressional district centered on Canton, Ohio, McKinley was a protectionist in a much different light than most people think today. Protectionism was needed, in his view, to enable American capitalism to flourish in a world dominated by international monopolies. In 1882, in Congress, McKinley answered free traders in debate:

---

73 D. A. Irwin, "Great Tariff Debate of 1888," *Journal of Economic History*, March, 1998

"England wants it [free trade], demands it—not for our good but for hers; for she is more anxious to maintain her old position of supremacy than she is to promote the interests and welfare of the people of this republic, and a great party in this country voices her interest.... She would manufacture for us, and permit us to raise wheat and corn for her. We are satisfied to do the latter, but unwilling to concede to her the monopoly of the former."

The growth of American industries was not limited to tinplate. The American glass industry was crushed after the War of 1812 by a flood of imports. By 1820, a once vibrant glass company in Western Pennsylvania saw their output decrease 85% and employment 76%. Then the strong Republican tariffs from 1860 to 1890 caused a boom in American manufacture. Glass tariffs peaked in 1880 at 55 percent of the imported value on average. In 1880 there were twice as many glasshouses as there had been in 1860, and their output was 2.4 times greater. When tariffs moved from revenue levels to McKinley protective levels, new segments of the glass industry developed. In 1860 there was no domestic production of rough plate glass, but by 1890, 97% of the domestic consumption was supplied by American glass houses. Polished glass went from zero in 1870 to 82% of the domestic market in 1890.[74] Total glass factories went from 169 firms in 1879 to 355 in 1899. Like other protected industries, annual wages increased from $479 a year in 1890 to $521 in 1900. Of course, this increase was much lower than the increase in profits, but profits were also invested in new equipment and research. America would revolutionize glassmaking by 1910.

While economists argue free trade versus protectionism on a case-by-case basis, manufacturers point to the massive economic growth of the era of McKinley tariff protection from 1880 to 1910. In 1880 the American steel industry was struggling to expand against the supremacy of British steel, but it flourished under the McKinley Tariff Act of 1890. Steel production went from 1.3 million tons in 1880 to 11.2 million tons in 1900 to 28.3 million tons in 1910. In 1898 the American steel industry surpassed Britain in pig iron production. By 1900, America was making more steel than Britain and Germany together. The U.S. gross national product grew from an estimated $11 billion in 1880 to $18.7 billion in 1890 to $35.3 billion in 1910.[75] During the peak tariff years of 1896 to 1901 under President McKinley, steel production increased 111%, electrical equipment production increased 271%, and farm equipment increased 149%. During the same

---

74 Warren Scoville, *Revolution in Glassmaking*, (Cambridge: Harvard University Press, 1948), 51
75 *Historical Statistics of the United States, Colonial Times to 1970*, (Washington DC: Bureau of the Census)

period, wages increased 10% and employment 20%.[76] Prices also fell as productivity and innovation mushroomed.

How do most economists explain the industrial growth and manufacturing expansion through the period of 1865 to 1913? Certainly innovation and invention are offered up first. The impetus for such innovation was not unrelated to tariffs. Stable prices and potential future markets encourage investment in research and development. The period saw the Bessemer process revolutionize steel, the automatic bottle machine revolutionize glass, refining revolutionize oil, AC current revolutionize electric lighting and the application of AC current change the power industry, and the transportation industry also boomed. A manufacturer will argue that these innovations came into being as a result of tariffs. Price increases allowed for good profit margins, which encouraged investment back into the business. Carnegie, Libbey, Owens, and Rockefeller all demonstrated this. High employment pushed domestic consumption, as Henry Ford demonstrated. Both manufacturers and economists can agree that 1865-1913 was one America's most inventive periods. Charles Murray argues that science and technology actually peaked during this period and has declined since.[77]

Protectionism took the blame in part for the 1930s depression, but the real worldwide problems had more to do with competitive nationalism than protection that created world economic problems. Free trade disciples have controlled both parties since World War II. Reagan was a free trader, but with the heart of McKinley, putting tariffs on machine tools, cars, and steel. Reagan also championed a 50 percent tariff to save Harley–Davidson, which responded with a manufacturing miracle of new efficiency. In return Reagan saw a rebirth of the old McKinley working class alliance with his party. Since Reagan, however, free trade economics have ruled Washington regardless of party. The period of 1865 to 1913 stands out statistically for manufacturing growth and demands more economic study. The Warren Scoville economic study of the glass industry from 1880 to 1920 supports the manufacturers' view.

William Scoville's study of the glass industry in Ohio offers one of the most complete economic studies of the period[78] from 1880 to 1920. The glass industry advanced in exports, production, employment, and innovation under the McKinley tariffs. Scoville clearly shows that the tariffs protected the glass industry from lower cost foreign competition. The response was a price decline, employment

76 *Historical Statistics of the United States, 1789 –1945* (Washington DC: U.S. Department of Commerce

77 Charles Murray, *Human Accomplishment: The Pursuit of Excellence in the Arts and Sciences 800 B.C. to 1950*, (New York: HarperCollins, 2003)

78 Warren C. Scoville, *Revolution of Glassmaking: Entrepreneurship and Technological Change in the American Industry,' 1880 to 1920* (Cambridge: Harvard University Press, 1948)

boom, and heavy reinvestment of the profits, and automatic glassmaking machinery for the first time in 3000 years. Scoville's study even suggests a possible linkage between tariffs and glass innovation; that is, the tariffs encouraged more risk taking in research and development.[79] Edward Libbey and Michael Owens created a research company in 1898 to develop automated glass making equipment. As we have seen with textile, steel, and woodworking, high tariffs actually increased exports. American ingenuity created automated processes that made quality product so cheap that Europe had no choice but to buy the automated machinery. By 1920, 95% of the world's glass bottles were produced on an Owens bottle-making machine.

The American glass revolution during the McKinley tariffs was nothing short of a miracle. Economist Scoville stated: "High tariffs gave domestic manufacturers continued protection from foreign producers, and as a result, innovators may have felt a little more reckless in their schemes than they would have otherwise." McKinley was not an economist and showed little interest in theory, but he knew manufacturing. As we have seen, McKinley argued for protectionism before entering politics based on his Ohio iron industry experiences. McKinley believed that foreign dumping could actually be used to suppress innovation. Clay had documented that the English had successfully suppressed the iron and textile industry in the 1810s. The simplest of economic principles seem to apply; high prices will result in invention and innovation.

Perhaps more importantly, tariffs stabilized the industry and allowed more investment in plants because of the good return on investment. Libbey in the glass industry reinvested in Toledo Glass, a company dedicated to research and development that changed the nature of glass making in a decade. Stabilization and investment can also be seen in the increase in annual patents issued from 12,903 in 1880 to 24,644 in 1900. Technology cut prices and increased markets. Bessemer steel rail price dropped from $68 a ton in 1880 to $32 a ton in 1890. Carnegie invested massive profits into bigger furnaces and new equipment. Blast furnaces that stood at seventy feet in 1880 were built to heights of a hundred feet by 1900. Daily output of these furnaces increased ten-fold. Carnegie gutted and rebuilt five-year-old mills to gain more efficiency. Tariffs assured the stable markets needed to make that type of long-term investment. Concern over future market volume is a major deterrent to capital investment.

In 1885, Congressman McKinley gave his classic defense of protectionism at Petersburg, Virginia. Petersburg had once been the industrial Pittsburgh of the Confederacy. McKinley's argument was simple:

---

79 Warren C. Scoville, *Revolution of Glassmaking: Entrepreneurship and Technological Change in the American Industry, 1880 to 1920* (Cambridge: Harvard University Press, 1948)

"Do you think there would be an idle man in America if we manufac-tured anything that Americans use? Do you think if we didn't buy anything from abroad at all, but made everything we needed, that everyman would not be employed in the United States, and employed at a profitable remu-neration? Why, everybody is benefited by protection, even the people who do not believe in it — for they get great benefit out of it, but will not confess it; and that is what is the matter of Virginia, heretofore she has not believed in it. You have not a public man that I know of in Washington for twenty-five years, save one, except the Republicans, who did not vote against the great doctrine of American protection. American industries, and Ameri-can labor; and do you imagine that anybody is coming to Virginia with his money to build a mill, or a factory, or a furnace, and develop your coal and your ore — bring his money down here when you vote every time against his interests and don't let those who favor them vote at all? No! If you think so you might just as well be undeceived now, for they will not come."

To some, this old and often-used argument may seem too simplistic; yet it is no more simplistic than Adam Smith's examples of village shoemakers and tai-lors. It is interesting that simple solutions are favored in most endeavors except economics.

Many believed that McKinley's success and views were based on his being an Ohio politician and his Ohio instincts tended to be right. McKinley's eco-nomic theories came from his Ohio middle class experience, like Adam Smith's came from the great traders of Glasgow, Scotland. Both theories affirmed the success of their market of origin. Of course, free traders argued that tariff pro-tection would lead to elimination of exports. In fact, the Republican period of tariffs (1865 to 1900) saw exports quadrupled, and during the high tariff years of 1897 to 1900 exports surged, more than doubling. American industry gained both technological and economy of scale advantages over foreign competition from tariffs. McKinley actually encouraged foreign imports but only on an equal footing and never at a disadvantage to America. He fully believed that fairness would prevent trade wars.

In 1892, as governor of Ohio, William McKinley gave a speech in Boston to slow the Democrats' effort to reduce the Tariff Act of 1890 during the Democratic administration of Grover Cleveland. McKinley used an example of the clothing buttons that would be popular in New England:

"We used to buy our buttons made in Austria by the prison labor. We are buying our buttons today made by the free labor of America. We had 11 button factories before 1890; we have 85 now. We employed 500 men before 1890, at $12 to $15 a week; we employ 8,000 men now at $18 to $35 a week."

Overall it is hard to dispute the success of McKinley protectionism in the aggregate. It was a popular policy as well. McKinley built an alliance of capital-ists and laborers in the industrial areas of the United States. The strength of this voting alliance has never been achieved since. Remnants of this alliance would still be seen in voting trends in industrial cities such as Pittsburgh as late as the 1950s. Pittsburgh and the steel industry were great benefactors of the McKinley Tariff.

During the 1891 governor's race, McKinley's Democratic opponent James Campbell made an un-researched claim that the tariffs had favored illegal aliens in the glass industry, not Americans. The northwest Ohio glass industry was booming and that required skilled craftsmen from key parts of Europe. In the early 1800s, American glass manufacturers actually had to smuggle master glass-makers in from Europe, as it was illegal in most European countries for glass-makers to emigrate to the United States. The cylinder glass towns of northwest Ohio such as Maumee and Findlay needed skilled glass blowers. Campbell was in particular referring to the Belgian cylinder glassblowers. Many were natural-ized aliens. McKinley correctly pointed out that the wages of American cylinder glassblower were six times higher than those of Belgium. The difference had al-lowed American companies to readily attract these skilled blowers who made up a small percent of the overall workforce created by the tariffs. Campbell had ignorantly focused on one of the success stories of the McKinley tariffs. Glass manufacturing countries such as Italy and Belgium had made it illegal for glass-blowers to emigrate in order to protect their own glassmaking industry. Venice had even built a guarded island for glassmakers.

The steel industry in the America of the 1890s dominated the world in every measure due to the McKinley tariffs. Carnegie Steel of Pittsburgh, in particular, prospered. Producing 4.3 million tons in 1890 and 10.2 in 1900. Profits went from 5.3 million to 40 million in 1900. The huge jump in profits came not from price (which actually declined) but from a doubling of productivity. Profits per ingot ton went from $4.56 in 1890 to $7.88 in 1900. Wages paid went from $7.6 million in 1890 to $10.9 in 1900.[80] Carnegie Steel averaged about a million dollars a year in plant improvements during the period, which most anti-tariff supporters sug-gested would never happen. Carnegie purchased a two-year-old Bessemer steel plant and completely gutted it to install better technology. The return from plant investment far outpaced that of other investments.

Under the Cleveland administration in 1894, the Democrats were able to re-duce the tariffs. While the Democrats in general opposed the tariffs, many indus-trial state Democrats sided with the McKinley approach. Some Democrats join-ing the Republican opposition mitigated the Wilson Tariff Bill of 1894 (a tariff reduction). President Cleveland was disappointed that the bill fell short of his

---

80 Kenneth Warren, *Triumphant Capitalism*, (Pittsburgh: University of Pittsburgh Press, 1996)

requests and allowed the bill to become law without his signature. The timing of the reduction was extreme as America was already in the 1893 recession. Tariff reductions in coal, iron, and steel helped the Republicans build a new labor-capital coalition in Pennsylvania and Ohio, which would win the presidency for McKinley in 1896. One of the first things President McKinley did was to call for an extra session of Congress in 1897 to restore the tariffs of 1890. The restoration was known as the Dingley Act (named again after the chair of the Ways and Means Committee).

McKinley protectionism created in reality the industrial self-sufficiency that Jefferson had dreamed of in American agriculture. Basically the booming steel, glass, electrical equipment, iron, and machinery industries were busy supplying American growth. The late 1880s saw a boom in American industry. American industry was meeting all of America's domestic demand and creating a surplus by 1898. Companies like Westinghouse Air Brake and Toledo Glass dominated world markets based on the technology they had developed under protective tariffs. In most of these industries, exporting was not needed or considered until 1900. The roots of McKinley protectionism ran deep in industrial America. In August 22, 1878, the *Times of London* hailed the American manufacturer: "The American mechanizes as an old Greek sculpted, as a Venetian painted." A few years earlier, the *Atlantic Monthly* had proclaimed that engineering was the national genius of America. It is the decline of American manufacturing that today heralds a loss of American core achievement for the world.

McKinley's full dinner pail policy was a unique blend of capitalism, manifest destiny, American exceptionalism, and protectionism. As a boy he saw the ups and downs of his father's iron business dependent on import levels. As a quartermaster in the Civil War, he well understood the need for domestic industries in time of war. McKinley's policies were based more on his economic experiences rather than economic theory. It was a bread-and-butter approach forged in industrial cities, not by economists. The laborer and manager became part of the same team, which went further than economics; McKinley saw the relationship as a social philosophy as well. The rise of socialists and anarchists in the 1870s and 1880s had caused anxiety at many levels of government. The nations' workshops, Pittsburgh and Chicago, had forced even Democratic politicians to support military intervention in 1886 and 1892. McKinley's simple solution was the expansion of American industry, jobs, and wages. The basis of the policy is really an expansion of Henry Clay's "American System."

McKinley's use of protectionism as a social and economic policy was also a brilliant political strategy. That found support among labor and capital in the Eastern and Midwestern states. His tariff policy (which was also anti-British) drew in the Irish in industrial cities, who previously had been Democrats. McKinley even captured a high percentage of the blue-collar Catholic vote, a Republican feat not duplicated until the election of Ronald Reagan in the 1980s. McKinley made protectionism the only real issue that crossed religious and party loyalty lines. The policy of protectionism is often linked with the support of "Big Business" for McKinley, but there was a strong contingent of businessmen that wanted free trade. These included the great railroad trust, exporters, importers, and merchants. Another was the banking industry, including J. P. Morgan who was behind the railroad trust. Railroads benefited in moving imported product from the docks across the country. J. P. Morgan actually had a closer relationship with President Grover Cleveland. Still, McKinley's weakness was his belief that capitalists would put nation ahead of profit. Often this was a bad assumption, but even so McKinley was attuned to the welfare of the workingman. He knew as a boy that the greatest fear of factory workers was not poor conditions, high prices, or low pay, but unemployment.

McKinley's approach to protectionism was pure nationalism covering both the American laborer and capitalist. McKinley's greatest speech on the need for a protective tariff came in an 1888 speech in opposition to the Mills Bill:

> Free Trade in the United States is founded upon a community of equalities and reciprocities. It is like the unrestricted freedom and reciprocal relations and obligations of a family. Here we are one country, one language, one allegiance, one standard of citizenship, one flag, one constitution, one Nation, one destiny. It is otherwise with foreign nations, each a separate organism, a distinct, and independent political society, organized for its own, to protect its own, and work out its own destiny. We deny to those foreign nations free trade with us upon equal to equality with our own. He is not amenable to our laws. There are resting upon him none of the obligations of citizenship. He pays no taxes. He performs no civil service; he is subject to no demands for military service. He is exempt from State, county, and municipal obligations. He contributes nothing to the support, the privileges and profits in our markets with our producers, our labor and our taxpayers? Let the gentlemen who follows me answer. We put a burden upon his productions, we discriminate against his merchandise, because he is alien to us and our interests, and we do it to protect our own, defend our own, preserve our own, who are always with us in adversity and prosperity, in sympathy and purpose, and, if necessary, in sacrifice. That is the principle which governs us. I submit it is a patriotic and righteous one. In our country each citizen competes with the other in free and unresentful rivalry, while with the rest of the world all are united and together in resisting outside competition as we would foreign interference.

This powerful speech, reminiscent of the reasoning of Adam Smith, refutes the words of Adam Smith's free trade argument with a justification for American protectionism. Biographer Marshall Everett called this speech "the greatest ever delivered on a purely economic question in the halls of the American Congress."

It goes to the heart of protectionism as fair and honorable. It defines a new right, the right of Americans to supply their own market. It defends a new American right — a right to participate in American prosperity. Furthermore, it promotes protectionism as embodied in the rights of every American. McKinley argues that trade is not for political gain but for the gain of our working citizens. Our jobs must be protected because it is the American citizen that bears the burden and cost of freedom. It is not anti-foreign but accepts the premise that only free societies can compete freely. He recognizes that Americans broke free of England for economic reasons, and that unfair trade is tyranny. McKinley went on to state "Free foreign trade admits the foreigner to equal privileges with our own citizens. It invites the product of foreign cheap labor to this market in competition with domestic product, representing higher and better paid labor." McKinley had given five years of his life in the service and believed these sacrifices of citizens for liberty required the government to put citizens first.

Another strength of McKinley's protectionism was its application of scientific management of the time. McKinley's approach had evolved by hard study and statistical follow up. In the 1880s, McKinley took the idea of reciprocity from James Blaine and incorporated it. McKinley believed duties needed review annually, and favored a permanent review committee if Congress. He believed jobs were the first consideration for duties, but a point would be reached based on industry success where profits went into capitalist's pockets versus investment. He consistently reduced steel tariffs from the 1807s to 1900. His approach was far from blind protectionism; it was protectionism with a goal of American growth. His scientific management and review of duties eliminated any potential trade wars. He never believed that in a complex world trade could be truly free.

Until the last fifty years, there was always a struggle in Washington DC over free trade and protectionism. The roots of this struggle go back to colonial times and were even an underlying factor in the Civil War. Generally, the farmers and merchants of the nation favored free trade while the urban and industrial areas favored protectionism. Another generalization is that the South and West favored free trade, while the East, Mid-Atlantic, and Midwest favored protectionism. International pressure came from Great Britain and France, which favored free trade. Great Britain's view of free trade was based on the writings of Adam Smith, but it was far from a purist approach. Adam Smith's *Wealth of Nations* is often referred to in free trade debates even today. *Wealth of Nations* was published in 1776 to great acclaim in Great Britain. While Adam Smith's theories are often hailed as the basis of capitalism, they are uniquely suited for Great Britain. Smith argues the supremacy of free trade and capitalism based on human instincts. It remains a powerful thesis tested in over two hundred years of debate. It assumes, however, that humans will be allowed to freely act. This is far from true when we view the world as a whole. The least quoted part of the book is Smith's concession of conditions where tariffs might apply.

Adam Smith had argued that tariffs make sense when applied to defense related industries. This exception was popular and, of course, applied to the huge shipping and shipbuilding industries of Britain of the time. Smith also made concessions for some "core" national industries. This thesis favored Britain more than any other nation at the time. Smith argues as well that some nations are better suited for certain types of manufacture. While no one can refute the conclusions of Smith based on his own view of economics, his thesis clearly favored Britain in its international application. The basic premises of Smith's theories were objected to early on in America. As an extension of American independence, the founding fathers argued economic self-sufficiency. For many years, Thomas Jefferson's view of American agrarian self-sufficiency ruled the American political view.

The application of Jefferson's agrarian self-sufficiency to American industry began with the ascendancy of Henry Clay of Kentucky to Speaker of the House in 1812. The period of 1812 was again ripe for nationalistic economics and self-sufficiency. The first protective tariff was passed in 1816 on iron, wool, and cotton goods. It was hailed in the mills of New England and by the iron producers of Mid-Atlantic States and opposed by the south, which exported cotton to British mills. As Speaker of House, Henry Clay stacked committees with protectionists and extended the tariffs in the 1820s. In a two-day speech in March of 1824, Henry Clay wailed against free trade, planting the roots of what would be known as the American System:

> Are we doomed to behold our industry languish and decay yet more and more? But there is a remedy, and that remedy consists in modifying our foreign policy, and in adopting a genuine American system. We must naturalize the arts in our country, and we must naturalize them by the only means, which the wisdom of nations has yet discovered to be effectual — by adequate protection against the otherwise overwhelming influence of foreigners. This is only to be accomplished by the establishment of a tariff.[81]

Clay's American system was nationalistic capitalism based on America's higher moral ground and manifest destiny. The basic beliefs were shared by Abraham Lincoln and William McKinley years later. Of course, it came with regional and segment opposition from the South and some farmers who remained opposed even through McKinley's era. McKinley held the same underlying beliefs of the American System. McKinley was unashamed of his nationalistic approach to trade. He also believed that America and its workers were especially destined to be a beacon of freedom for the world. Americans, therefore, should

---

81 Robert Remini, *Henry Clay: Statesman for the Union*, (New York: Norton & Company, 1991), 230

have priority in their own markets. He assumed manifest destiny, but his economic principles were forged in the industrial valleys of Ohio. He early on saw the struggles of his father's iron business against British iron imports. Iron and iron products flooded the American market, keeping the development of the American iron industry restricted well into the 1800s. Even the Confederates learned the hard lesson of depending on imported iron in war. His home district of Canton, Ohio also was struggling to become a center of American manufacture during the period.

McKinley's basic belief in the American System was deeply personal. He was not a friend of the robber barons of the time as many tried to frame him as. J.P. Morgan had financially backed McKinley, but feared his weak commitment to the gold standard. J. P. Morgan also favored free trade. In fact, prior to the establishment of the Federal Reserve, all presidents including the great trustbuster Teddy Roosevelt had to bow to the influence of J. P. Morgan. McKinley is often criticized for his lack of trust busting, but that was more related to his belief that business strength was good for all. McKinley also believed that government should act more as a referee than a judge or law enforcement arm. Democrats of the time tried to paint him as anti-union and labor because of his low key use of government, but the facts support a different assessment.

Early in his career, McKinley had supported miner strikes in Ohio. He supported tough immigration laws to prevent the flow of cheap labor into the country, which undercut American wages. His strong support against immigration was consistent with his "full dinner pail" strategy. He had fought hard for industrial safety laws, particularly those for railroad workers. Most importantly, he believed that American labor deserved protection and higher wages because they were investors and stakeholders in democracy. McKinley felt America was the world's beacon of hope for all workers. His favorite industrialist was George Westinghouse of Pittsburgh. Westinghouse and McKinley became friends when McKinley was Chairman of the Ways and Means Committee in the 1880s. Both men worked on the implementation of air brakes and signaling systems in the railroad industry. They took an immediate liking to each other based on their shared Christian beliefs and respect for the American laborer. Westinghouse had been a supporter of the Democratic administration of Grover Cleveland but was won over to McKinley Republicanism. McKinley would often call Westinghouse to Washington to get his views on industry. During the McKinley administration, Westinghouse purchased the James Blaine House on Dupont Circle as a winter home so he would be more available for such discussions. McKinley often visited Westinghouse at his Pittsburgh home and summer home in the Berkshires. Westinghouse and McKinley were like-minded on how the American

System should function. In the 1880s, Westinghouse was a major manufacturer of railroad products such as air brakes. Of course, Westinghouse would go on to be a major manufacturer of electrical equipment as well. Westinghouse supplied the world air brakes out of his Pittsburgh manufacturing shops. He was unaffected by national tariff battles because he supplied a technologically superior product.

Westinghouse was also the antithesis of the robber baron of the times. He had gone out of his way to promote the welfare of workers in his plants. Westinghouse pioneered things like pensions and health care. He built the model town of Wilmerding outside of Pittsburgh, supplying well-kept houses to his workers. Westinghouse's basic application of the Golden Rule to labor relations was what McKinley believed should be the norm and believed (somewhat naively) that capitalists would follow. Both men were concerned over the rise of socialism because of poor treatment of laborers as well as lack of work. Both men had been appalled by the deaths in the Railroad Strike of 1877, the Haymarket Riot of 1886, and the Homestead Strike of 1892. The rise of socialism, however, was causing a red scare in industrial circles. The country's leaders looked for a political and social solution. Like Westinghouse, McKinley believed lack of employment and good wages would promote the rise of socialism more than a belief in socialistic doctrine. McKinley's view was simplistic, but he never complicated it with other factors. High employment and industrial growth was the social tonic needed by America. In the end McKinley saw it correctly, the American worker had no real interest in socialism as a working framework. Teddy Roosevelt, on the other hand, like so many in the upper classes, believed socialism was a political threat.

While McKinley understood the root cause of socialist popularity, he missed the problems of the abuses of capitalism such as monopolies and trusts early in his presidency. McKinley never felt the need to challenge the trusts of the time. He watched closely to assure no price abuses or wage abuses resulted in the protected industries. The statistics of the 1890–1910 period or even the broader protectionist period of 1880 to 1920 show that wages outpaced wholesale prices throughout the period.[82] All statistics suggest that manufacturers not only increased wages but poured money back in capital investment and research. All major industries showed major jumps in both technology and productivity. America's greatest inventors such as Edison, Westinghouse, Michael Owens, Tesla, and others evolved during the period. Capitalists like Carnegie in steel and

---

82 *History of Wages, Colonial Times to 1928,* (Washington DC: United Statistics Bureau of Statistics)

Libbey in glass found greater returns in investing in manufacturing versus the bank.

While McKinley rarely applied the Sherman Anti-Trust Act in his administration, he had been key to its passage in 1890. During 1890, then Chair of the House Ways and Means Committee, McKinley forged a compromise that passed both the Sherman Act and the Tariff Act of 1890. President Grover Cleveland had attacked tariffs in 1887 as the "mother of trusts." McKinley realized that the public had a negative opinion of trusts; the passage of the Sherman Act with the Tariff Act helped dampen criticism and united the Republican Party. McKinley was also well aware that trusts could readily be tempted to abuse their position. McKinley's industrial employment ushered in the great technological advances of the period, but his ambivalence towards trusts is a fair criticism. He favored anything that he believed would expand or favor America. The growth of trusts and monopolies was tolerated to some extent because their technological breakthroughs actually allowed for increased competition. Technology also helped reduce prices. A recent study of the period argues: "The American economy was at just that point experiencing vigorous expansions of output, firms were aggressively lowering prices, bidding up real wages, introducing new products and industrial techniques, and drastically shifting cost curves downward... causing dramatic structural changes in the U.S. economic landscape such that the exploitation opportunities of local monopolies were everywhere evaporating."[83] The fact is that in glass, iron, steel, and many other industries new technology actually increased competition. Technological breakthroughs were in many cases the direct result of corporate investment in research and development.

McKinley's full implementation of Henry Clay's American System was a political masterpiece. His great Tariff of 1890 passed Congress by satisfying many Democrats with the counter balance of the Sherman Anti-trust Act and Interstate Commerce Act. As a third term congressman in 1880, McKinley hailed and supported President Chester Arthur's federal tariff commission. The Tariff Commission actively monitored the tariffs and their impact. The records of this commission throughout the latter half of the 19th century testify to its activity. McKinley adapted the trade policy of reciprocity of President Garfield's Secretary of State James Blaine. McKinley opposed bankers, favoring slight inflation because he believed it helped the laborer. This led him to support bimetallism against the demands of the Eastern bankers, who favored free trade.

McKinley did much more than implement the ideas of Henry Clay and Alexander Hamilton; he added to and improved the "American System." Pig Iron

83 William Baxter, *The Political Economy of Antitrust*, (Lexington: Lexington Books, 1980)

Kelly certainly influenced McKinley. For almost twenty years, McKinley was the protégé of Pennsylvania's Pig Iron Kelly on the House Ways and Means Committee. Kelly influenced McKinley in seeing that democracy and capitalism are interrelated in America; they combine to form the "American System." Kelly had championed black suffrage because equality and opportunity are the foundation of American capitalism. Capitalism without opportunity, upward mobility, and civil rights is no better than tyranny. Kelly had also fought for the shorter work-week and better working conditions. McKinley incorporated all of this into his vision. It was Clay's system adapted for the Industrial Revolution.

Ohio was where cornfields surrounded steel mills, and Wall Street finance clashed with Western speculation. The East supported the gold standard to prevent inflation while the West wanted a silver standard to support growth. McKinley with other Ohio Republicans forged a gold standard within a silver equivalent framework known as "buckeye bimetallism." McKinley worked with Western Democrats to pass bimetallism as a compromise, the Sherman Silver Purchase Act of 1890. In the presidential elections of 1896, McKinley's bimetal-lism would help him win some of the Border States which had voted Republican. McKinley had moved the party from the "party of piety" to the "party of prosperity."

McKinley Republicanism was a true movement based on the American System. His presidential victories of 1896 and 1900 were victories for the protectionists. Industries boomed as never before, as the steel, glass, and oil industries of America outproduced the world's competition. The stock market rose 70% from 1896 to 1899. The government ran a surplus and in 1899 exports were double that of imports. McKinley won both national elections by a wide margin. His coat-tails carried the Republican Party, controlling both houses and winning both midterm elections. The Republican Party held or captured all the non-Southern governorships as well. The only comparable electoral revolution was that of Franklin Roosevelt's New Deal. Lewis Gould, one of McKinley's biographers, described McKinley's presence in the 1890s: "He stood at the top of American politics as a result of his own skill and because he was such a dominant personality of his time, as Franklin Roosevelt would become in the 1930s."

McKinley is often criticized for his favoritism of big business, but his relationship with the great trust builder J. P. Morgan was weak compared to that of Grover Cleveland prior to him and even Teddy Roosevelt after him. Morgan's main concern was the maintenance of the gold standard, which McKinley reluctantly supported although he doubted the theory behind it. Because of his invalid wife, monastic type living, and personal beliefs, he rarely socialized with industrialists. The blueblood Republicans looked upon him as a commoner. Generally,

McKinley allowed his friend and advisor Mark Hanna to work out deals with bankers and industrialists. In fact, McKinley was not a wealthy man and bordered on bankruptcy in the 1880s. He was never fond of the power he wielded as president, defining his happiest days as being a major in the Union Army under General Hayes (future president of the United States). In many ways, McKinley was our first President from the middle class. His only political passion was the extension of the American System, which he had debated since his youth, and believed it was his personal destiny to advance. It was clear to McKinley that the American System and protectionism would be his legacy.

He had started to rein in big business at the time of his death. He had taken on Carnegie Steel armor contacts for their high price and low quality in 1898. In addition, treatment of labor was becoming a concern. In his early days in the Congress, McKinley had quietly brought a bill for a national arbitration system, and as governor he implemented a statewide system in Ohio. Governor McKinley would often call fighting labor and capitalists to his office to resolve disputes without politics. In 1901, McKinley started to build a national system for improved labor relations. He formed the joint government–labor commission called the National Civic Federation with Samuel Gompers as vice president. He pushed the Erdman Act of 1898, which assured wage arbitration for railroad workers. McKinley went further than Congress and formed an executive branch tariff commission in 1898. He often sent Mark Hanna for behind-the-scene negotiations with big business as opposed to the headline-grabbing trust busting of Teddy Roosevelt.

McKinley did realize in his second term that the American System might need to be modified to meet the emerging international role of America and the booming surplus of American industry. In his Pan-American Exposition speech a few days before his death, McKinley proclaimed, "Isolation is no longer possible or desirable." In addition, the McKinley tariffs had built a robust American industry with high capacity and an excess of production. Again he noted in his Pan-American speech, "Our capacity to produce has developed so enormously and our products have so multiplied that the problem of more markets requires our urgent and immediate attention." In his new administration of 1900, McKinley looked into opening up trade to further stimulate American industry and productivity. His own success had created some inherent blockages to selling the mounting American industrial surplus. The American shipping and merchant marine industry was all but dead. He needed a mechanism to open trade without causing an import flood, and an Isthmian Canal was needed to expand shipping and trade. Furthermore, he wanted to expand the merchant marine.

In the late 1880s, McKinley had started a policy of trade reciprocity. Like all of his policies, it was based on common sense bread-and-butter issues. Trade reciprocity would be based on the minimum requirement of equality in trade. McKinley believed that America's unique combination of freedom, democracy, capitalism, and Christianity gave it a favored position in the world. Reciprocity in McKinley's view was to be economic, not political. McKinley actually appointed reciprocity commissioner John Kasson to work on trade relationships after the passage of the Dingley Tariff Bill. The French agreements have already been noted, but there were agreements with Argentina and Jamaica. In Argentina, American wool manufacturers got lower duties, while Argentinean farmers got lower duties on their citrus fruits. Overall McKinley had limited reciprocity agreement successes, but he forged a new and pioneering approach. The policy alone helped prevent retaliatory trade wars.

McKinley also was innovative in his 1890 bill which included a special reciprocity clause. The bill allowed for 99% free of the duties collected on raw materials imported, then exported as finished goods to foreign markets. This was a creative approach to allow cheap raw materials to manufacturers, while promoting American manufacturing aboard. This would allow South American wool and raw sugar to flow in and be converted by American manufacturers into clothing and refined sugar without duties to South America. McKinley also showed flexibility and discernment as he moved from opposing to incorporating the reciprocity ideas of James Blaine. McKinley realized that the reciprocity along with scientific schedule review was an essential tool for fair trade, and it could defuse the argument of a risk of trade wars. Trade wars never developed on McKinley's watch. McKinley's approach required hard work by both the legislative and executive branches as well as constant monitoring — something future Congresses and Presidents chose not to do. McKinley's years of study and review keep paying dividends as he fined tuned his approach to protectionism and tariffs. He demonstrated a unique ability to blend politics into an American strategy for tariffs.

As President, he pushed for reciprocity arrangements through treaties in the 1897 Dingley tariff. Many conservatives were concerned that McKinley's reciprocity arrangements would lead to an erosion of protectionism, but McKinley believed it was necessary for the future. American surplus was becoming an issue, and McKinley wanted to allow for a boom in exports. In his last speech, at Buffalo, McKinley defined his vision: "A system which provides a mutual exchange of commodities is manifestly essential to continued and healthful growth of our export trade. . . . Reciprocity is the natural outgrowth of our wonderful industrial development under the domestic policy now firmly established. . . .

The expansion of our trade and commerce is a pressing problem. Commercial wars are unprofitable. A policy of good will and friendly trade relations will prevent reprisals. Reciprocity treaties are in harmony with the spirit of the times; measures of retaliation are not."

Economists today still search for reasons other than tariffs for the McKinley boom. It's a frightening proposition to free traders that scientific tariff management could be an option. The McKinley boom was as deep and broad as any in the nation's history. Milton Friedman suggests that the gold production from worldwide finds increased the money supply as much as 80% form 1898 to 1902.[84] Certainly this would explain a boom, but where was the inflation that would have resulted? For Friedman's period, food prices went up 3.6% but many manufactured items like clothing actually came down by 3.7%. Real wages in manufacturing went up as much as 12%. While the money supply increased, it was only one factor. McKinley's reciprocity had proved that scientific tariffs could increase exports of production surplus, and hold prices down. At the very least this period deserves more study.

McKinley's assassination in 1901 brought a change toward trade with the administration of Teddy Roosevelt. Roosevelt extended reciprocity to include the achievement of political objectives in trade for economic favors. Protectionism remained in vogue until the late 1920s, when economists blamed it for a worldwide depression. Many historians today still view the tariffs and protectionism of the McKinley era in light of trusts, robber barons, and muckraking. They clearly miss the passion of William McKinley on this issue. For McKinley, this was an American issue. He believed that Americans should be willing to fight for their system of government and that in return the government should fight for American jobs. McKinley saw manufacturing as America's God-given destiny. He had no interest in economic theories, only a belief in the American System. He refused to trade American manufacturing and jobs for global political goals without economic reciprocity. McKinley was an expansionist and an exceptionalist in that he believed that America and its style of capitalism were destined to dominate the world economically. He did not believe that capitalism and free trade were synonymous, but felt free trade was a deterrent to capitalism. He did believe that democracy and capitalism were synonymous.

---

84 Philips, 113

CHAPTER 16. MCKINLEY'S LABOR ALLIANCE — THE PEOPLE'S LEGACY

The growth of trusts and wealth during the McKinley boom is often given more attention than the growth of unions during this period. The fact is that union membership, which had declined during the Cleveland recession, quadrupled from 1898 to 1903. The organization and structure of labor unions reflected capitalistic society itself from 1860 to 1900. Unions represented the skilled workers in the majority of cases, leaving laborers, children, blacks, and women underrepresented. Pay within union jobs followed the Pareto distribution with the top wage being four times the lowest. Laborers made up from 30% to 40% of the manufacturing workforce and generally had no union to lobby for better treatment. The wage for laborers varied from $0.50 a day (women, children) to $1.50 a day during this period. Laborers were dependent on the government for protection from abusive hiring and wage practices. When they could, laborers worked to save money and move up to the middle class and the opportunity for social mobility was an important difference between Europe and America.

McKinley had come from a middle class industrial family, and he carried this perspective throughout his life. As a young lawyer, he moved into labor law (against the advice of many). He passionately believed in labor as the barometer of the health of the nation. He expressed this as president: "The labor of the country constitutes its strength and its wealth; and the better that labor is conditioned, the higher its rewards, the wider its opportunities, and the greater its comforts and refinements, the more sacred will be our homes, the more capable will be our children and the nobler will be the destiny that awaits us."

McKinley had no deep roots with capitalists; he saw them as necessary for the improvement of working conditions. He was not their first choice when he ran for his party's nomination. The king of finance, J. P. Morgan, was closer to McKinley's Democratic predecessor, Glover Cleveland, and his successor, Teddy Roosevelt. McKinley benefited little from his support of the capitalists; he had to borrow money to pay for his presidential inauguration suit and left an estate that was nearly bankrupt. His homes were middle class cottages; and for much of his life, he was a renter. He lived a simple life. In the army, he worked his way through battlefield promotions from the rank of private to major, where most upper class family members started. He borrowed money to go to law school. He was a pioneer in securing civil rights for blacks and women. In summary, his life was more representative of an ironworker than a captain of industry. At a McKinley Day dinner in 1907, McKinley's friend professor Mattoon Curtis called him "the representative American."

Tariffs provided the cornerstone of the strategic alliance between labor and management. Tariffs favor employment at home; it is only an exaggerated emphasis on profits alone that can make the process financially inefficient. It is fair to look at the McKinley's tariff approach as trickle-down economics. It will work, but some dollars are lost to the rich as well. McKinley's scientific approach and tariff review was aimed at making the trickle-down process more efficient. He believed government's role was to assure fairness to the employees in tariff application. The tariff argument boils down to some trends on which both free traders and protectionists can agree. Tariffs cause higher prices, higher employment, and higher production; they foster economic independence, spur domestic innovation plus investment, and can cause retaliation in international markets. By contrast, free trade brings prices down, lowers employment, lowers production, reduces domestic investment, fosters outside dependency, and increases world free trade.

McKinley applied scientific management to optimize the opposing trends. Congress formed a watchdog commission and President McKinley formed an executive commission to assure review and fairness (which would have appalled Adam Smith who would have viewed this as government interference). Bottom line, McKinley believed in favoring labor employment over other factors.

Another part of McKinley's unique political alliance was his belief that the heart of America was its middle class. McKinley believed that upward mobility to the middle class was the most important factor in checking the rise of socialism that was sweeping Europe. While he received support from laborers and in the capitalists, his core was the middle class. At the dinner in 1907, Mattoon pointed out: "No nation is stronger than its middle class. McKinley saw this, and we should all realize it. He did all in his power to preserve and augment the great body of industrious and frugal citizenship. Anything that tends to decrease the number and power of our great middle class is a direct attack not only against our government but against the health and prosperity of society." Where many politicians focused on breaking the rich or advancing the poor, McKinley's vision embraced growing the middle class to have the power to achieve the same goals. He and Ronald Reagan remain among the few presidents to have focused on America's middle class.

Such a political strategy required a strong economy as well as restraints on the capitalists and bankers (which, taken at face value, inevitably would represent a deviation from true capitalism). This approach, however, was a success for the nation as a whole. McKinley was the ideal man to strike such a balance. Intermediates such as Mark Hanna helped rein in the bankers and trusts. Even so, there was an incremental strengthening of the trusts, and McKinley feared he would have to use legal means to control them. The legal options at the time were limited since Supreme Court decisions had actually green-lighted trust formation. The bankers also had the upper hand in that without a national banking system, the nation depended on them to adjust the money supply. In major depressions, prior to the formation of the Federal Reserve, presidents had to knock on the door of J. P. Morgan. McKinley never had to do this. McKinley allowed rapid trust growth to assure a strong economy; his successor Teddy Roosevelt would have to address the problem after McKinley's death.

Perhaps just as important were McKinley's efforts to protect the laboring class from its own government. During the fight for the 1890 Tariff Bill, McKinley faced tough opposition from the Republican Administration of Harrison and his aggressive Secretary of State, James Blaine. Blaine had wanted reciprocity amendments, which would allow the president to "trade" favors for reciprocity arrangements. These are the "fast track" arrangements that presidents today enjoy. McKinley wisely saw the potential for politics and internationalism to enter trade agreements. McKinley fought against the Senate and Blaine on full presidential powers, pulling support from conservative Republicans. The compromise approved allowed the president to apply penalties for unfair trade but not to apply political favors. McKinley maintained that tariffs should be the domain of Congress and committee review. McKinley's compromise and experience would help him form a new approach for reciprocity to reduce tariffs while protecting American industries. Basically, the McKinley approach would assure a balance of trade, except where imports would be needed for the growth of American industry. To England and Europe, McKinley's tariff views were nationalistic, and McKinley would not argue with their criticism.

The problem, however, was a lack of regard for the laboring class in the 1800s by the owners and even the public. Immigrant workers were extremely hard working and usually submissive, and the corporations often took advantage of their weakness. Working conditions, long hours, and variable wages headed the list, but even the simple paycheck and a reliable payday were problematic. A survey of Michigan factory workers in the 1880s showed that more than a quarter had no regular payday and often waited up to 60 to 90 days for pay. Over 75% worked more than 60 hours a week and about 25% worked more than 10 hours daily.[85] The twelve-hour day was common in the textile mills of New England and the steel mills of Pittsburgh as well as the steel mills of the Mahoning Valley in McKinley's district. In coal mines, workers often worked 14 hours or more. New York bakers worked 16 hours a day, six days a week. McKinley's legal support of Ohio coal miners had reflected that he was outraged by the working conditions of the period. As governor of Ohio, McKinley had pushed state legislation to improve industrial safety, worker rights, and child labor laws. He believed protected industry should share prosperity with the laborer, rather than bankers. Far ahead of his time, McKinley pioneered the idea of employees as stakeholders on a par with shareholders.

McKinley had supported the eight-hour day from his earliest days, and in 1890 promoted a federal bill for the eight-hour day for government workers. McKinley had often talked with Samuel Gompers on the expansion of the eight-hour day to industry and included it in the 1900 platform. But on the eight-hour day he had stiff resistance from many top tier capitalists such as Andrew Carnegie and J. P. Morgan. Throughout his career he promoted safety acts at the federal and state level to protect miners, railroad, and streetcar workers. He promoted bills for the formation of unions. In Ohio, he passed arbitration bills to assure the fair treatment of labor and the right to impartial tribunals. As governor he used his own funds to help hungry striking miners. He correctly envisioned the American union/management system as an option to either violence or socialism. He would not allow violence and only used overwhelming force when necessary, but he often publicly rebuked owners. He hoped for an age of cooperation, at the same time realizing that laws would be needed to address abuses.

McKinley as governor of Ohio had supported several laws and organizations to offer a mechanism to resolve labor disputes and had personally lobbied the Ohio state legislators to pass an arbitration law. Labor fairness and peace

---

85 Page Smith, *The Rise of Industrial America*, (New York: Penguin Books, 1984), 217

were already part of his overall economic strategy. McKinley did the same thing as president, helping to achieve the passage of the Erdman Act of 1898. Senator Hanna played a key role in this effort as well. The bill passed in McKinley style with little fanfare. The Erdman Act set up wage mediation for the interstate railroad system. McKinley understood that as tariffs protected industries, there was a tendency to strike for higher wages. McKinley wanted labor and capital to both benefit in an orderly fashion. He also worried about the rise of socialism because of capitalist abuse.

Throughout his career, McKinley always enjoyed strong labor support in Ohio and in industrial districts nationally. Yet, McKinley as Ohio's governor resisted any effort of violence by labor. In the 1894 Ohio miners strike, he called in John McBride, President of the United Mine Workers, to warn him that he would use the National Guard to keep the peace. The union called a national strike, and coal trains were being attacked throughout Ohio. When violence continued, McKinley used an overwhelming show of force to end it, including machine guns placed on trains. The overall affect brought peace quickly. Most of the Ohio and national press referred to the miners as anarchists, bridge burners, and troublemakers. McKinley, however, placed the blame on the operators in a press statement: "If some coal operators in the craze of competition did not forget that coal miners are human beings." During the course of his earlier experiences in the legal defense of rioting miners, McKinley had found working conditions in the mines abhorrent. Hanna changed his view to support better conditions.

McKinley broke with American capitalists and manufacturers in his belief that unions were a necessity. Even the most progressive manufacturers such as George Westinghouse and H. J. Heinz sought to do away with unions. McKinley's law background and government experience seem to have convinced him that management and union could coexist and even be the basis of a management–labor system. The union could act as a buffer or safety valve for the workers against the abuses of capitalism; then government in some form could act as the final arbitrator. Such a system, of course, is what we have today, and McKinley more than any president can be considered its originator.

McKinley also earned the respect of the national union leaders. Unlike Harrison and Cleveland, McKinley personally warned the union of his intention to use troops. As governor, he often dispatched Mark Hanna to convince the owners to step down or to argue the case for better wages and conditions. His strong support of labor won him the support of many Catholic bishops as well. Again, McKinley broke with mainstream Republicans on his support from labor, immigrants, and Catholics. McKinley's vision of the ideal American working society and manufacturing economy was unique in its coverage and in the alliance of labor and capitalists. On a campaign tour in 1899, he was made an honorary member of the Brick Layers and Stonemasons' International Union. Part of this honor was the result of McKinley's strides in appointing union members to government jobs and arbitration boards.

McKinley used labor leaders as White House consultants, and often assigned them to committee investigations. When he signed the Erdman Act, he assigned labor leaders to arbitration boards. Former AFL chief Samuel Gompers and former chief of the railway union, Frank Sargent were assigned to his Industrial Commission to study trusts and tariffs. M. M. Garland, who had been President of the amalgamated Iron and Steel Workers during the Homestead Strike, was assigned as a duty commissioner. Terence Powdery, former head of the Knights of Labor, was made General Commissioner of Immigration. McKinley also gave many lower level government jobs to midlevel labor leaders. McKinley's "Full Dinner Pail" policy required the cooperation of labor and capital, and McKinley did his best to maintain this balance in government.

McKinley looked at his Tariff Bill of 1890 as a victory for labor. He argued: "The law of 1890 was enacted for the American people and the American home. Whatever mistakes were made in it were all made in favor of the occupations and the firesides of the American people." McKinley can stand on this in his accomplishment record against his own party during the battle for the tariff. He rejected political reciprocity as designed by the Republican administration that would have reduced American labor. McKinley stated it in an 1892 speech: "It didn't take away a single day's work from a solitary American workingman. It did it by establishing new and great industries in this country, which increased the demand for the skill and handiwork of our laborers everywhere. It had no friends in Europe. It gave their industries no stimulus. It gave no employment to their labor at the expense of our own." McKinley was always simplistic in his patriotic roots and that was the strength of his political alliances. Nationalism provided common ground. His critics often misunderstood the strength of a simplicity, which allowed him to unite farmer, capitalist, owner, laborer, and the middle class as Americans above all. He used patriotism as his ethical rule to rein in the abuses of capitalists, gaining the respect of many capitalists that disagreed with him.

McKinley's protection speeches always included wage charts, as he felt that the issue of wages was the focus of protectionism. In a typical congressional debate in 1883, he used a familiar line: "He who would break down the manufactures of this country strikes a fatal blow at labor. It is labor that I protect." [86] Even

---

86 William McKinley, *Speeches and Addresses of William McKinley*, (New York: Doubleday, 1900)

his critics believed his sincerity, preferring to call him a naïve puppet or political hack of the capitalists rather than one who was on the take. In fact, he benefited very little personally from his support of business interests. Furthermore, in an age of almost daily scandals and corruption, McKinley and his administrations were scandal free. McKinley tastes, lifestyle, and economic ambitions never rose above those of the middle class. He actually found enjoyment sitting on the front porch. His personal devotion to his invalid wife left time for only the most necessary socializing. As a researcher, discovering this laid-back lifestyle was an eye-opener, making some of the accusations of later historians ridiculous. This was a man who truly wanted to live a middle class life in Canton, Ohio. Of course, he was ambitious (no president can be otherwise), but he was not pretentious.

McKinley followed the pulse of laborer and the middle class in his Congressional debates. The following is from McKinley's floor speech in support of his 1890 bill:

> The accumulation of the laborers of the country have increased, and the working classes of no nation in the world have such splendid deposits in savings banks as the working classes of the United States. . . . The savings banks of nine States have in nineteen years increased their deposits $628,000,000. The English banks in thirty-four years increased theirs $350,000,000. Our operative deposits $7 to the English operative's $1. The vast sums represent the savings of the men whose labor has been employed under the protective policy which gives, as experience has shown, the largest possible reward to labor.[87]

It was an important argument that the savings of laborers and the middle class were tied to protective tariffs. It is an argument lost today as free trade policies have at least coincided with a deep reduction in the American savings rate.

Savings for industrial workers, through small, became the foundation of their lives. Many were saving to buy land or bring their families from Europe. Many, like the Czolgosz family, wanted to purchase a saloon, a "hotel," small farm, or at least a yard large enough to raise chickens. Land ownership was possible only if the family of the laborers pulled together, like the Czolgosz family, as an economic unit. H. J. Heinz, Edward Libbey, and George Westinghouse pioneered in providing good jobs for women. Westinghouse plants in East Pittsburgh employed many wives and young single immigrant women for short-term labor. These women worked less than four years to add to the family savings. Children were also considered economic contributors to the family. In the 1890s, large families moved to the glass towns of Ohio and West Virginia where the children could be fully employed. Young Italian, Slav, and Hungarian bachelor laborers piled into rented boarding houses to save money to start a family. In addition,

---

87 Merritt, 156

ethnic and social clubs became sources of help for the ethnic laborers. McKinley had often addressed the problems of laborers, fighting for the eight-hour day, child labor laws, and fair wages.

The idea that Mark Hanna created McKinley's image for Big Business interests doesn't fit the facts. Typical of liberal, modern historians is the following view: "Hanna decided to groom for the presidency a man of impeccable protectionist sentiments. . . . McKinley was a good-natured man, ruled by simple notions; if not a party hack, he was certainly a party war horse. . . . His achievements were relatively modest — his heroism, as hardy a boy, . . . McKinley had a gift, invaluable to a politician of narrow vision and limited understanding, of emitting sonorous platitudes as though they were recently discovered truths."[88] Some go further to view him as a harmless buffoon. The real issue was his simple middle class lifestyle, Christianity, belief in capitalism, and passion for protectionism. His speeches often attacked the academics of the time, which never endeared him to college historians. McKinley studied economics as few did, only to conclude that economics is best understood in the city street. Interestingly, Adam Smith arrived at the same conclusion, but at the time there were mainly villages. McKinley's reputation suffered from the earlier scandals in his party and from his belonging to an age known for social problems. Some of the historical bias goes back to the dirty campaigns of the time. The personal attacks, spinning, and outright lies were worse than today! In McKinley's case, the jury may still be out as the free trade debate continues into our time.

A more recent biographer is a bit more fair: "Of course, this is the hidden McKinley, the egalitarian who ran with the Grangers and promoted women's rights, the 'people's candidate' who beat the Eastern bosses, the man who wouldn't have a lobbyist in his cabinet, the cautious reformer who was on the verge of leading a fight to curb the trusts, reform the tariff system, and reenact a progressive income tax. This is the McKinley that brings the hints of Lincoln and FDR to the second tier credentials of the Republican consolidators. This is the McKinley that might have surprised Americans in that second term he had barely started."[89] McKinley was in every way a middle class president. Though he lacked the charisma of Teddy Roosevelt, the education of a John Kennedy, the intellectual power of Thomas Jefferson, and the political power of FDR, he was every bit as popular. He was one of their own, and there had been few from the middle class.

McKinley's fully employed and protected American manufacturing at first may seem too simplistic, nationalistic, and naïve for today's economic moderns.

88 Smith, 547
89 Phillips, 159

Some might argue that we have unemployment insurance and social security as a safety net, and we don't need to cater to capitalists to support labor. It is true there are many ways to help labor such as socialism. For most of the 1800s it was the "boss system" that played that role. The political bosses were located in cities and industrial areas. They provided a safety net by finding jobs, creating jobs, and directing gifts of money to the poor. The boss would send a Christmas goose or get a hospital bed for an injured laborer. A disabled family head might be given a low-level government job. In return, the poor delivered the votes. The bosses then could "sell" a block of votes to wealthy capitalists or politicians. The boss system created a type of codependency or plantation mentality. The boss system was costly and inefficient, but it did redistribute the wealth and really was socialism on a local level. Still it played an important role to offset the abuses of capitalists and push some wealth downward. Bosses were particularly strong in the East where they had ties with Big Money as well.

The boss system, of course, required a type of labor co-dependency that was full of abuses. It preyed on immigrants, the poor, Catholics, and the struggling. In the late 1880s the regional bosses started to form a combine that could control both party nominations. In 1896, McKinley ran "against the bosses", using the capitalists' money to offset the government money and graft of the bosses. The bosses traded votes and living necessities, but in the progress the dream of advancing to the middle class was given up by the laborer. McKinley opposed this system, preferring manufacturing to supply the wealth and needs of the workers. He fully believed this on the same level that Jefferson had believed in his agrarian vision. McKinley's idealism was powerful enough to fracture boss voting blocks in Pittsburgh, Chicago, Cleveland, and New York. The problem would always be capitalists who abused the system such as George Pullman, Henry Clay Frick, Andrew Carnegie, and Vanderbilt. These men envisioned a paternal capitalism which would redistribute the wealth downward, but it abused labor in the process. McKinley found allies in his beliefs in many second tier capitalists such as Mark Hanna, Myron Herrick, and George Westinghouse. McKinley's approach also appealed to certain nationalities, such as the Germans and Irish, who dreamed of becoming middle class citizens. These nationalities, in particular, didn't want to be dependent on politicians.

A key ingredient of McKinley's success was his ecumenicalism, which helped him find support among the laboring Roman Catholic vote. His tolerance had developed in Democratic Stark County where no Republican could win without strong crossover votes from the Democrats. McKinley had stood firmly against the native and anti-Catholic wing of his party. He had gained a reputation of overpopulating appointments with Roman Catholics. The American Protective Association, which was both anti-Catholic and anti-immigrant, had tried everything to prevent his nomination for 1896. The opposition of the American Protective Association had tried in 1894 to vote him out as governor. Many even believed McKinley had discriminated against American Protestants as governor and pointed to his refusal to remove two prison guards because they were Catholic. McKinley refused even though the A.P.A. had 63,000-plus members (most of which were Republicans) in Ohio and he had only won the 1891 by only 21,511 votes. A number of Catholic bishops and priests came to his aid by going to Catholic parishes to support McKinley. One of the priests was Father Vattmann, who had been appointed by President Harrison at the request of McKinley. He won the election by 81,995, picking up many Ohio Catholic votes.[90] Another stand as governor was freedom for Catholics to worship in public owned institutions. He had heard of a young Catholic in the Columbus Deaf and Dumb school who had been deprived of a priest till she lay on her deathbed. McKinley penned the following to the superintendent: "I need not say to you, what I am sure you will appreciate — that the public institutions of the State are nonsectarian and that pupils should be privileged to worship according to their beliefs."

McKinley's aggressive support and selection of Catholics in government positions was not only consistent with his beliefs but won him Catholic Church support. He appointed Judge Joseph McKenna, a Roman Catholic, as his Attorney General and then to a spot on the Supreme Court. McKinley developed a strong following among the Irish Catholics as well. While Catholics made up about 30% of the vote in 1896, McKinley carried about 45% of their vote. Only Ronald Reagan and George Bush in recent times have come that close to carrying such a block of Irish Catholic votes. The Irish and German Catholic votes McKinley lost were mostly related to his strict liquor laws. The glass and steel industries that his tariffs protected were predominantly manned by Irish laborers who gave some support to McKinley, but local Irish bosses held the overall Irish vote Democratic.

McKinley's funeral at Canton had many representatives including cardinals and bishops. No president, let alone a Republican president, had ever reached out to Catholics in such a way. His behavior and mannerisms demonstrated a sincerity that few national politicians had shown. A grief-stricken New York Archbishop Corrigan said this at the funeral: "He was a man of large faith in God and deep religious sense. He was devoid of bigotry. During two summers spent away from Washington, he spent his vacation at Lake Champlain in the immediate vicinity of the Catholic Summer School, and the courtesy and kindness he

---

90 H. H. Kohlsaat, *From McKinley to Harding: Personal Recollections of Our Presidents*, (New York: Charles Scribner's Sons, 1923), 18-21

showed was such as to bring him nearer to hearts of all people there and make him seem as if he was one of them." He was the first President to put Catholics in high positions on the cabinet and the Supreme Court. Throughout his career, he hired Catholics for any position against the wishes of party officials. Catholics went further in hailing him as a role model Christian. Cardinal Gibbon's eulogy stated: "How different was the life of our Chief Magistrate! No court in Europe or in the civilized world was more conspicuous for moral rectitude and purity, or freer from the breath of scandal, than the official home of President McKinley. He would have adorned any court in Christendom by his civic virtues."

McKinley's support of blacks was equally strong, but he did have critics. Like most revaluations of McKinley, his actions seem to speak for themselves. McKinley, as president, appointed more blacks to government positions than all his predecessors combined. The 1899 statistics remain impressive: "200 black Americans employed in the Interior Department, 168 in the government Printing Office, and 10,050 were serving in the US Army." In the Philippines over the War Department objections, he required that black regiments have their own officers. McKinley had spoken often for blacks to be given all rights, privileges, and opportunities of any citizen. In his first political speech for Republican candidates in 1867, he stumped for the passage of black suffrage for men. In an 1880 speech he preached: "the whole power of the Federal Government must be exhausted in securing every citizen, black and white, rich and poor, everywhere within the limits of the Union, every right, civil and political, guaranteed by the Constitution and the laws. Nothing short of this will satisfy public conscience, public morals, and public justice."[91]

McKinley's belief in the need for full civil rights for blacks centered on the record of blacks during the Civil War. He stated of black service in the war, "They enlisted in our armies and were made soldiers...they served with distinction in the field, they marched, countermarched, and fought side by side with white soldiers. They were not only soldiers, but see the service they rendered as guides to our armies, as spies to the enemy's camp, and the greatness of all their kindness, sympathy and assistance to our soldiers' attempting to escape from the prison hells of the South. I tell you, was there nothing else to recommend them, their services alone should be sufficient." He fought hard to assure equal treatment for black veterans, feeling anything less was un-American. He was one of a number of politicians, which made the veterans' organization, The Grand Army of the Republic, fully integrated by the 1890s. He might have fallen short of the mark politically, but never personally. In Southern cities, he changed hotels if

---

91 Armstrong, 114

the refused to allow blacks to meet with him at the hotel. He stood out in a time when the Supreme Court and public wanted more segregation.

As governor, McKinley had worked closely with black politician John Green, an attorney from Cleveland who had served in the Ohio legislature. Green had been a strong supporter of McKinley's. In the 1890s, Green was promoting a bill to make Labor Day a legal holiday in Ohio. McKinley was also a strong supporter of the bill. Both Green and McKinley were asked to speak on September 1, 1890, at the Cincinnati Labor Day celebration. At the time Green was running for state senator and McKinley for governor. Green was denied a room at the Gibson House, where McKinley was staying. McKinley canceled his reservation and moved to where Green was staying. The next day, both rode together in the parade to loud cheers from the black population.[92] This behavior is consistent with the belief that equal opportunity was to be the foundation of the American democracy. McKinley was the most aggressive state governor on attacking the rising tide of lynching in the 1890s. Lynchings clearly were appalling to McKinley, and he promoted tough legislation at the state and federal levels.

McKinley often added black suffrage to his speeches. He was more and more upset by the treatment of blacks, whose real freedom he believed was the purpose of the Civil War. McKinley would define himself as a Lincoln Republican. In an Ironton, Ohio speech in 1885, he clearly stated his belief: "Free and impartial suffrage in one section of our country is of little value if it be withheld, denied or suppressed in another section. The equality of citizenships at all elections is the bedrock upon which our institutions rest, the rock of national safety and safeguard of the future of the Republic." Race relations were strained again in the 1890s with violence, and McKinley was again ahead of his time on equal opportunity. This belief fit into McKinley's overall view of upward social mobility as the cornerstone of internal peace throughout the nation, and a strong middle class stood as an arsenal against race violence, class warfare, religious hatred, and socialism. The Democrats often used white supremacy as a vote-getting technique, but McKinley always held the high ground. If the blacks had had the vote in 1896, McKinley would have carried many Southern states.

---

92 Armstrong, 117

Chapter 17. A New Middle Class and the American System

In Thomas Jefferson's agrarian vision, the American middle class was a group of merchants, small business owners, and craftsmen. The realization of Clay's industrial America added a new group to the middle class. This group consisted of the corporate manager, supervisor, clerk, and foreman (of which McKinley's father was one). It also included a broader group of highly skilled craftsmen, such as machinists, molders, founders, and mechanics. This new industrial supervisory group earned about $2.50 to $3.00 dollars per day in 1880. The highly skilled craftsman made about $2.50 to $3.00 a day in 1880; this compared to a day laborer, who made about $1.00 per day. Even the ambitious industrial worker could move into the middle class, since pay was often productivity based. Pennsylvania coal miners in the rich seams could mine four to six tons of coal at a $1.00 a ton, making their day wage as high as $6 in 1880 (of course a day was 12 hours long.) The miners' wages were reduced by the fact that they had to pay $.75 per month for tool sharpening, $.60 a gallon for lamp oil, and $2.25 a keg for blasting powder. The miner's rate, moreover, as seen in the Panic of 1873, was dependent on the overall economy and in bad times the wage was reduced by the payment for material goods from the company store. During the Panic of 1873, mine wages dropped to as low as $.50 a ton.

In 1878 the state of Ohio called $1.00 a day the poverty level. Boom industries tended to have higher wages in the Gilded Age. A railroad clerk earned around $1.5 a day, conductors $2.80 a day, and engineers $4.20 a day. Pay in the trades varied by type, as seen in this 1874 survey:

Trade	Wage per Day in 1874
Bricklayer	$3.06
Blacksmith	$3.02
Stonecutter	$2.89
Plasterer	$2.65
Blacksmith	$2.30
Tailor	$2.30
Carpenters	$2.30

As industrialization led to increased urbanization, other subgroups arose to support urban living; schoolteachers could make $2 to $7 a day. A private school superintendent could make as much as $600 a month or $20 a day. These wages emphasized the value that the emerging middle class placed on education. Store clerks made $.25 to $.60 per day. A telegraph boy, which is how Andrew Carnegie started out, made about $.50 a day.

The industrial world of the factory was a bit different. An employee manager might make $5 a day. The new position of the factory foreman paid around $3 per day ($21 per week) in 1880. The skilled workers working under him made around $2 per day ($14 per week) and the unskilled worker around a $1 a day ($7 per week). Company "white collar" clerks earned around $1.50 per day and were part of the growing industrial based middle class although at the lower end of the class. Boys made about $.50 per day and women about the same. The real drawback was that most worked 60 hours a week or more to earn those wages.

A survey of industrial workers in 1900 showed little change:

Trade	Wage per Day in 1900
Average factory worker	$1.38
Boiler makers	$2.08
Foundry work	$ 1.30
Machine operator	$1.92
Foreman	$10.00
Accounting clerk	$3.00
Woman in a sewing factory	$0.35

The skilled worker had a different set up. A roller or steel puddler, which represented the highest level of skill, might approach or even exceed the wages of foremen. These top industrial jobs represented part of the new middle class. The union reinforced the structure and offered a path for the industry worker to rise into the middle class; for some even a path into the upper class. Rollers, at the top of the worker ladder, could reach $10 to $15 per day in the 1880s.[93] It was this opportunity that kept immigrants leaving Europe for these jobs. Many of Carnegie's millionaire managers had risen through the ranks. Carnegie started as a boy laborer at $1.25 a week. Charles Schwab, future president of United States Steel, started as a fifteen-year-old boy carrying survey rods for a dollar a day in 1880. Of course, this was an improvement of $3 a week as an errand boy for a Braddock storekeeper. It may even be argued, that the upward mobility of the uneducated lower class was much greater than today. Lack of education or degrees offered no barrier to moving up and through the management ranks. McKinley had known this opportunity as he moved through the ranks of the military from private to major. He felt deeply throughout his life that upward mobility was critical to the proper functioning of capitalism.

Based on 1880, the following living expenses might be required:

$2.44 per week for food
$1.25 per week for clothes
$1.38 per week for other necessities
$1.50 per week for rent

Some typical food prices were corned beef $.06 a pound, coffee $.14 a pound, flour $.02 a pound, and butter $.22 per pound. Bread was around $.05 a loaf and potatoes $.39 a bushel. Poverty level in 1880 was considered to be $500 a year. Numbers are very difficult to find because of regional variations. Industrial slums were common in the cities. These areas overcharged for rent, in many cases. A two-room apartment might run $7 – 11 per month without toilets, baths, or heat.

Based on an 1890 survey of steelworkers at Homestead, the following statistics stand out. Of the 3800 employees at the Homestead Mill: rollers, which represented less than .5% of the workforce earned $7 to $7.50 a day; 109 skilled laborers (2.9%) earned between $4 to $7 a day; and 800 skilled workers (21%) earned $2.50 to $4 a day. The balance was represented by an unskilled group of 32% earning $1.68 to $2.50 a day, with the remaining 43% earning less $1.40 and working twelve hours. A family budget from the same Homestead study is enlightening. The average Homestead steel family took in $663.58 annually, of which $85 was from other members in the family. For example, young boys as well as the women might pick up some day work. The budget consisted of 45.1%

---

93 David Montgomery, *The Fall of the House of Labor*, (Cambridge: Cambridge Press, 1987), 32

for food, 19.5% for clothing, 15.3 % for rent, 6.6% for tobacco and alcohol, 11.6% for things such as books, entertainment, and newspapers. This left a surplus of 15% for the family income, which could be applied to savings.[94] Often steelworkers working at Homestead lived in nearby burghs, which were connected by an extensive streetcar system. The rail fare was estimated at $3.50 month or as high as 6% of the income of a non-Homestead family.

The above budget and wage information can help put a perspective on the problems of labor. The 15% surplus is certainly a respectable number and would allow for substantial savings; however, work was not consistent for long-term savings. Workers lived in crowded quarters with vegetable gardens and live chickens (and sometimes pigs) to supplement the food supply. Economic slowdowns and strikes were common, and both of these drained savings. The implementation of the Carnegie and Frick sliding scales in Homestead reduced wages by 50% on the high end and 15% on the low end before the 1892 strike. Assuming an average of 20%, this would cause a great deal of stress in the family budget. The data also suggests the importance of consistent work, something that was lacking over the years. McKinley was very attuned to this need of the laborers. Strikes rarely occurred in slow economic periods. What workers feared most were the long periods of poor economic conditions. Conditions might be poor and wages low, but it was the ability to work every day that was paramount to the family budget.

McKinley was keenly attuned to this bottom-line concern. One of his biographers put it best: "None decried more than he the money-getting of the age. He prized the homely virtues of honestly, diligence, thrift, and individualism, all of which were symbolized for him by economic wealth protected by the tariff. These virtues had made him successful; they could do the same for others." McKinley had found happiness in the middle class. He longed for the simple life of porch sitting and reading the local paper. His economic view was to uphold the working classes within the capitalist system, thus reducing the urge to move to full socialism.

McKinley had always argued that protectionism resulted in an increased savings rate by laborers and the middle class. McKinley saw savings as a tool for entry into the middle class, and he believed that wages should not only cover basic needs but also enable workers to save. As a former banker during the Panic of 1873, he well understood the relationship of savings and the economy. Early in his career he represented one of the many small banks dependent on the laborer and middle class for their existence. Thrift was considered a fundamental virtue,

---

94 Gerald Eggert, *Steelmasters and Labor Reform 1886-1923*, (Pittsburgh: University of Pittsburgh Press, 1981), 13

although, McKinley himself proved to be a poor personal money manager. Furthermore, McKinley was one of the few presidents for whom the salary of the time ($50,000) represented a major step up financially.

McKinley was consistent in his concern for the middle class in all arenas. As governor, he had fought for a re-distribution of taxes away from the middle class. He had fought hard for a safe work place. He was the middle class's politician. A close friend noted: "His nearness to the people, his closeness to the very sympathies and hearts of the masses of the American people, has not been excelled by the experience of any American within the memory of man."[95] That closeness can be attributed to the fact that as a congressman, governor, and president, he never rose financially beyond the middle class. He understood their fear of debt and even unemployment. He was the darling of the middle class reporters that followed him. In a time of corruption, even his critics were in awe of his honesty and virtue. Almost every biographer was struck by his virtue. Even to later biographers, he appeared almost too good to be true. It's easier to understand men of greed or the virtues of the saints, but virtues of a middle class president seem to good to be true.

Perspectives on the class differences of the Gilded Age are often distorted by wealth distribution figures. The richest one percent of the nation controlled 26 percent of the wealth (which was the same in 1962). Today the number is even higher, with one percent controlling 34 percent.

While the numbers have shock value, the distribution of wealth in all countries tends to follow this Pareto distribution. It is not surprising that a very small percent of the population controls a large percentage of the wealth. Occupational mobility tells a better story of class contentment and opportunity. Studies of the Gilded Age reveal that between 30 to 40 percent of low-level workers moved into higher-level jobs during their lifetimes. Even more telling was upward mobility between generations, with 40 percent of blue-collar sons moving to white-collar work.[96] Upward mobility in Europe was almost non-existent. This is the allure for the working class in capitalistic societies. Entry into the middle class probably required an annual salary of $800. Walt Whitman put the middle class test at $1000 per year. The new white-collar jobs of the 1890s put many into the middle class.

Some salaries for the Gilded Age are givin in the next table.

---

95 Halstead, 133
96 Morris, 166

Skilled Craftsman	$800 per year
Department Store Buyer	$1200
Bookkeeper	$2000
Insurance Agent	$1200
Railroad Clerk	$800
Warehouse Clerk	$1100
Editor	$2500
Schoolteacher	$500

For these clerical and lower-management jobs work was steady, unlike factory work.

The middle class, who tended to spend a high percentage of their income (whereas the rich invested), became the driving force of the economic engine. Houses were the first interest of the emerging middle class of the Gilded Age. Skilled workers in the Pittsburgh area could get a "cottage"-style six-room, one-story house for $1200 to $2000 with help from Westinghouse Company. Homestead (mill town near Pittsburgh) had four-room cottages for $1500 and five-room worker cottages for $2000 without company help. Middle class homes in Philadelphia could be built for $3500. These homes, which had three floors and 3,400 square feet of living space, were bigger than the median house of today. McKinley's house in Canton had a value of $6000, a typical upper middle class home. Again, what is striking is that immigrant families who started in mill slum housing might own a house a generation later. It was even common for immigrants to make the leap within a generation. Immigrant families tended to work as an economic unit including the wife and kids. Often a young girl or wife might take a job for a few years to build savings for a house. Westinghouse Electric hired thousands of immigrant women, who worked for less than four years at light production jobs with wages at $700 a year. These women were either married, saving for a house, or single and saving for marriage. The middle class tended to move to the suburbs and commute to work via the streetcar system of the 1890s. Many of the immigrants considered their initial mill jobs as a form of purgatory — high suffering with an assured future. None of the mill families would have returned to Europe because of the hope and mobility possible in America. It was this hope and mobility that prevented socialism and anarchism from getting deep roots.

The movement up the class ladder was visual in the steel mill towns of Braddock and Homestead around Pittsburgh. The steel mills were built on the shores of rivers in deep valleys. New immigrants would enter into low rent districts and slums. Locals talked about those from "below the tracks." Railroads followed the rivers but up at 100 to 400 yards distance to avoid flooding. The slums were near the river and mill gates. Moving up in society meant moving "up the hill." The higher up the hill, the higher the level of society. The average stay in the slums was about a generation or less. There were various uniquely American ways to move up. Some, such as the early Irish, used the illegal rackets. More commonly, laborers moved up the skilled crafts ladder. Slavs and Germans tended to buy bars, saloons, and hotels to enter the middle class. Then, of course, there were the NBA-type stars of the period, men like Carnegie, Schwab, and others who started in the slums and rose to corporate offices. These stories were popular with many writers, but the odds were long. Still upward mobility was the characteristic that gave the impetus of hope to these laborers. Actually, the uneducated probably had much more upward mobility than they do today.

The trusts and large corporations themselves provided another part of middle class and upper middle class growth. The steel industry created a new class of salaried technical employees such as chemists, metallurgists, and mechanical engineers. Standard Oil and Dupont created the new field of chemical engineering. The electrical industry's big companies such as Westinghouse Electric and General Electric caused a boom in high paying electrical technician and engineering jobs. These large companies had the capital to invest in research and development. The demand for engineers and technicians created a plethora of engineering colleges and universities. MIT and the University of Pennsylvania started a four-year degree in chemical engineering in the late 1880s. MIT and Cornell started electrical engineering degrees in 1892. By 1895 the University of Michigan had a full engineering college with over 300 students. Capitalists poured money into these science and engineering schools to produce engineers for their companies. Technical institutes such as Carnegie Institute of Technology were created, as industry's demand for engineers could not be met. In 1900, private funds had built universities such as Carnegie, Case, Stevens, and Worchester (MIT led the way in 1866). By 1900 there were 45,000 engineers employed by Big Business. These were upper middle class jobs. Engineering graduates increased from 3,878 in 1890 to 10,430 in 1900.

Educational opportunities grew rapidly in the decade of the 1890s as manufacturing money poured into families and communities. The growth of business was a key factor in the growth of American education. Enrolments in secondary education and colleges more than doubled from 43,731 in 1890 to 94,883 in 1900. There was a philanthropic movement to establish a type of technical community college or advanced secondary technical education, resulting in schools like Drexel Institute of Philadelphia, Armour Institute of Technology in Chicago,

Pratt Institute of Brooklyn, and the Tuskegee Institute, which McKinley visited as president.

Another type of college emerged in the 1890s as a result of the growth of business. This was the "commercial" or business college. These schools focused on bookkeeping, business arithmetic, typewriting, and stenography. Schools like Duff's Business School in Pittsburgh supplied clerks and future managers for Carnegie Steel, many of which became company officers. Andrew Carnegie and H. J. Heinz took their first and only business courses at Duff's. These schools operated at night for working students and offered a path to the middle class. Records are limited, but many working immigrants attended these schools. One estimate in 1897 suggested there were 341 such business schools with at 77,000 students (the number was probably closer to 100,000).

Before 1880, colleges focused on a liberal arts education for the wealthy and privileged classes. The rise of technical education changed all that. The social demographics in higher education changed with the shift toward a technolog-ically-oriented curriculum. The president of MIT reported in 1894: "An unusu-ally large proportion of our students come from families of moderate means who never consider the possibility of first going to a classical college and then to a professional school."[97]

Engineers could earn $1200 to $2200 a year in the 1890s, and wages improved with experience. Experienced engineers earned from $3000 to $12,000. The top engineering salary in 1893 for mining engineers was $25,000! Bertha Lamme got her electrical engineering degree from Ohio State in 1893 and joined Westing-house Electric as the first woman engineer. Her salary allowed her to live in the suburbs and commute on the same train as the owner George Westinghouse. Big Business and industry funded scientific management departments that would lead to future business schools. Companies like Westinghouse and Carnegie Steel started cooperative study programs with the universities. Westinghouse Electric offered employee technical courses to prepare for advanced studies. Companies also offered in-house trade schools to produce electricians, metal-workers, and technicians, not only for themselves but also for their customers and suppliers. Even high school technical schools were funded and in some cases donated by capitalists such as Charles Schwab. This new wealth helped spur consumerism.

Even in dismal slums, consumerism was apparent. While the immigrants were very adroit at distilling alcohol for home consumption, they preferred to drink at bars because they provided a form of entertainment. A common first

---

97 Sunny Auyang, *Engineering-An Endless Frontier*, (Cambridge: Harvard University Press, 2004), 121

step for immigrants out of the mills and factories was to open a saloon, small store, or "hotel." Department stores evolved even in these mill towns to service the needs of the laborers. After basic housing and food, new immigrant laborers purchased good clothes (compared to their European counterparts). Historian Daniel Boorstin called it the "Democracy of Clothing." Laborers loved to dress up for weddings, Saturday night socials, and church. Travelers from Europe were amazed to see that the working class could be hard to identify because of the "overdressing." By the 1890s, most American clothing appeared as "ready-to-wear" styles sold in department stores. In 1890, the value of ready-to-wear clothing was over $1.5 billion. By then, 75% of America's wool production was going into ready-to-wear clothing. Ready-to-wear shoes boomed by 1890, creating a huge new industry. Rapid style change was a uniquely American phenomenon and kept the clothing factories going flat out, while hand-me-downs were much more common in Europe. The clothing industry created a consumer society that was unknown in Europe. Protective tariffs allowed American companies to operate at high volume and achieve economies of scale. This led to a decrease in prices, while profits rose.

The purchasing power of the laborers, skilled craftsmen, and middle class created new industries, which boomed with the economy and drove industrial growth. From 1890 to 1900, employment in the wool industry increased from 20,888 to 76,565; in the cotton industry from 68,991 to 143,369; and in the shoe industry from 40,773 to 78,861. Another industry made possible by the expanded base of potential purchasers was the manufacture of sewing machines. The sewing machine was a common household necessity at $150 to $300 a machine. A historian noted: "The sewing-machine is one of the means by which the industrious laborer is as well clad as any millionaire need be, and by which working-girls are enabled safely to gratify their woman's instinct of decoration."[98] With sewing machines, adjustments to ready-to-wear clothing could be made with ease, creating more demand for manufactured clothing. Sewing machines also mechanized the clothing industry, bringing prices down. The cost of clothing decreased 20% from 1890 to 1900, driven by demand volume and improved manufacturing.

In the 1870s, H. J. Heinz revolutionized the food industry by tapping into the new customer base. Heinz started with bottled grated horseradish. This common and easily grown root required tedious grating that bruised knuckles, and its pungent oil stung the eyes. As a boy, Heinz had discovered a market for grated horseradish as a convenience product; housewives would pay to reduce difficult kitchen labor. He wasn't the first to realize that grated horseradish was market-

---

98 Boorstin, 97

able, but he was the first to envision fully a national market for it. By the 1890s, Heinz was selling bottled pickles and sauerkraut, saving more kitchen time for the housewives. The growth rate of Heinz's company dwarfed that of the steel industry.

The rise of the middle class, in itself, created new industries, such as clothing, prepared food, and personal products. Steelworkers' wives buying bottled pickles created a booming glass jar industry. The rise of worker consumerism helped the department store. The department store made luxury available to a broad segment of society, thus becoming another engine of the economy. Streetcar systems grew to take mill workers from their boroughs and towns to the core city. Factory families within a ten to twenty mile orbit of the city could ride for five cents with free transfers. The boom in department stores caused a boom in newspaper circulation, since daily advertising was part of the consumer model. Heinz, for example, set aside a huge budget for advertising his food products. This advertising money freed the larger newspapers from the political control of past decades. Another side industry that developed from department stores was the plate glass industry for department store windows; and thanks to the McKinley tariffs, there was an American glass industry to meet the new demand for plate glass and bottle glass. Consumerism led also to the concept of the five-and-dime store, such as Woolworth. Woolworth created a new type of low-price temporary labor market; their clerks were paid $1.50 a week. It offered a place for women to make extra money for the family. Woolworth noted in 1892: "We must have cheap help . . . when a clerk gets so good she can get better wages elsewhere, let her go . . . we cannot afford to pay good wages and sell goods as we do now." The economic boom of the 1890s also brought mass consumerism to the farmers, via catalog companies such as Sears.

Consumerism, coupled with protected industries, stimulated a rise in the middle class. Consumer-driven industries such as textiles employed 112,900 in 1890 and 324,000 in 1900. The leather industry employed 6,000 in 1890 and 13,200 in 1900. Even more dramatic, foundries and machine shops employed 15,500 in 1889 and 145,400 in 1899. The extent of this economic boom is nothing short of amazing. The consumer market of America was the greatest in the world. The upward spiral of factories and consumers built a middle class that was rich compared to most countries. McKinley's industrial dream had been realized. Growth, however, seemed to drive more growth, and American industry needed new markets to sustain the growth rate of the 1890s.

McKinley saw the middle class as the barometer of national strength and the buffer of socialism. In a 1907 memorial speech at the Tippecanoe Club, Professor Mattoon Curtis defined McKinley's view:

McKinley's belief in democracy was supported by a profound grasp of the American situation and by what the future of our country demands. His democracy was complete. Voltaire once said that English society was like English ale — the bottom dregs, the top froth, and the middle excellent. American society is of the excellent middle class — froth and dregs are negligible factors...No nation is stronger than its middle class. McKinley saw this, and we should all realize it. He did all in his power to preserve and augment the great body of industrious and frugal citizenship. Anything that tends to decrease the number and power of our great middle class is a direct attack not only against our government but also against the health and prosperity of society.... McKinley grasped this great social truth in democracy, so he grasped its correspondingly great political truth, that political issues should divide the people vertically, not horizontally, that rich and poor, high and low should be found in both political parties. If there is anything un-American, if there is anything intrinsically pernicious in a democracy it is the effort to make horizontal political issues, to create classes and set classes against classes. This also calls for wise leadership — calls for men of the McKinley type.

McKinley deplored class segmentation, yet he was opposed to government schemes to effect wealth redistribution and even the philanthropic redistribution of wealth by the capitalists. He often used the Westinghouse quote: "The person who takes charity thinks himself inferior. The donor feels superior. I would rather give a man a chance to earn a dollar than give him five and make him feel he's a charity case." Most workers felt the same way; they wanted a chance to save for the future and personal improvement. His industrial democracy offered mobility and political equality. He stood firmly against any form of government redistribution of wealth via taxes or other methods. Fair wages and stable employment, coupled with democratic principles, he felt, would lead to opportunity and upward mobility. He was aware that the excesses of capitalists presented the greatest roadblock to his vision of an industrial democracy. The best check to the capitalists was peaceful arbitration with unions. Government's role was to facilitate this peaceful arbitration.

McKinley's vision of industrial democracy and the opportunity to move up in society was distinctive in its inclusiveness. Even Jefferson's agrarian vision excluded blacks, and Hamilton's industrial republic did not include the poor and lower classes. McKinley was more interested in a form of democracy that was fully inclusive. McKinley's industrial vision replaced that of Jefferson's agrarian society. His belief in equal opportunity among races, sexes, and religions was the next step after the freeing of the slaves, and set the direction toward the later civil rights movement. His belief that capitalists and laborers had common ground in their love of country was a cornerstone of his policy. The root of all his policies was that America had a grand calling to lead through democracy. He accepted neither the violent tactics of the trade union nor the social abuses of the owners. He believed in a social and economic equilibrium that could be achieved through industrial growth and mutual respect between capital and labor.

CHAPTER 18. McKINLEY, CAPITALISM, AND TRUSTS

> I hope we shall crush in its birth the aristocracy of our monied
> corporations, which dare already to challenge our government to a
> trial of strength, and bid defiance to the laws of our country.

— *Thomas Jefferson, 1816*

The struggle to find the best compromise between an agrarian democracy and an industrial republic is as old as this nation itself. It was at the heart of the Federalist and Jeffersonian struggle. It has defined the American two-party system. As the nation developed an industrial base, the industrial republic arose as a new vision. McKinley did not attack the agrarian model, but saw its role changing. Industrial prosperity would now drive both business and farming. McKinley's vision evolved through middle class eyes, and had the same idealism of Jefferson's agrarian Eden. One of the lasting criticisms of McKinley remains the growth of trusts, combinations, and holding companies during his administration. There is no doubt he was tolerant of many of these because they contributed to prosperity and employment. McKinley did not see anything inherently wrong with these combinations. J. P. Morgan saw them as more efficient and natural for capitalism, and McKinley seemed to have shared this pro-business approach. The idea of monopolistic price control, however, was the McKinley line in the sand. This was the abuse he had started to address in his second term. What no one, including McKinley, foresaw was the ultimate size of the economic boom created by American consumerism and protectionism.

When McKinley took office, America's oldest monopoly was America's biggest business, employing over a million. Railroads were the focus of the nation's business. With all their many faults, railroads managed to cut transportation costs in half from 1860 to 1900. Still, they had almost no popular support. Railroads since the 1870s had given big business a bad name. Corruption seemed natural to this industry, and newspapers had full-time reporters following it. Yet railroads were more efficient than the government-run canal system. The railroads were a national asset, an essential part of the infrastructure of business. In a sense, the railroads actually increased competition by breaking up regional monopolies of manufactured goods. They became very powerful and could control manufacturing as well. They also worked to the disadvantage of the small farmer. McKinley had understood this problem and had worked to restrict their abuse of power over his years in Congress.

The Pennsylvania Railroad and Standard Oil Corp. illustrate both the power and weaknesses of the railroad monopolies. Initially, the Pennsylvania Railroad allowed more distant and small refiners in New York, Philadelphia, and Pittsburgh to compete with Rockefeller's Cleveland refiners. In general, the railroads had actually acted to control the rise of local monopolies by reducing the handicap of distance. At one point in the 1870s, Thomas Scott, President of the Pennsylvania Railroad, vowed to crush Standard Oil. The Pennsylvania Railroad wanted to move product on their roads to Philadelphia from the oil fields in northwest Pennsylvania. The Erie Railroad was tied to moving it to Cleveland to be refined, and the New York Central wanted to move it towards New York refiners. Rockefeller pulled off a combination agreement that favored his Cleveland refiners and secured a better freight schedule. This type of behind-the-scenes agreement became the problem of the trusts in the Gilded Age. The railroads were a necessity, but they seemed to bring out the worst in businessmen.

But the real hatred for the railroads was not from monopolistic dealings with the oil industry, but their rate schedule with the farmers. High rates had been a constant complaint of the farmers from the 1870s. The railroad had forced the growth of the farmers Grange to help fight high rates. As a congressman, McKinley had joined in to help the farmers with their fight with the railroads. He had supported the Interstate Commerce Act of 1887 to control railroad rates. As a logistics officer during the Civil War, he was well aware of the importance of transportation. He had seen how the railroads had made possible the growth of the steel industry. McKinley had reasoned, like Henry Clay and Alexander Hamilton before him, that control of the transportation infrastructure was a federal duty. Furthermore, the great railroad riots of 1877 had hardened the public towards railroads. McKinley opposed railroad control over the growth of American industry. But as with any government intervention, this often resulted in slow or no response from the McKinley administration as freight rates declined during the 1890s.

The idea of a trust evolved after the Civil War. Prior to the 1890s, corporations used pools and trade associations to control markets. These pools were commonly secret arrangements that set prices. Pools were beyond the arena of the law, but they were obviously a constraint of free trade. From a business standpoint, pools had limited success in controlling prices because of the individual profit motive. Railroads and steel companies would break the agreement if they could gain market. The profit motive and greed tended to make pools inefficient in their ability to control prices. Often a company would break out of the pool and a price war would result. The truth is capitalists were disappointed with pools as a means to control prices because they could not trust each other. The Supreme Court decision in 1899 came down hard on pools and cartels, pushing corporations to mergers and trusts. Trusts were a formal arrangement of corporations, by which corporations were joined together under one board of trustees. The board of trustees could set market share and price. Trusts offered the capitalists better control than secret pools. Since there was a common board of directors, a trust functioned as one large corporation. Trust certificates made the agreement formal and board control binding. It was a bit different in that bankers and financiers, who made the trust arrangements, became directors. Bankers like J. P. Morgan and August Belmont became corporate moguls.

The anti-trust movement of the 1890 Congress appeared to be more precautionary, driven by the press and a rise of popular socialism. There was a valid concern that protected trusts would control prices. The Sherman Anti-Trust Law of 1890 was created by the Republicans to pave the way for tariffs. The statistics suggest that monopolistic price control in the 1880s did not exist, or else the efficiencies of the combinations overwhelmed it. Another possibility is that the high demand created by consumerism made profits more volume-driven than price driven. In that decade the price of sugar fell 20%, the price of lead 12%, coal prices remained steady, and economies of scale (and technology investment) reduced the price of steel rails 53%. Capitalists like Carnegie became focused on volume as a means of increasing profits rather than raising prices.

A decade earlier, Standard Oil showed the same economies of scale, volume growth, and efficiencies, which resulted in lowered prices. The cost of refining oil to kerosene went from 3 cents a gallon in 1869 to half a cent a gallon in 1885. The price to the consumer went from 30 cents in 1869 to 8 cents in 1885. Rockefeller used his size to drive down costs in various ways. Standard Oil, like Wal Mart today, demanded suppliers and others, including the Pennsylvania Railroad, give him big volume discounts. Andrew Carnegie had also taken on the giant (and his major customer), by building his own railroad to the Cleveland iron ore ports when the Pennsylvania Railroad charged too high a price. Railroad charges actually decreased around 40% over the period from 1880 to 1890, but uneven charges and special deals resulted in a general sense of unfair treatment by the railroads.

On the surface, these trusts were huge by 1900, and they controlled industries such as whiskey, coal, cotton, steel, copper, lead, railroads, sugar, lumber, and oil. They were monopolistic, and with no competitors in sight they could set prices as high as they wanted. Their success did vary; J.P. Morgan was the most successful at it. Price control abuse became an even bigger issue shortly after the McKinley era. In McKinley's day, even America's largest trust, United States Corporation, controlled less than 60% of the steel market. The McKinley Administration threatened to go into the armor business in response to the high prices quoted to the government.

Some trusts, like some mergers today, did offer efficiencies in production and sales. Cartels in Europe in the 1890s were common, and actually had government involvement for the very reason of gaining efficiencies. Many times production improvements made it possible to reduce prices. The stable market favored investment back into the business as well. Carnegie in particular invested enormous amounts of capital back into the business, as did Rockefeller. Carnegie created a huge number of jobs, although mostly at low wages. However, when bankers, rather than operators such as Carnegie and Rockefeller, formed these huge combinations, such efficiencies of scale did not generally result.

The term "trust" is actually a misnomer after the 1880s. The trusts were killed by state action; they were soon replaced by "holding companies". Federal court rulings in 1895 actually encouraged the holding company. The facts suggest these late century mergers reduced competition but never achieved monopolistic price control. The main reason these holding companies and "trusts" provoked distrust seems to have been the huge profits they brought in, and the arrogance of the bankers who put the mergers together. In the 1880s, the control of these giant corporations passed from inventors and operators to bankers. Men like J. P. Morgan replaced the founders such as Edison in General Electric, Carnegie in steel, and Vanderbilt in railroading. The years 1899, 1900, and 1901 were the peak years of combinations. Ralph Nelson, who did the most detailed study of mergers during that period, concluded that the growth of these combinations was not based on price-fixing or economies of scale, but on the capital market. Nelson stated: "The high correlation between merger activity and stock prices suggests that much of the merger activity of the period had its origin or was influenced by the stock market. Further examination indicated that capital market factors overrode the level of industrial activity in influencing merger activity." There is also evidence that these new financial combinations were more aggressive in trying to control prices through market control. The loss of control by the old manufacturing lions shifted the means by which the fierce competition went on, and market control was a new tool. This raised a new threat to McKinley's manufacturing view of prosperity.

The formation of United States Steel is an example of the generation of nonproductive capital. The real assets of US Steel were $682 million, against which J. P. Morgan offered the paper capital of $303 million of bonds, $510 million of preferred stock, and $508 million of common stock. In addition, J. P. Morgan earned a fee of $12.5 million and subscription promoters took another $50 million. One estimate is that it took $150 million to float the deal.[99] This money built no blast furnaces or rolling mills, but created wealth on Wall Street. In 1900, industry could still be viewed as an overall positive influence. McKinley had no problem with money being made by the owners, who often poured it back into the business that generated jobs. What was different about the combinations of the late 1890s was the domination of bankers.

Carnegie Steel had been aggressively combining since the 1880s, but these combinations were different from J. P. Morgan's great steel trust of United States Steel. First, Carnegie was a ferocious competitor within the industry. He took over Homestead Works (then Pittsburgh Bessemer) from rivals, who were overtaken in union problems in 1883. Carnegie went on to gut and rebuild the almost new mill. He added the latest furnace technology from Germany, that of Open-Hearth. He built the largest plate mill in the world within a few years. Profits and employment soared. In 1891, a state of the art rail mill at Duquesne, Pennsylvania challenged Carnegie's supremacy in rails. Carnegie launched a spurious marketing strategy to discredit the new technology. He also dropped prices to drive them out of business. In the end, he forced Duquesne Works to sell out to him, but again he invested in the plant.

By contrast, Morgan's United States Steel combination took money out of plant investment and reduced jobs. Morgan replaced top management with lawyers and accountants, investing in dollar generation versus plant improvement. Both approaches were predatory, but the manufacturers, at least, invested in the plants.

Bank-driven combinations were the real problem. Oilmen, avoiding banker and financial underwriters, had at least put the old Standard Oil Trust of the 1880s together. There were no promotional profits, and when the trust was bro-

---

99 Robert Heilbroner, *The Worldly Philosophers*, (New York: Touchstone Books, 1953), 237

ken up in 1892, it was worth much more than its original capitalization. Records clearly show that McKinley was concerned about combinations that sent the advantages of tariffs to banking directors. He believed in full protection if the protective tariff dollars went to investment, jobs, and technology. McKinley himself had imposed a duty on the Sugar Trust in his 1890 Tariff because of alleged profiteering. McKinley gave tacit approval to a Republican call to reduce duties on the products of the newly formed United States Steel. McKinley's tariff policy had always been based on job creation, not corporate profits. Banking involvement and Wall Street arrangements in these late 1890s trusts were problematic in his view. McKinley realized before his death that this new abuse of the trusts would have to be addressed, and he realized it long before the public in general did because of his understanding of the protective tariffs.

At least in McKinley's era the record of trusts with the unions was mixed. Generally bank driven combinations resulted in a loss of jobs through the closing of overlapping and inefficient operations. Morgan and Judge Gary resisted the union, trying to offer an alternative known as welfare capitalism, while maintaining the 12-hour day and low wages. Judge Gary offered employees stock options, but few had the money to join the plan. William Dickson, an ex-Carnegie steel officer and steel industry reformer, even complained, "I cannot believe that the present status of labor can be maintained permanently by the United States Steel Corporation, however benevolent in intentions and practice. In effect a few men (really Judge Gary, George Baker, and J. P. Morgan) have absolute control over half the steel industry and all persons affected by it. This is repugnant to the spirit of our institutions." McKinley had foreseen this, but his deliberation over the issue took too long.

Sometimes an overlooked element was the large creation of new middle class jobs. These included managers, foremen, and supervisors, and a whole new class of industrial scientists and engineers. Carnegie Steel basically created the new careers of industrial chemists, chemical engineers, and metallurgical engineers. Carnegie Steel donated the funds to create these departments at universities. Westinghouse similarly created the first demand for college-educated electrical engineers. Fredrick Taylor at Midvale Steel created the new field of industrial engineering in the1890s. Again, the stability of the McKinley market assured a future in these career fields as well. The increase in profits of some companies in the late 1800s created new corporate functions such as research and development. By the late 1890s, companies like Edison General Electric and Westinghouse Electric had large research functions. Another middle class job created was that of industrial technician, which fostered the growth of technical trade schools funded by large corporations. Small industry never had the funds to support such functions.

Trusts and combinations have some inherent advantages. J. P. Morgan's argument of major efficiencies is a fact. Economics of scale can and did give American manufacturing a global advantage by the end of the 19th century. In the debate over the Sherman Anti-Trust Act in 1890, most agreed that the area of steel, zinc, lead, sugar, coal, and petroleum production all had a form of monopoly. These monopolies, however, would result in major price reductions in the decade of 1890 to 1900. Steel dropped 20%, refined sugar dropped from 7 cents a pound in 1890 to 4.5 cents in 1900, and coal dropped from $3.10 a pound in 1890 to $2.20 in 1900.[100] These came after similar reductions a decade earlier. The petroleum industry, after the railroad, was America's largest monopoly, and oil prices dropped from $12 a barrel in 1870 to $1 a barrel in 1890. Technologies like the telephone and electric lighting grew exponentially as well during this period. The fact is that monopolies in the growth phase often result in price reduction and gain market share by efficiency. Once growth turns to maturity, monopolies tend to raise prices to maintain profit growth. McKinley worried only about the danger of mature monopolies. Of course, greed was always a factor that could come into play early on as well.

Senator Mark Hanna came to believe, like Morgan, that large combinations resulted in efficiencies and were good for the country. Of course, this might have been convenient thinking since they were a source of campaign funding. By 1898, Hanna had shown little concern for the growth of trusts, while McKinley worried. McKinley had to counsel and discipline Hanna a number of times about trusts. During one speech in Chicago, Hanna went too far with the following: "There is not a trust in the United States. There is a national law, and in every state there is a law against trusts. They cannot exist, and every law against trusts, national or state, has been the product of Republican lawyers." It also angered Hanna that McKinley allowed Roosevelt to speak against trusts. Hanna was in the middle of a Midwestern campaign tour when McKinley pulled him in and gave him a heart-to-heart talk at the White House. McKinley had also cautioned him on his Senate support for trusts. Hanna was a loyal and true friend, and once confronted, he brought his views in line with McKinley's. McKinley had clearly supported the Republican platform that called for legislation against the trusts and had been actively involved in writing it. He did try to use his strength in influencing legislation, supporting a bill to reduce tariffs on the competing products of newly formed United States Steel in 1901.

100 Jim Powell, *Bully Boy*, (New York: Crown Forum, 2006), 79

The concern wasn't so much over prices and monopolies as labor. Monopolies clearly had demonstrated efficiencies and reduced production costs. The problem was that they reduced prices to increase market, while at the same time holding wages down. In 1892, while Carnegie's new steel mill at Homestead gained efficiencies so incredible that he took in $10,000 a day while his workforce was being asked to take pay cuts. The coal industry had behaved similarly over the years. It was this difference that McKinley preached against. So many of the bloody strikes and riots could have been avoided over the years by a little more sharing. This gap caused political opposition and the rise of a modest socialist movement.

Bryan had tried to make trusts an issue in 1900, but it was hard to blame their existence on McKinley or Republicanism. A biographer of the time noted: "The trust issue proved of little more cogency. The great combinations of capital, which were increasing with alarming rapidity, no doubt excited widespread dread and distrust. But the attempt to convert the Trust question into a political one could not be sustained. It was a business issue, pure and simple, for which neither party could justly be held responsible. The effort to saddle it on the back of Republicanism necessarily failed." Both parties had a history of opposing the formation of trusts, and the only legislation that had been pushed through was by a Republican Congress. In 1900, the trusts promoted fear, but lacked the reality of monopolistic behavior. Their inability to attain monopolistic control wasn't because of lack of trying, but because market factors prevented it for the time being.

The formation of trusts meant little to the average worker in the 1890s, but the perceived differences in wealth did arouse resentment. Labor didn't resent profits; the question is always where to draw the line. When the difference between high corporate or owner profits and low pay is extreme, the question of fairness arises. A company cannot function without workmen any more than it can without investment capital. Carnegie's idea of a sliding wage scale made little sense if the capitalists made profits even in bad times. The behavior of some wealthy capitalists was reminiscent of the royalty of Europe, whereas the laborer wanted an opportunity to increase his wages and move up in class. George Westinghouse in the 1890s was competing against the Morgan trust of General Electric while giving his workers pensions, good wages, and insurance. George Westinghouse lived well but he proved one can make a good profit and take care of the workforce at the same time. Samuel Gompers went so far as to say that if capitalists behaved like Westinghouse, there would be no need for unions.

Statistics for the 1890 to 1900 decade support the conclusion that prices came down, profits rose, and wages held or slightly increased. Average annual manufacturing income went from $425 a year and $1.44 a day in 1890 to $432 a year and $1.50 a day in 1900. The average day in manufacturing remained around 10 hours. Heavily protected industries such as steel fared slightly better with wages. The cost-of-living index fell during the decade from 91 to 84, or about 8%. The clothing cost of living dropped even more from 134 to 108 or 19%. Food stayed about the same, but the cost of protected sugar dropped around 25%. The bottom line is that real wage (adjusted for cost-of-living index) rose from $1.58 a day to $1.77 a day in 1900 or about a 12% increase.[101] This was the real positive of the McKinley approach, but still too much of the profits were being held by a few owners or bankers. Trickle down economics was inefficient, but it did deliver better wages.

Writing about the capitalists of the McKinley era is a difficult task because the historical paradigm is so entrenched. The capitalists of the time were demonized in the press and that remains in the historical framework. Noting the positive side or defending these capitalists runs hard against the picture that we have come to accept. Men like Carnegie, Rockefeller, Frick, Mellon, Morgan, and others are remembered for their exploitation of workers. McKinley, while not a member of the club, suffers from association. McKinley deplored their attitude and lack of sharing with labor, but he also saw their important role in the functioning of the economy. At times these men could even display virtues that were the best of mankind. While they were rich as kings, they were not the aristocracy. Many had started poor, and most gave back in their own ways to society. They were fiercely patriotic and as passionate about capitalism as the socialists were about socialism. My purpose is not to justify their mistakes but to better understand their human complexity.

Greed was and remains part of history's characterization of them. Still, during the formation of the Dingley Tariff of 1897, steel men such as Henry Clay Frick, Carnegie, and Swank came out to say that their industry had enough protection and did not need an increase. Senator Nelson Aldrich of Rhode Island surveyed Frick and Swank about higher steel tariffs. The surprising answer came by letter form Frick: "The undervaluations going on are scandalous and rapidly driving honest importers out of business. Speaking broadly, we do not know anything in the Iron and Steel Schedule that requires increased duties."[102] Frick also noted the importance of product specific duties to American manufacturers, which had always been McKinley's scientific approach, versus across the board

101 Albert Rees, *Real Wages in Manufacturing 1890-1914,* (Princeton: Princeton University Press, 1961)
102 Harvey, 297

revenue tariffs. Carnegie even suggested higher tariffs on luxury items as a means to tax the wealthy. Protection still bred trusts, and abuse seemed to follow.

McKinley rejected the idea of welfare capitalism, so popular among capitalists, such as Carnegie, Pullman, and Rockefeller. Carnegie expressed it as the responsibility of the wealthy to redistribute a portion of their wealth. Carnegie and Rockefeller can be credited with the giving of libraries, museums, and schools, but did this justify low wages to make such profits? Carnegie actually believed that this sort of philanthropy was part of his mission. Depending on capitalists to redistribute the wealth made little sense in the Gilded Age. This was no better than industrial feudalism, and there were many capitalists who did not want to play the feudal lord. They wanted to enjoy the money themselves. Henry Clay Frick, J. P. Morgan, August Belmont, and Charles Schwab had no interest in welfare capitalism. For McKinley, fair wages and benefits were the best means of re-distributing wealth. Thus the decision of how the money was spent was not to be determined by the capitalists (as Carnegie wanted), the government (as the socialists wanted), the unions (as radicals such as Eugene Debs wanted), or by "nature," as the anarchists wanted — but by the reasonable and justified needs of the worker. By 1900, McKinley was starting to fear that tariff dollars were going into bankers' pockets and welfare capitalism.

McKinley, Treasury Secretary Gage, and Comptroller of the Currency Dawes, all became aware of the rapid rise of trusts in 1898–1899. Gage and Dawes had long been advocates of trust monitoring and restrictions. While Gage felt there was no method to control the trusts, Dawes argued for legal action. Dawes noted in his journal several discussions with the President on the abuses of the growing trusts. As early as March of 1899, McKinley and Dawes had come to the conclusion: "The enormous capitalization of industrial concerns and combinations in apparent effort to control and raise prices is deeply stirring the people, and will force the question of further legislation on this subject into the next campaign."[103] McKinley pushed Congress for review and legislation. He did not pursue aggressive legal action because his Attorney General felt recent court rulings on the Sherman Anti-Trust Act had precluded it. Even on the legislation front, Senator Mark Hanna did not see too much of a role. McKinley was not persuaded, and he challenged Congress in his annual address, followed by a call for legislation in the 1900 Republican Platform.

McKinley was consistent in his belief that tariffs should be designed to build American manufacturing and jobs, not monopolies. His tariff schedules, while fiercely protective of infant and defense-related industries, showed less need in

103 Dawes, March 6, 1899, p185

the large mature industries. In the 1897 Dingley Tariff, he asked not to increase duties on steel because of America's dominance in the industry. McKinley's view on protectionism was modified by his discussions with industry leaders. Both Henry Clay Frick and Andrew Carnegie believed in the late 1890s they were strong enough to take on any world competitor even without increased tariffs. Carnegie also grew so confident that he felt tariffs were unnecessary, but Carnegie was alone in this view. Still, McKinley realized that there was a point of diminishing returns with tariffs, or a point where tariff protection went to personal profits versus job creation. McKinley's scientific approach required that industry be evaluated every few years.

He also consistently applied his pro-manufacturing, anti-monopoly strategy to the mother of all trusts, the Sugar Trust. McKinley struggled with the sugar duty in 1890. He wanted to protect the sugar industry but was critical of their monopolistic practices. He tried in 1890 for a compromise with a small two-cent a pound duty, but the amendment was voted down and free sugar won. The Sugar Trust wanted free raw sugar. Effort was made again in the 1897 Dingley Tariff, but again the Sugar Trust was too powerful in Congress. The Sugar Trust was one of the few trusts which had open Democratic support. McKinley was open to possible reciprocity treaties. In 1899, when Puerto Rico became a territory, the Sugar Trust wanted a tariff to protect them from Puerto Rican sugar. McKinley argued that as an American territory, they deserved all rights of America; again he lost the battle to the Sugar Trust. In this battle McKinley put American citizenship, rights, and law above any protection of manufacturing. Still, the pressure may well be the reason for a fall in sugar prices from 1890 to 1900.

McKinley had even broken with Mark Hanna on trusts. Hanna chose to ignore the issue, believing the growing trusts were a sign of economic health. As a senator, Hanna consistently argued their necessity. Hanna had opposed the addition to the 1900 platform of a call for legislation against the trusts. When the 1900 campaign started, Hanna was called to the White House for a reprimand about his support of trusts. McKinley further angered Hanna by letting Roosevelt loose on the trusts — which were making campaign contributions.

McKinley was clear about the problem of trusts by 1898, and he was searching for a way to limit them. He saw trusts as a threat to the overall program of protection. Politically, the Democrats had embraced it as the number one issue in the 1900 elections. McKinley correctly saw tariffs, reciprocity, and the growth of trusts as a single issue. He knew well it could stimulate labor unrest and could certainly become a factor in the growth of the socialist party through boom times.

The criticism that McKinley failed to take action on the trusts is, however, valid. McKinley studied the issue to death, as he had the currency issue. When his Attorney General could not see any legal means to tackle the trusts, he studied the Supreme Court rulings himself. Discussion with the Cabinet and advisors got nowhere as they were split on the issue. Charles Dawes and Secretary Gage were vocal against trusts as was his Vice President. Hanna and other conservative senators chose to avoid the issue or to support trusts as a necessary, if regrettable, component of prosperity. Cartoons attributed McKinley's inaction to the influence of Hanna. McKinley was not so much unsure that trusts were harmful as he was uncertain of the method to control them. The Democrats even backed down on the issue in the campaign in order to focus on imperialism. He is also faulted because Roosevelt, as President, used the Sherman Anti-Trust Act, where McKinley had hesitated. All three of his Attorneys General appear to have delayed McKinley's decision, but ultimately the responsibility lies with McKinley. His indecisiveness had been a problem since his slowness to join the military. His indecisiveness on the gold issue actually worked to his advantage, but with the trusts it worked against him.

His pick of Philander Knox as Attorney General in his second term is highly questionable, although Knox got the job after McKinley's first choice, Joseph Chocate, turned him down. Knox, of Pennsylvania, had close ties to the steel trusts as well as to capitalists such as Andrew Carnegie and Henry Clay Frick. McKinley had known him since Knox's college days in Alliance. Knox had also came to McKinley's aid financially. Before his death, McKinley warned Hanna that anti-trust action was inevitable against the Northern Securities Company. Knox was new on the job and hesitated, himself, but under Teddy Roosevelt he would bring suit against them.

Another abuse that McKinley was almost alone in opposing in the 1890s was child labor. The corporations depended on cheap child labor. The Glass Industry was about 35–40% child labor and represented the nation's biggest abuser. This was also a major factor in Ohio industries. Mining used about 20% child labor, followed by the steel industry. The year 1900 showed 790,000 working children aged ten to thirteen, and 960,000 aged fourteen to fifteen. Children worked for around $.50 an hour versus $1 an hour for unskilled adult labor. The lowest pay for dangerous work was for "breaker boys" in the mining industry at $.35 a day! Typically, they worked ten to twelve hours. A large number of these children were "outcast, homeless, and orphaned." The Children's Aid Society estimated they processed 300,000 of children in 1889. McKinley had always been concerned about child labor, safety, and working conditions in the factories. As governor he hired more inspectors to enforce state laws and his was the only state to have an age limit set at thirteen. As the inspectors found more violations, the judiciary refused to enforce the fines and punishments. Until the 1890s, there was little interest even in the unions concerning child labor. Unions such as the American Flint Glass Workers Union represented the more skilled workforce and focused on wages and hours. The glass industry was the largest abuser and often used "orphan trains" to bring children from New York into the glass factories of Ohio and West Virginia. Some families needed these wages to augment their finances, and that was part of the problem.

Another issue on which McKinley had often stood alone was industrial safety. McKinley had led the effort in Congress to have air brakes applied to trains in the 1880s. Over 1,000 brakemen were killed and over 5,000 were injured annually! It took years to gain the necessary railroad safety legislation. He also worked to have a signaling system implemented to avoid the horrific train crashes of the later 1800s. The manufacturing industry was not much better, with a typical large steel mill in the Pittsburgh area having 80 fatalities a year and thousands of injuries. Safety, like child labor, was a cost issue for industry and generally required government regulation in order to improve. McKinley had worked in the iron industry and was well aware of the dangers and the impact on families.

The needed push for child labor laws and safety laws was left to reformers and socialists, who saw these issues as inherent abuses of capitalistic nations. One of the most vocal 1890s reformers was Florence Kelly, the daughter of Pennsylvania's "Pig Iron Kelly" (McKinley's early mentor).

McKinley felt child labor law was the responsibility of government, and he actually wanted to raise the age limits throughout his career. McKinley had pushed hard to have the age limit raised during his career. This was extremely unpopular with the business barons, who claimed that child labor was a necessity. McKinley worked hard with Samuel Gompers to build national support, lacking any political support from business and the unions. Ohio was the exception in restricting boys to thirteen years or older, but the state lacked enforcement and violations were common. McKinley wanted change with a national law and strong enforcement. His concern about children was another example of the inclusiveness of McKinley's industrial democracy. It wasn't until 1916 that Federal Law helped end child labor abuses.

With women, like blacks, McKinley's views were encompassing and ahead of his times. McKinley's support of women's suffrage had gone back to his earliest Canton days. His support continued throughout his career; biographer Kevin Phillips noted he was the only nineteenth-century president to receive honorary doctorates from two women's colleges. As governor, McKinley helped Ohio women win the vote in school board elections. While he never made it a campaign issue, McKinley openly supported voting rights for women. McKinley showed little bias in gender, race, or religion. Cleveland, for example, had openly opposed women's suffrage. Exclusion of women in the vote had been a major issue with the socialists.

One area where McKinley lacked inclusiveness was immigration. His view on immigration was consistent with the union view. Business was more interested in cheap labor to run the mills and factories. Business had also used cheap immigrant labor to break strikes. The immigration issue has many similarities today. Opponents of immigration pointed to the influx of anarchists, criminals, and socialists. Native opponents would add Catholics to the list of degenerates. McKinley's view evolved more from labor. He stated the following in 1896 acceptance speech: "The declaration of the platform touching foreign immigration is one of peculiar importance at this time, when our laboring people are in such distress. I am in hearty sympathy with the present legislation restricting foreign immigration and favor such extension of the laws as will secure the United States from invasion by the debased and criminal classes of the Old World." This was basically Bryan's stand in the election of 1896. Democrats tended to be pro-immigration because of their immigrant-voting base, but there was a mixed view. Irish, for example, had bitterly opposed Chinese laborers immigrating and taking away their railroad jobs in the 1870s and 1880s. Both parties wanted some immigration, but the grassroots in America opposed "new" immigration.

Again, McKinley's views were out of step with the Robber Barons. Frick had commonly used immigrants to break strikes and drive wages down. At the turn of the century, Carnegie Steel was cited with a systematic approach to hiring immigrants to reduce wages and break strikes.[104] A Pittsburgh Survey noted the following in regard to Carnegie Steel: "It is a common opinion in the district that some employers of labor give the Slavs and Italians preference because of their docility, their habit of silent submission . . . and their willingness to work long hours and overtime without a murmur. Foreigners as a rule earn the lowest wages and work the full stint of hours." The Republicans, led by Henry Cabot Lodge, pushed for a bill that would have required immigrants to speak English, which would have shut off immigration. Grover Cleveland vetoed it in 1896, and the Congress failed to resurrect it under McKinley. McKinley seemed to let Congress have its way, as his hands were full with foreign policy issues. Immigration was a topic all politicians avoided, if possible.

104 Matthew Josephson, *The Robber Barons*, (New York: Harvest, 1934), 362

CHAPTER 19. MCKINLEY'S PLACE IN HISTORY

> McKinley's desire to heal, renew prosperity, and reunite, deserve a
> subcategory and criteria of their own. Of these, McKinley, also a re-
> aligner seems most deserving of promotion into near-great ranks.

> — *Kevin Phillips, 2003 Biographer of McKinley*

The biographies of McKinley have had little middle ground until recently.
The earliest tend to be hagiographic, followed by a stream of biographies that
belittle him. Some border on the ridiculous. McKinley is often portrayed as lucky
to have managed to dress himself each morning or as a total creation of capitalist Mark Hanna, even though Hanna's relationship came late in his career. Most
agree in his concentration on the tariff issue, but even here some liberal historians perceive him as dealing only on an emotional level with the tariff issue. These
historians have chosen to ignore the endless statistics found in his speeches and
writings. His papers are filled with statistics to the point of tedium, as were his
speeches. A free trade bias seems to have clouded historians' view of McKinley's
success.

His amazing efforts to promote black suffrage are compared to today's advances and found wanting. His five years of military service is written off as him
being a "cook." This popular President gets some of the lowest marks in intel-
ligence (with the possible exception of George Bush). His simple background
seems to rule out any possibility of comparison to the presidential graduates of
Harvard and Yale. The criticisms are old, most originating from his opponents
in political campaigns. His simple tastes seem backward to many historians.

Things, however, are changing as recent biographers have found him to be in a second tier of "near-great" presidents.

Let's look first at McKinley, the person. Some of the hagiography of "Saint McKinley" appear close to the truth. He certainly would be an oddity today or at least would be viewed as one by the press. The years of commitment to his troubled wife are almost unbelievable and would be difficult to make up. Habits like reading the bible to her each night are hard for today's Americans to grasp. His wife remained his closest friend, and they preferred to be together on the front porch rather than attend parties. They phoned, telegraphed, or signaled each other everyday. On being shot, his first concern was for his wife. In an era of scandals, capitalistic excesses, and political favors, McKinley was never touched by a serious scandal. Even his worst critics found his virtues (while naive) beyond reproach. On a moral level it would be hard to find a president on his level with the exception of Abraham Lincoln (one of McKinley's presidential idols). The most persistent myth that haunts the McKinley administration to this day is that he was a tool of the capitalists. The facts are much different.

The greatest capitalist of the day, J. P. Morgan, was not a supporter of McKinley except by default. Morgan's terms of "nauseating," "having the backbone of a Jellyfish," and "Wobblie-Willie" are hardly supportive. McKinley had a lower opinion of Morgan. When McKinley's friend George Perkins asked him for advice about joining Morgan, McKinley advised against it, saying such employment would "squeeze the humanities of him." Morgan never had personal meetings with McKinley as he did often with President Cleveland and President Roosevelt. Furthermore, other than a tacit agreement on the platform, McKinley never made the type of national agreements Morgan made with Cleveland and Roosevelt. Morgan opposed McKinley's war with Spain and McKinley's support for the Panama Canal. Morgan supported the Republican ticket, but he had combined with the Eastern bosses to defeat McKinley's nomination. Morgan was a close friend with Boss Thomas Platt, a decided enemy of McKinley. The tariff question meant little to Morgan, whose railroads profited from trade, as did his banking interests

McKinley fared not much better with America's second biggest capitalist. Carnegie, like Morgan, felt McKinley was a weak man and a wobbly supporter of gold in 1890s. Earlier he had sharply criticized McKinley's bimetallism. McKinley could have made almost every capitalist happy and found limitless support by simply declaring for the gold standard outright. Hanna was instrumental in bringing Carnegie into the fold, despite their differences on gold. Initially, Carnegie abhorred McKinley's indecisiveness, but that changed to concern over his support for war. Carnegie, a fierce anti-imperialist, withdrew all financial support for McKinley's second run for the presidency. Carnegie became a bitter enemy, feeling that McKinley was at best mentally ill. Carnegie started to go public with his attacks on McKinley, arguing, "He lacked backbone." [105]

Probably fifth on the list of capitalists was Carnegie's partner Henry Clay Frick, who may in fact have been McKinley's biggest single campaign contributor. But again, they were hardly friends. Prior to the Republican national convention, Frick was a solid supporter of Thomas Reed for president. In a letter to "Bet-a-Million Gates," both Frick and Gates agreed on Thomas Reed in 1896,[106] Gates being one of the top ten capitalists himself. They seem to hoave thought little of McKinley, although his rank and file support was clear to them. Frick was also a close friend of McKinley's enemy, Boss Matthew Quay. The fact is that McKinley was not the choice of the first tier capitalists and bankers. It took Hanna to get contributions out of them.

Where does the myth come from? First, both Morgan and Carnegie are on record for personal donations of $250,000 to McKinley's 1896 campaign; this is equivalent to the entire estimated donations to the Democratic Party. Rockefeller and Frick were also $250,000 donators. The motivation was a fear of free silver Bryan being elected. Bryan struck panic into the businessmen across the nation, resulting in huge donations to McKinley. Carnegie had donated to McKinley's debt relief fund due to the arm-twisting of Hanna. McKinley had strong support among the second tier of capitalists as well as top tier capitalists such as George Westinghouse and Henry Clay Frick. But even here, McKinley's beliefs on gold differed. Hanna is often considered a boss who controlled McKinley. The fact is that Hanna was a wealthy industrialist and a brilliant campaign manager, not a political boss. Although Hanna aspired to be a political boss in the mold of Matthew Quay and Thomas Platt, he never quite achieved that dream. Hanna did become one of America's best known campaign managers.

Clearly, McKinley's support for business, intended to create American jobs, made him appear to be a front for the capitalists. But McKinley had a symbiotic relationship with Big Business; neither had control of the other. While conservative historians favorable to protectionism wrote the initial biographies of McKinley, more recent biographies are by global free-trade historians. The difference in the view of McKinley is striking. Teddy Roosevelt, on the other hand, gets high marks from historians as a globalist and "trustbuster."

Teddy Roosevelt, the trustbuster, actually received over $600,000 from J. P. Morgan and associates. Roosevelt also got $500,000 from George Gould.[107]

105 Peter Krass, *Carnegie*, (Hoboken: John Wiley & Sons, 2002), 386
106 George Harvey, *Henry Clay Frick*, (Privately printed 1936), 293, Frick Collection
107 Patricia Beard, *After the Ball*, (New York: Harper Collins, 2003), 146

Roosevelt's array of donators was actually larger than McKinley's. Teddy Roosevelt gets credit for the "progressive era" that broke up the trusts, but it was McKinley who set the groundwork. Many progressives such as Teddy Roosevelt, Roosevelt's vice president Charles Fairbanks, and Robert La Follette were first McKinley lieutenants. McKinley's selection of Gage as Secretary of the Treasury showed his opposition to trusts. Gage had even opposed parts of McKinley's tariffs because they aided trusts. It might be argued that McKinley's behind-the-scenes approach was more effective than Roosevelt's headlines.[108] There is also evidence that McKinley would have become more aggressive in his second term. Roosevelt met frequently with Morgan, who escaped the brunt of Roosevelt's trust busting. In any case, Roosevelt clearly cut deals during the Panic of 1907 with J. P. Morgan that allowed Morgan to create a steel monopoly and destroy Westinghouse Electric (Morgan's General Electric's only competition). In addition, Roosevelt became a personal friend of Henry Clay Frick, visiting him at his mansion in Pittsburgh. Roosevelt also developed relationships with Morgan's steel trust manager, Judge Gary.

A more recent biographer, Kevin Phillips, put it best: "The William McKinley who sought and won the Republican nomination in 1896 was no Eastern Wall Street backer or apologist for the burgeoning trusts. He was too much of a Middle West democrat and Lincolnian. That was part of why he enjoyed so much popularity among Americans and rank-and-file Republicans alike." McKinley merely found common ground with the capitalist. He was a believer in the power of democracy and capitalism, but was well aware of their shortcomings. He detested the approach of paternal capitalism as well as socialism. In many ways, he was more Whig and Federalist than a Gilded Age Republican. He believed that a strong American economy could solve many problems. McKinley often publicly attacked the abuses and excesses of the business owners.

McKinley had very little social or even business contact with the top tier capitalists. George Westinghouse was the one exception; Westinghouse had a winter home in Washington during the McKinley Administration (Westinghouse purchased the former home of James Blaine in Dupont Circle). McKinley praised Westinghouse publicly, hoping that other capitalists would emulate him. Westinghouse believed in fair pay versus community philanthropy, welfare capitalism, and paternal control. He pioneered employee pensions and saved payroll money for bad times to avoid layoffs. Westinghouse felt wages were better than charity. Westinghouse was a man of principles, much like McKinley. They shared much on a personal level as well. Both were from middle class manu-

---

108 Jim Powell, *Bully Boy*, (New York: Crown Forum, 2006)

facturing backgrounds. They both were Civil War veterans, and both started as privates working their way into the officer ranks. Both had faced bankruptcy in mid-career. Both were active in the YMCA and the Grand Army of the Republic. They were both ecumenical in their outlook toward other religions. Both men had high praise from labor and its leadership. Both men feared the potential abuses of monopolies and the trusts as abuses. Both men disliked the power of the Eastern bankers. In the end, the bankers and Morgan would break Westinghouse in the Panic of 1907.

Another part of the myth that McKinley was a tool of the trusts and bankers was the support and admiration of bad boy Henry Clay Frick. Frick had given freely to McKinley's first campaign and had commissioned a painting of the elected president. We had seen that McKinley was far from Frick's initial pick, but Frick grew to admire and respect him. Frick had actually been a major supporter of McKinley's enemy, Matthew Quay. Frick, however, had a deep hatred of the Democratic Party and would support any Republican over a Democrat. At first, Frick and McKinley seem unlikely bedfellows, but they shared a belief in capitalism. Frick represented the classic capitalist. He had built a coal empire and had become Andrew Carnegie's partner, but the latter's handling of the Homestead strike marked him forever. He broke off from Carnegie in 1898 and became an associate of J. P. Morgan. He was one of America's richest men and a verbal advocate of capitalism. While he and McKinley were never close friends, Frick respected few people as much as McKinley. Their views on capitalism differed but their commitment to the principles were equally strong. At McKinley's death, Frick was one of the first to join Hanna with a major donation for a McKinley Memorial and Library at Niles. The Frick bronze bust is centrally and prominently displayed there. Frick had been denied such an honor in his hometown of Pittsburgh. Frick was said to have privately visited the Memorial a number of times, drawing "inspiration" from it.

McKinley seemed to have this effect on capitalists. McKinley's idealist vision of capitalism seemed to inspire them to better things and maybe to have shamed them a little. There was a type of awe in McKinley's belief in capitalism, despite his lack of participation in its bounties. It had to be difficult for men like Frick and Carnegie to understand. J. P. Morgan looked at McKinley as naive and foolish. Frick, with all his faults, was an ideal husband and father, something he shared with McKinley. Unlike most of the politicians whom Frick dealt with, McKinley was not a political boss. McKinley also kept a distance, with Hanna collecting the donations. Frick wrote a letter to McKinley asking him to name Knox as Secretary of the Treasury, and so did Carnegie. The very fact they had to write letters is telling. McKinley insiders (of which there were few) dealt directly. McKinley, in fact, disliked letter writing, preferring to communicate through associates.

History, like his contemporary critics, searched for a conspiracy between the expansion of American territory and Big Business. In other words, there is a view that American imperialism was part of the growth plan for American business. Again, the facts certainly don't support any such conspiracy, but McKinley did believe in the growth of the American industrial empire. McKinley supported the annexation of Hawaii and the construction of a Pan-American canal before the Spanish American War, but Puerto Rico, Cuba, and the Philippines were thrust on him. He hesitated and studied before moving into the war. His Cabinet was split on war as were many of the Republican capitalists. Hawaii and the Canal were key to expanding American exports and trade, and the Philippines offered a naval port for the East. McKinley was convinced that America needed new markets for its surplus, but he never envisioned gaining them by territorial conquest. McKinley and business magnates were much more interested in trade with China than the Philippines. He favored some relationship with the Philippines, but never was fully clear on what it should be in the long run. With Cuba he resisted the popular belief, going back to Jefferson, that Cuba's annexation was America's "manifest destiny." The very fact that McKinley did not support annexation of the Philippines and Cuba is the basis of the independence of those countries today. Teddy Roosevelt, on the other hand, was an unapologetic expansionist and imperialist. While business pressured him to take more action with China, McKinley stuck to the goal of open trade versus territorial expansion.

Another common attack and myth was that McKinley was a creation of Mark Hanna. Hanna actually came late in joining McKinley around 1892. They had often been on opposing sides in the Republican Party. Hanna for years was a supporter and manager of John Sherman, while McKinley supported Blaine's presidential run. They became close friends, but McKinley made the policy decisions. Hanna was a brilliant campaign manager, but he wanted and did move out on his own in politics as an Ohio Senator and party boss. Thomas Platt, no friend of either McKinley or Hanna, described the relationship: "Hanna was a lovable character, personally. His heart was as big as the house in which he lived. McKinley and he were as brothers. McKinley's tragic death quite broke Hanna's heart, and hastened his own demise. The opposition to McKinley was bitter and reminiscent of today. McKinley is the pliant tool of Mark Hanna, the most vicious, carnal, and unrelenting oppressor of labor and crusher of its organizations in existence. He is a man who would stop at nothing — not even murder if he could do it."[109]

The relationship between Hanna and McKinley is perplexing. They were extremely close, as brothers can be, or father and son, but often had disagreements about such things as the gold standard, trade reciprocity, Roosevelt, the approach and nature of trusts. The arguments never resulted in a break in their friendship. Hanna, after having his say and allowing his anger to diffuse, would acquiesce to McKinley's directions. While McKinley let Hanna run the campaigns, he did set limits. McKinley set the front porch campaign, but Hanna turned it into a success. There is evidence that McKinley had to review ethics with Hanna from time to time.[110] Hanna was always closer to the capitalists, being one himself and having responsibility for the campaign funds. McKinley used Hanna as a buffer; he needed their support but was leery of being asked for political favors. Yet Hanna would often be the man that McKinley talked to, into the late hours of the morning, after the Cabinet had disbanded. The record shows McKinley as the dominant partner, however. He reprimanded Hanna a number of times, in a fatherly manner. The type of admiration McKinley aroused in all capitalists seemed to be the result of the ethical standard that he represented. McKinley's death hit Hanna harder than anyone other than Ida. Many believe Hanna was never the same after McKinley's death, and that depression led to Hanna's own death a few years later.

Lewis Gould, who penned the most definitive study of the McKinley presidency, summed it up best: "McKinley was not elected president in 1896 because of the guiding genius of his associate Mark Hanna, because of coerced voters and Republican cash, or simply because of Democratic errors. He stood at the top of American politics as the result of his own masterful skill." Another biographer, Kevin Phillips, compared him to Franklin Roosevelt as well. McKinley's strategy of inclusive pluralism was a lifetime time of progress; Hanna merely packaged a lifetime of achievement. Hanna's political career after McKinley was less than mediocre.

Research into the papers and notes of McKinley suggest that it was he who manipulated Hanna. This was not a type of dominant control, but a subtle control. Hanna doesn't seem to have aspired to be policy maker but a power broker similar to a party boss like Thomas Platt or Henry Cabot Lodge. John Hay, a Republican liberal and blueblood, noted that McKinley had two masks. After Hay's visit to McKinley's campaign headquarters in Canton, he wrote his liberal Democratic friend Henry Adams: "I was more struck than ever with his mask.

109 People's Party Paper, July 3, 1896.
110 Gould, 224

It is a genuine Italian ecclesiastical face of the fifteenth century. And there are idiots who think Mark Hanna will run him!" Hanna really dominated in political tactics; McKinley alone made strategic decisions and policy. McKinley's passive reserve in public was one of his masks that misled many analysts. Yet the critics hammered home the perception of Hanna being the sculptor of McKinley. McKinley was consistent with his basic views throughout his career, long before Hanna appeared. In fact, McKinley had opposed Hanna's candidates such as Sherman over the years. With the possible exception of the gold issue, it was McKinley who wrote policy into his speeches. Hanna acted more as a publisher versus an editor.

McKinley's simple tastes and living style were things most capitalists couldn't understand. His only luxuries on the new presidential salary were some badly needed suits and some jewelry for his wife. He preferred to sit on the front porch in Canton rather than go to parties. He just didn't fit into their world. They had a personal reason to support the theory of capitalism, but McKinley had none. He lived a middle class life. For men like Hanna, Frick, and Rockefeller, his lifestyle forced them to look at themselves. Roosevelt and "Old Money" looked at McKinley as lacking in class. McKinley was a rarity in the world of capitalists. Even the best of the capitalists, George Westinghouse and H. J. Heinz, had a hard time meeting his virtues. There is no question that these tycoons looked up to McKinley with a bit of disbelief.

Most historians have looked at the 1896 election as the rise of the "populist" William Jennings Bryan. It was McKinley, however, that represented the real populist movement. McKinley rose through a blueblood and Eastern establishment controlled Republican Party. He won the nomination by out-smarting America's most powerful political bosses and richest capitalists. McKinley united the second tier nouveau riche capitalists with the middle class and working class, offering vision rather than mere handouts from the bosses. Neither J. P. Morgan nor Andrew Carnegie liked him, yet he brought them into the fold. While he acquiesced to the demands for gold, he never put his full passion behind it until it proved a stimulant to the economy. He never socialized with the party bluebloods, and appointed Catholics and blacks to key positions. His social circle was family, Ohio friends, and his cabinet. He preferred to read his hometown newspaper to the national giants. His middle class living was an embarrassment to blueblood party Republicans, who often looked at him as the lesser of two evils.

McKinley stands almost alone as truly middle class throughout his life. Other middle class presidents such as Eisenhower, Nixon, Grant, and Reagan found success and some wealth prior to the presidency, although Harry Truman and

Abe Lincoln might challenge McKinley. Few presidents died as poor, with the possible exception of Washington (in terms of cash position). Republican blue-bloods of the time saw him as a bit of a hillbilly, yet by bringing in the middle class McKinley gave the Republican Party the majority. McKinley's political strength was that he was middle class. He was born and belonged to the middle class. He loved middle class pleasures such as reading the hometown paper and sitting on the front porch. His favorite memories were from his military service. Personally a devout Christian, he was ecumenical in all aspects of his politics and missionary in his behavior. The presidential salary was a huge increase for McKinley, whereas historically it has been a step down. McKinley's Dinner-Pail Republicanism was completely middle class. McKinley represented an important realignment nationally and within the Republican Party. He brought in the middle class and working class to his alliance. Like Reagan, McKinley was opposed by the bluebloods of the party, yet without the McKinley realignment, the Republican Party could never have dominated for so many years. Much of McKinley's strength came from the American red blood laborers usually found in the Democratic Party. He was shamelessly patriotic and nationalistic.

McKinley's "dinner-pail industrialism" is clearly on a par with Jefferson's Agrarian Vision, Clay's American System, and Roosevelt's New deal. All these, at least for the period, gave results. Protectionism and tariffs have come to seem like an anti-intellectual position in a complex world. Protectionism was a conservative principle until the 1960s, and now it is a concept lost to both parties. Economic reciprocity has lost to political reciprocity in trade arrangements. Part of the issue is tied to the death of nationalism, which was a component of McKinley's vision. Furthermore, the main pillar of McKinley's Dinner-Pail Republicanism was American exceptionalism, which passed away in the 1970s. Today the heart geographically of McKinley's political strength is called the "rust bowl." The once great factories of the industrial heartland have broken windows as Henry Clay had predicted in 1814. The great bronze busts of the pantheon at the McKinley Niles Memorial are no longer recognizable to young visitors.

Bibliography

Books

Adams, Henry. *The Education of Henry Adams.* New York: Library of America, 1968.

Adams, Henry. *Letters of John Hay,* ed. Henry Adams. Washington: 1908.

Adams, James. *The Epic of America.* New York: Triangle Books, 1931.

Andrew Byron. *Life and Speeches of William McKinley and Garret Hobart.* Chicago: F. Tennyson Neely, 1896.

Allen, Frederick Lewis. *The Great Pierpont Morgan.* New York: Harper and Brothers, 1949.

Armstrong, William. *Major McKinley: William McKinley and the Civil War,* Kent: Kent State University Press, 2000.

Barnard, Harry. *Rutherford B. Hayes and his America,* New York: Bobbs-Merrill, 1954.

Beer, Thomas. *Hanna, Crane and the Mauve Decade.* New York: Knopf, 1941.

Brandes, Stuart. *American Welfare Capitalism.* Chicago: University of Chicago Press, 1976.

Burn, Duncan. *The Economic History of Steelmaking, 1869-1939.* Cambridge. Cambridge University Press, 1940.

Carnegie, Andrew. *Autobiography of Andrew Carnegie.* Boston: Houghton Mifflin, 1920.

Clark, James. *The Presidential Battle of 1896.* Philadelphia: Globe Bible Publishing, 1896.

Clay, Henry. *The Papers of Henry Clay.* Lexington: University of Kentucky Press, 1959.

Cochran, Thomas. *Frontiers of Change,* New York: Oxford University Press, 1981.

Colman, Edna. *White House Gossip.* New York: Doubleday, 1927.

Croly, Herbert. *Marcus Alonzo Hanna.* New York: Chelsea House,1983.

Dawes, Charles. *A Journal of the McKinley Years.* Chicago: The Lakeside Press, 1950.

Depew, Chauncey. *My Memories of 80 Years.* New York: Charles Scribner's Sons, 1924.

Everett, Marshall. *Complete Life of William McKinley.* Memorial Edition, 1901.

Fallows, Samuel. *Life of William McKinley — Our Martyred President.* Chicago: Regan Printing House, 1901.

Friedman, Milton. *Money Mischief: Episodes in Monetary History.* New York: Harcourt Brace Jovanovich, 1992.

Glad, Paul. *McKinley, Bryan, and the People.* Chicago: Ivan R. Dee, 1991.

Green, James. *Death in the Haymarket.* New York: Pantheon Books, 2006.

Gould, Lewis. *The Presidency of William McKinley.* Lawrence: University Press of Kansas, 1980.

Gould, Lewis. *The Spanish-American War and President McKinley.* Lawrence: University Press of Kansas, 1984.

Hacker, Louis. *The World of Andrew Carnegie: 1865-1901.* New York: J. B. Lippincott, 1968.

Halstead, Murat. *Life and Distinguished Services of William McKinley.* Memorial Association, 1901.

Harpine, William. *From the Front Porch to the Front Page.* College Station: Texas A&M Press, 2005.

Harvey, George. *Henry Clay Frick: The Man.* New York: Charles Scribner's Sons, 1928.

Hay, John. *William McKinley: Memorial.* New York: Crowell, 1902.

Hay, John. *Abraham Lincoln: A History.* New York: Century Company, 1886.

Heald, T. Edward. *William McKinley Story.* Canton: Stark Country Historical Society, 1964.

Hessen, Robert. *Steel Titan: The Life of Charles Schwab.* New York: Oxford University Press, 1975.

Jensen, Richard. *The Winning of the Midwest, 1888-96.* Chicago: The University of Chicago Press, 1971.

Jessup, Philip. *Elihu Root.* New York: Dodd & Mead, 1938.

Jones, Stanley. *The Presidential Election of 1896.* Madison: University of Wisconsin Press. 1964.

Kasson, John. *Civilizing the Machine: Technology and Republican Values in America, 1776-1900.* New York: Grossman Publishers, 1976.

Kenny, Christopher. *The McKinley Monument: A Tribute to a Fallen President.* Charleston: History Press, 2006.

Koenig, Louis William. *Bryan: A Political Biography of William Jennings Bryan.* New York: Putman Publishing, 1971.

Laughlin, Laurence. *History of Bimetallism in the United States.* New York: Greenwood Press, 1968.

Leech, Margaret. *In the Days of McKinley.* New York: Harper and Brothers, 1959.

Lehman, John. *A Standard History of Stark County, Ohio.* Chicago: The Lewis Publishing Company, 1916.

Livesay, Harold. *Andrew Carnegie and the Rise of Big Business.* Boston: Little Brown, 1975.

McClure, Alexander and Charles Morris. *The Authentic Life of William McKinley.* Washington: Office of the Library of Congress, 1901.

McElroy, Richard. *William McKinley and Our America.* Stark County Historical Society, 1996.

McElroy, Robert. *Grover Cleveland: The Man and the Statesman.* New York: Harper and Brothers, 1923.

McKinley, William. *Speeches and Addresses of William McKinley.* New York: Doubleday, 1900.

May, Earl. *Principio to Wheeling: A Pageant of Iron and Steel.* New York: Harper & Brothers, 1945.

Montgomery, David. *Beyond Equality: Labor and the Radical Republicans,* Urbana: University of Illinois Press, 1981.

Morgan, H. Wayne. *William McKinley and His America.* Syracuse: Syracuse University Press, 1962.

Morgan, H. Wayne. *From Hayes to McKinley: National Party Politics.* Syracuse: Syracuse University Press, 1969.

Nelson, Ralph. *Merger Movements in American Industry 1895-1956.* Princeton: Princeton University Press, 1959.

Olcott, Charles. *The Life of William McKinley.* Boston: Houghton Mifflin, 1916.

Phillips, Kevin. *William McKinley.* New York: Henry Holt, 2003.

Rauchway, Eric. *Murdering McKinley.* New York: Hill and Wang, 2003.

Rhodes, James Ford. *The McKinley and Roosevelt Administrations,* New York: Macmillan, 1922.

Skrabec, Quentin. *The Boys of Braddock.* Westminster: Heritage Books, 2004.

Skrabec, Quentin. *Metallurgic Age.* Jefferson: McFarland & Co., 2006.

Skrabec, Quentin. *George Westinghouse: Gentle Genius.* New York: Algora Publishing, 2007.

Standiford, Les. *Meet You in Hell: Andrew Carnegie, Henry Clay Frick, and the Bitter Partnership that Transformed America.* New York: Crown Publishers, 2003.

Taft, Philip. *Organized Labor in American History,* New York: Harper and Row, 1964.

Tarbell, Ida. *The Life of Elbert H. Gary.* New York: D. Appleton, 1925.

Timmons, Bascom. *Portrait of an American: Charles G. Dawes.* New York: Henry Holt and Company, 1963.

Wall, Joseph. *Andrew Carnegie.* New York: Oxford University Press, 1970.

Welch, Robert. *The Presidencies of Grover Cleveland.* Lawrence: University of Kansas Press, 1988.

Williams, Harry. *Hayes of the Twenty-Third.* Lincoln: University of Nebraska Press, 1965.

Wilson, Woodrow. *Congressional Government.* New York, 1900.

Zieger, Robert. *Republicans and Labor.* Lexington: University of Kentucky Press, 1969.

Manuscripts and Archives

Library of Congress, McKinley Papers

Presidential Library and Museum, Canton, Ohio

Niles McKinley Library, Niles, Ohio

Hayes Presidential Library, Fremont, Ohio

Library of Congress, Carnegie Papers, William Day papers, and Cortelyou papers

King Library of the University of Kentucky, Clay Papers

INDEX